From political violence to negotiated settlement

Perspectives in British–Irish Studies
General Editors: JOHN COAKLEY and JENNIFER TODD

Other titles in this series:

*Changing shades of orange and green: redefining
the union and the nation in contemporary Ireland*
edited by JOHN COAKLEY

*Renovation or revolution? New territorial politics
in Ireland and the United Kingdom*
edited by JOHN COAKLEY, BRIGID LAFFAN
and JENNIFER TODD (forthcoming)

From political violence to negotiated settlement

The winding path to peace in
twentieth-century Ireland

edited by
Maurice J. Bric and John Coakley

University College Dublin Press

Preas Choláiste Ollscoile
Bhaile Átha Cliath

in association with the Institute for
British–Irish Studies, University College Dublin

First published 2004
by University College Dublin Press
Newman House
86 St Stephen's Green
Dublin 2
Ireland

www.ucdpress.ie

Published in association with the
Institute for British–Irish Studies,
University College Dublin

ISBN 1–900621–84–3
ISSN 1649–2390

Cataloguing in Publication data
available from the British Library

Typeset in Ireland in Adobe Garamond and
Trade Gothic by Elaine Shiels, Bantry, Co. Cork
Text design by Lyn Davies
Printed in Ireland on acid-free paper
by ColourBooks, Dublin

Contents

Tables and Figures

Tables

Figures

Contributors to this volume

PAUL BEW is Professor of Politics at Queen's University, Belfast. His publications include *Charles Stewart Parnell* (2nd edn, Gill & Macmillan, 1991); *Ideology and the Irish question: Ulster unionism and Irish nationalism 1912–1916* (Clarendon, 1994); *Between war and peace: the political future of Northern Ireland* (co-author, Lawrence & Wishart, 1997); *Northern Ireland: a chronology of the troubles 1968–1999* (co-author, Gill & Macmillan, 1999); and *Northern Ireland 1921–96: political forces and social classes* (co-author; rev. edn, Serif, 2001).

MAURICE J. BRIC is a senior lecturer in history at University College Dublin. He has published on the history and culture of eighteenth-century Ireland and America and *Ireland and America: the economy of an emigration, 1760–1800* (forthcoming). He is a member of the Royal Irish Academy and Chairperson of the Irish Research Council for the Humanities and Social Sciences.

GENERAL JOHN DE CHASTELAIN has had a distinguished career in the Canadian Army where he rose to the rank of General and the position of Chief of the Defence Staff. He also served as Canada's ambassador to the United States. Since 1995 he has been involved in the Northern Ireland peace talks which led to the Good Friday Agreement on 10 April 1998. He is currently Chairman of the Independent International Commission on Decommissioning in Northern Ireland.

JOHN COAKLEY is an associate professor of politics at University College Dublin and is director of the Institute for British–Irish Studies. He has edited *The social origins of nationalist movements* (Sage, 1992); *Politics in the Republic of Ireland* (with Michael Gallagher, 3rd edn, Routledge, 1999); *Changing shades of orange and green: redefining the union and the nation in contemporary Ireland* (UCD Press, 2002); and *The territorial management of ethnic conflict* (2nd edn, Frank Cass, 2003).

PAUL DIXON is a lecturer in politics at the University of Ulster, Jordanstown. He specialises in the areas of Northern Ireland politics (particularly British policy towards Northern Ireland and the peace process), British politics and comparative conflict, and has published extensively in these areas. His most recent publications include *Northern Ireland: the politics of war and peace* (Palgrave, 2001).

RONAN FANNING is Professor of Modern History at University College Dublin and is a specialist in the fields of British–Irish relations and Irish foreign policy. Among his publications are *The Irish Department of Finance: 1922–58* (Institute of Public Administration, 1978) and *Independent Ireland* (Helicon, 1983). He is a member of the Royal Irish Academy and co-editor of *Documents on Irish foreign policy*, vols 1–3 (Royal Irish Academy, 1998, 2000, 2002).

ALVIN JACKSON is Professor of Modern Irish History at Queen's University, Belfast. He has been lecturer in modern history at University College Dublin, John Burns Visiting Professor at Boston College and a British Academy Research Reader. His most recent books include *Home rule: an Irish history, 1800-2000* (Weidenfeld & Nicolson, 2003) and *Ireland 1798–1998: politics and war* (Blackwell, 1999).

MICHAEL LAFFAN is a senior lecturer in history at University College Dublin where he is also chairperson of the School of History. He has published a number of articles on nineteenth- and twentieth-century Ireland and his most recent book is *The resurrection of Ireland: the Sinn Féin party 1916–1923* (Cambridge University Press, 1999).

EUNAN O'HALPIN is Professor of Contemporary Irish History at Trinity College, Dublin. His books include *Defending Ireland: the Irish state and its enemies since 1922* (Oxford University Press, 1999), *Ireland and the Council of Europe: from isolation towards integration* (with Michael Kennedy, Council of Europe, 2000), and *Documents on Irish foreign policy*, vols 1–3 (co-editor, Royal Irish Academy, 1998, 2000, 2002).

JOSEPH RUANE is a senior lecturer in sociology at University College Cork. He is author or co-author of over 30 articles and books on Irish development, the Northern Irish conflict and the changing European context including *The dynamics of conflict in Northern Ireland: power, conflict and emancipation* (co-author, Cambridge University Press, 1996), *After the Good Friday Agreement: analysing political change in Northern Ireland* (co-editor, UCD Press, 1999), 'The politics of transition', *Political Studies* (2001), and *Europe's old states in the new world order* (co-editor, UCD Press, 2003).

Foreword

Ireland's presidency of the European Union has given us a unique opportunity to play a role in building and establishing a stable constitutional framework for a new Europe.

This great initiative has been matched by developments closer to home.

The agreement that was reached on Good Friday 1998 between parties and governments provided a basis for a lasting solution to a conflict that has cast a shadow over the lives of several generations. New institutional arrangements for the government of Northern Ireland and interlocking institutions covering the North–South and East–West dimensions have provided a dynamic new structure for the consolidation of peace. Not all the elements in this blueprint for peace are finally in place. However, what is more remarkable than the few remaining hurdles which remain to be jumped is the set of wide bridges which have already been crossed.

This collection of essays is a timely reminder of one of the biggest obstacles on the road to a lasting peace. The gun has long been associated with Irish politics, and much of our history has been taken up with a struggle between two approaches: parliamentary politics and the armed struggle. The essays in this volume draw attention to the deep historical roots of this tension. The distinguished contributors to this volume are to be congratulated for addressing such a complex issue.

I would also like to pay tribute to the Institute for British–Irish Studies at University College Dublin. Since its establishment in 1999, the Institute has played an invaluable role in bringing academics and policy-makers together to analyse the nature of the British–Irish relationship and to evaluate mechanisms that can help in resolving the challenges which arise from it. I hope that the work of the Institute, through its lectures, conferences and seminars, will continue to make a contribution in an area where the link between the academic and political worlds remains vitally important.

BERTIE AHERN, TD
Taoiseach

Preface

The essays that are brought together in this volume began their collective life at a conference organised by the Institute for British–Irish Studies at University College Dublin on 23 March 2001. At the time of the conference, controversy over the decommissioning of paramilitary weapons was at its height; and as this volume goes to press, three years later, the matter has still not been resolved.

The issue of decommissioning is not a simple one, as became clear from the contribution of the distinguished chair of the decommissioning body, General John de Chastelain; and, indeed, the continued existence of this body six years after the Good Friday agreement bears this out. This makes it all the more important to seek to set this almost intractable difficulty in context, and the turbulent course of Irish political history is the most important context of which we need to be aware. The speakers at the conference, and the essays presented here, attempt to do precisely this, by exploring the tension between paramilitary and electoral politics. The revised texts of the lectures have been supplemented by two introductory chapters, a conclusion and an appendix.

The editors wish to record their warmest thanks to the authors of the contributions included here for their patience in dealing with editorial queries and for their commitment in taking time out of busy schedules to work on their texts. Thanks are also due to four other people who assisted by chairing sessions in the course of the conference – Mr Noel Dorr, Chair of the Institute for British-Irish Studies, Professor Mary E. Daly, Dr Jennifer Todd and Dr Maurice Manning – and to the then President of UCD, Dr Art Cosgrove, who opened the conference. We owe a particular debt of gratitude to those whose work caused the conference to run smoothly or who have contributed in other ways to the preparation of this book: to Carmel Coyle and Karen Lang, and to Jean Brennan, Kevin Howard, Michael Kennedy, Claire Mitchell, Hazel Moloney, Lone Pålshaugen, Brid Reason and Anna Visser. Finally, a word of thanks is due to Barbara Mennell of UCD Press for the care with which she piloted this book through its production stage.

MAURICE J. BRIC
JOHN COAKLEY
April 2004

Chapter 1

The roots of militant politics in Ireland

Maurice J. Bric and John Coakley

Introduction

Writing on 1 September 1994, the day the IRA ceasefire came into effect, the veteran Northern Ireland correspondent David McKittrick commented that

> This may not be the end: there will probably be more deaths before it is all over and before armed conflict can finally be replaced by mere political controversy. But a momentous point has been passed in this painful process: the IRA has stopped and does not intend to start again (quoted in McKittrick, 1996: 3).

Ten years after the ceasefire, the IRA's guns appear to have been definitively silenced. However, dissident republicans and loyalists continue to threaten the peace, and the prospect of long-term political stability is not yet guaranteed. As we mark the ninetieth anniversary of another momentous development in Ireland's history, the enactment of home rule in 1914, it is salutary to remember the lessons of history.

Even before 1914, the legitimacy of conventional politics was periodically challenged by those who attached greater significance to armed force than to popular majorities. Since then, the tension between these two views has continued, although this is neither a distinctively Irish phenomenon nor one that is peculiar to the nationalist tradition. Even within liberal democracies, the notion that some values are so sacred that they cannot be overridden by conventional decision making is not uncommon. This raises important questions about how political decisions are made in the first place: normative questions about the appropriateness of particular formulas and practices, and empirical and analytical questions about the value system that underlies the political framework itself, as well as the various political movements and parties which claim a place within it. It is important to consider these fundamental questions further before we turn to the manner in which they are addressed in the chapters that follow.

Dilemmas of political violence

Any attempt to apply the dichotomy between militaristic strategies and the norms of conventional or 'constitutional' politics is complicated by three general considerations. First, this dichotomy is useful only when it is seen as an ideal type, one which describes two poles of a continuum rather than two sets of mutually exclusive actors. Second, it depends very much on context: the experience of many countries shows that while most democrats accept the rules of liberal democracy as leading them to potential political success and victory, some may be disposed to revert to more militant strategies if they do not. Third, the political discourse of 'constitutional' politics can often be embedded in a history which lends itself to different interpretations and ambiguities – a point that is particularly relevant in Ireland.

Our first point has to do with the nature of the gradient that lies between militant and conventional politics. Historical experience suggests that while even the most uncompromising militants may occasionally see the ballot box as an effective political instrument, committed liberal democrats may also think of resorting to extraordinary measures, especially if they regard the integrity of the state as being under threat, although they usually define any such measures as compatible with the constitution and the laws. Moreover, between violent rebellion and conventional party politics, a range of strategies can depart in varying degrees from the two poles of the continuum. Among these are campaigns of civil disobedience, politically organised strikes, various types of political intimidation, and strategies which by encouraging electoral abstention or the spoiling of ballot papers are designed to de-legitimise public institutions.

Our second point relates to the importance of political context in defining the probability that particular groups will opt for militant strategies. While majorities usually favour the principles of liberal democracy, they may also consider other options when their hegemony is endangered. For minorities who subscribe to the principles of liberal democracy, the implied recognition of majority rule can cause its own pain, and it can promote a mood to consider less conventional methods. Some useful evidence to illustrate this point may be taken from the Northern Ireland Life and Times Survey conducted between October 2002 and January 2003, which looked at attitudes towards the Good Friday Agreement – a settlement which suggested a new model for associating 'majority' and 'minority' within conventional structures and institutions. In general terms, the survey has to be read with the usual *caveat* that Sinn Féin emerges with only 11 per cent of the total party vote and 28 per cent of the nationalist vote. This is obviously an understatement of the party's real strength; neither is it particularly surprising, given that survey respondents are typically reluctant to indicate their support for radical movements.[1] The survey shows that 98 per cent of nationalist respondents claimed to have voted for the agreement in 1998 and that 97 per cent of them would do so if the referendum were held again. Only 64 per cent of unionist respondents claimed to have voted 'yes' in 1998, while as few as 40 per cent would be prepared to do so again at the time of the survey.[2] While this decline in unionist support for the agreement reflects a view that unionists 'lost out' in the process, there are other significant differences between the communities that are relevant for the theme of this book, the most telling of which are presented in table 1.1.

Table 1.1 **Disposition to accept defeat on long-term goals, by party, Northern Ireland, 2002**

Party	Position of party supporters (percentages):			No. of cases
Unionist parties	Support Irish unity	Would accept / live with Irish unity	Almost impossible to accept Irish unity	
Ulster Unionist Party	2.9	71.7	25.4	441
Democratic Unionist Party	1.5	45.6	52.9	206
Alliance Party	17.0	78.4	4.5	88
Nationalist parties	Support the Union	Would accept / live with the Union	Almost impossible to accept the Union	
SDLP	27.7	70.9	1.4	368
Sinn Féin	9.1	88.8	2.1	143

Note: 25 persons who responded 'don't know' have been excluded. The table presents responses to two questions: 'Do you think the long-term policy for Northern Ireland should be for it to remain part of the United Kingdom or to reunify with the rest of Ireland?'; for those supporting the union, 'If the majority of people in Northern Ireland ever voted to become part of a United Ireland do you think you would find this almost impossible to accept; would not like it, but would live with it if you had to; or, would happily accept the wishes of the majority?'; and, for those supporting Irish unity, 'If the majority of people in Northern Ireland never voted to become part of a United Ireland do you think you would find this almost impossible to accept; would not like it, but would live with it if you had to; or, would happily accept the wishes of the majority?'

Source: calculated from Northern Ireland Life and Times survey data, 2002–3.

The central point of this table is the set of varying reactions to a scenario where unionists' and nationalists' long-term goals were fundamentally rejected: where unionists were voted into a united Ireland, or nationalists were constrained to remain permanently in the United Kingdom. Among nationalists, the reported willingness to accept or at least to live with the majority decision is overwhelming. Even among Sinn Féin supporters, only two per cent stated that even if Irish unity never came about, this outcome would be 'almost impossible to accept'. Among unionists, though, 25 per cent of Ulster Unionist supporters and 53 per cent of Democratic Unionist supporters stated that they would find Irish unity 'almost impossible to accept', even if a majority supported this.[3] Thus, while it is true that one scenario (the constitutional status quo) is more likely to prevail than the other, the survey provides interesting evidence of the apparently greater long-term disposition of one community – the nationalist one – to accept the conventional norms of political decision making in this respect.[4]

These data, as well as the rhetorical shift on the part of the republican leadership over the past decade, suggest that most republicans are now reconciled to a new decision-making context, one that is much less favourable to them. They accept that it is not the people of Ireland, but the people of Northern Ireland (subject to consent on the part of the south) who will determine the future status of the province. This needs to be seen in the light of the well-known comment of Sir Ivor Jennings:

> Nearly forty years ago a Professor of Political Science who was also President of the United States, President Wilson, enunciated a doctrine which was ridiculous, but which was widely accepted as a sensible proposition, the doctrine of self-determination. On the surface it seemed reasonable: let the people decide. It was in fact ridiculous because the people cannot decide until somebody decides who are the people (Jennings, 1956: 55–6).

Recent events suggest, then, that Sinn Féin has accepted an historic shift, from seeing the people of Ireland as the decision-making unit (and seeing the IRA as the instrument for implementing the people's will, as expressed at the 1918 general election) to accepting the verdict of a popular majority within Northern Ireland (see Coakley, 2002). The unionist community has not had to confront a comparably distasteful political outcome, and if it did there is evidence to suggest that the range of strategic options would include those of the first period of unionist resistance in 1912–14.

The militant–conventional dichotomy also presents problems of terminology. In everyday speech, the parties which embrace conventional politics are commonly deemed to be 'constitutional'. But the term 'constitutional' has a certain resonance in the Irish political tradition, one that can leave its contemporary usage open to misinterpretation. Originally, the 'constitution' that featured so extensively in Irish political rhetoric was the 'constitution of 1688', the Williamite settlement that underpinned the Irish relationship with the British monarchy as well as the Protestant ascendancy on which it was based. From the early nineteenth century onwards, conservative political organisation was commonly expressed through 'constitutional' clubs, and the Irish unionist movement was powerfully linked to this concept. This was closely connected to the notion of a contract or covenant between people and ruler: between Irish (or, later, Ulster) Protestants and the monarchy, by which the one would give allegiance and the other would provide protection (see Farren and Mulvihill, 2000: 10–17). Defence of this 'constitution' was thus central to the unionist interest, and this term was part of mainstream unionist terminology. It is noteworthy that one of the first of the more recent unionist defensive organisations that anticipated the Northern Ireland troubles was Rev. Ian Paisley's Ulster Constitution Defence Committee, founded in 1966, whose own constitution described it in classic contractual language as 'one united society of Protestant patriots pledged by all lawful methods to uphold and maintain the Constitution of Northern Ireland as an integral part of the United Kingdom as long as the United Kingdom maintains a Protestant Monarchy and the terms of the Revolution Settlement' (quoted in Marrinan, 1973: 93–4).

In this sense, 'constitutional' parties were those which accepted the British constitution – perhaps fully, perhaps conditionally, depending on how one saw the maintenance of the union and the Protestant succession. However, the word 'constitutional' was also to acquire a second meaning – as embracing the conventional principles embedded in liberal democratic constitutions rather than rejecting them for the rule of force. It was in this second sense that Sean Lemass referred in 1928 to his party, Fianna Fáil, as being 'slightly constitutional'; within a few years, most would argue that it had become fully so. It was in this second sense, too, that only 'constitutional' parties were invited to participate in the talks that led to the Good Friday Agreement. These were defined as parties which were committed to 'exclusively peaceful and democratic means' and who rejected the use of violence.

It will be clear that parties that are 'constitutional' in the first sense are not necessarily so in the second sense, and vice versa. The two main unionist parties may claim to be 'constitutional' in the first sense; to be 'constitutional' in the second sense would arguably imply that they accept the principles of decision making as contained in the British constitution, and the democratic principles that were written into the Good Friday Agreement – in other words, in certain circumstances, to accept Irish unity. The corollary is the requirement that Sinn Féin accepts (though it does not, of course, necessarily like) membership of the United Kingdom for the indefinite future, a position towards which it has gradually been moving. The SDLP and the Alliance Party have, of course, from their foundation, been unambiguously 'constitutional' parties in this second sense – the sense in which we use the word below.

Militant politics in Ireland

As we have already emphasised, the interplay between militant or paramilitary strategies on the one hand and conventional or constitutional ones on the other constitutes a complex relationship, one whose full consequences have yet to become clear. Our major concern in this book is to explore the historical roots of the tension between these two approaches. Violence has indeed been a notable feature of public protest in Ireland and has always tested those who were looked to for leadership and authority. When it has suited them, governments have used it as a covert excuse to control the actions of even the most committed supporters of the constitutional process. For example, Daniel O'Connell was dismayed when he was imprisoned in 1844 for 'seditiously conspiring to raise and create discontent and disaffection amongst the Queen's subjects' (Shaw, 1844), and many other political leaders, nationalist and unionist, were to tread the same path over the decades that followed. It was a *sine qua non* of political organisation that in the continuously unfolding age of reform of the nineteenth and twentieth centuries public opinion was disposed to seek every outlet to express itself. For those grappling with popular democracy, it was not always easy to contain this process with a sense of comfort or predictability – a theme that the essays in this volume address.

The appropriate place to begin this analysis of the tension between para-militarism and politics is with its earlier history. In chapter 2, Maurice Bric traces the interaction between two types of movement, as well as between their respective leaders and organisations: those targeting political reform as a means towards greater social contentment and progress, and those focusing on agrarian concerns. This chapter suggests that it was among Daniel O'Connell's greatest challenges not only to confront these movements but also to incor-porate them within the ambit of constitutional procedure. It is worth observing that in this respect Parnell followed in O'Connell's footsteps during the later nineteenth century. However, the two men were also anxious to reinforce what they regarded as Ireland's 'natural leadership': the landlord class. Towards the middle of the century, a new political force emerged. As 'Catholic nationalism' pushed the Catholic bishops into a leadership role, they increasingly intruded on contemporary politics. Thus, to the older tensions between constitutionalism and militarism was added a new unease, as churchmen and secular politicians vied to set the course for contemporary Ireland. Towards the end of the century, cultural renewal added to the complexity of public protest, as unionists and nationalists began to suggest different versions of separatism, as well as to reassess the role of Westminster in legislating for the Ireland of the twentieth century.

The crucial events of the decade following the introduction of the third Home Rule Bill in 1912 are considered in three chapters. Ronan Fanning sets the scene in chapter 3, where he argues that as early as 1912 the British political system was neither willing nor able to deal with home rule. The Parliament Act of the previous year had effectively compromised the authority of the House of Commons, making the debates of 1912–13 'a meaningless charade'. In any event, Asquith was not as committed to home rule as Gladstone had been, and did not want to repeat the electoral humiliation of 1886 when the Liberals paid the price for breaking cross-party consensus on the issue. He had also come to agree with the Conservatives that to preserve the peace in Ireland, Ulster would have to be excluded from the third Home Rule Bill. Fanning points out that while racial and religious perspectives might have influenced this conclusion, the evidence is fragmentary. In this context, the integrity of parliament as an objective arbiter of a complex problem was made meaningless and Ulster Unionists took advantage of Asquith's 'wait-and-see' policy to assume 'interim control of the political agenda'. By 1916, republicans had written parliament off as an irrelevance in terms of promoting a settlement that was practical and acceptable. The differing reactions of the government to 'the reality of unionist sedition and the prospect of nationalist sedition' was stark, and suggested where the pragmatics of its policy lay. The Curragh mutiny of March 1914 highlighted the failures of parliamentary democracy itself. Fanning thus concludes that 'the downfall of Ireland's democratic nationalists had taken root before the Great War began'. Nationalist Ireland had lost faith in parliamentary democracy.

In analysing the republican response to these events in chapter 4, Michael Laffan accepts this interpretation, adding that given the circumstances in which the promised measure of home rule evaporated it was extraordinary that so many Irish voters still 'persevered with democratic procedures'. However, Irish nationalism was a diverse and unpredictable phenomenon. The firm British response to the Howth gunrunning by the Irish Volunteers in 1914 and the subsequent shootings at Bachelor's Walk confirmed the nationalist sense of injustice, and after Easter 1916 the enhanced reputation of the insurgents marginalised those who held more moderate views. The Irish Republican Brotherhood (IRB) thus became, 'even if surreptitiously', a part of mainstream nationalism, aided, ironically, by British and unionist actions which had the effect of undermining constitutional nationalism and stimulating radical rivals. Tensions between the military and civil levels of the new militant nationalist movement were perhaps inevitable. Sinn Féin provided a home for both, and helped to re-establish the 'normalcy' of the electoral process in 1922 – when a crucial election which saw the re-establishment of politicians rather than soldiers as the articulators of the public mood. This in effect also resulted, Laffan argues, in the containment of what were, on the face of it, uncompromising extremists.

Even if constitutional nationalism was electorally marginalised by Sinn Féin in 1918, it was not intellectually silenced, and Paul Bew analyses the writings of constitutional nationalists, and in particular their critique of republicanism, in chapter 5. It is true that leading members of the movement such as Stephen Gwynn argued that constitutional nationalists had marginalised themselves by failing to recognise the peculiar circumstances of Ulster. He cites, for example, the failure of John Redmond in March 1914 to accept Carson's offer of the exclusion of the six northern counties while leaving the way open for 'Irish unity on the basis of consent' – notwithstanding Redmond's own opposition to coercing Ulster unionism, and his party's adoption of this compromise position four years later. Gwynn also claimed that the violence of the Collins era, justified on counter-intelligence and broader political grounds, played a major role in shaping the 'sectarian institutions' of Northern Ireland. Bew links Gwynn's reflections on the 'self-defeating' aspects of Collins's strategy to the wider role of the British government, suggesting that between 1920 and 1922 Britain pursued a carrot-and-stick strategy designed to lead to the Treaty compromise of 1921. For its part, he argues, Sinn Féin had not sought a 'mandate for violence' in 1918, and as Ireland slid into armed conflict it had a polarising effect, marginalising moderate opinion which could not bring itself to side with London at a time when, in Horace Plunkett's words, 'a de jure government [was] repressing a de facto government'. The compromise of 1921 followed, although Bew cites C. H. Bretherton as observing in 1922 that nationalist Ireland was now getting no more than had been on offer in 1914.

It may not have been obvious in 1922, but what the southern Irish were granted at that time was categorically different from what had been on offer in 1914 (as modified by the introduction of partition in 1920). Autonomous status as a British dominion was altogether different from home rule within the United Kingdom, and this became clear in the divergent paths that the two parts of Ireland took subsequently. Southern Irish independence was expanded; but Northern Irish autonomy was ended with the imposition of direct rule in 1972. The threat from militant republicans pursuing their ideal of an independent, united Irish republic remained permanently in the background. The resources of this movement were not sufficient to offer a serious challenge to the status quo, and in chapter 6 Eunan O'Halpin focuses on the manner in which various republican alliances with forces outside Ireland have been analysed by the Irish, British and other states. On one level, such links promoted a familiar notion of 'England's difficulty as Ireland's opportunity' while, on another, it reflected an attachment to some vaguely defined transnational political ideology. More recently, however, the events of 11 September 2001 and alleged links between Columbia's FARC guerrillas and the IRA have powerfully challenged the American supporters of Sinn Féin and highlighted how the geopolitics of republican diplomacy have been influenced by a changing international landscape.

In Northern Ireland, the ending of autonomy in 1972 was followed in 1985 by a new arrangement between the two sovereign governments, the Anglo-Irish Agreement. This was seen by many Protestants as a breach of the unwritten contract between rulers and ruled – as giving Dublin an unacceptable voice in the internal affairs of Northern Ireland. In addition to more material supports, unionists possessed significant ideological resources that could be brought to bear in combating this perceived threat. In chapter 7, Alvin Jackson analyses unionist opposition to the third Home Rule Bill as a definite propaganda success – even if it was strategically flawed – and as providing the Northern Ireland state with an 'origin myth'. This drew on the resistance to home rule between 1912 and 1914, with Carson becoming 'an Orange Daniel O'Connell': the mobiliser, unifier and protector of his tribe. During subsequent times of crisis, unionist leaders used these images to legitimise their particular versions of events, as during the liberalising phase of the O'Neill era and following the fall of Stormont in 1972, as well as in opposition to the Anglo-Irish Agreement. However, this crucial historical episode was interpreted as these leaders saw fit, and it was used as an ideological instrument in the battle for legitimacy within unionism. Ian Paisley's celebration of Carson should be seen in this light, as should the ways in which both he and Terence O'Neill marked the fiftieth anniversary of the Larne gunrunning. However, as the past was carefully and even venerably marketed towards the political ends of the present and the future, Jackson argues that image triumphed over 'the complexity or elusiveness of their subject' as well as over 'the variety of unionist origins'. He thus concludes that the simplification of the past led to a certain sense of self-delusion and that 'Unionist Ulster failed partly because it was failed by its own past'. It is also clear that the failure of unionist opposition to the Anglo-Irish Agreement has stimulated a revision of the past and that, as a result, some Unionist leaders are rediscovering the pragmatism of its founding fathers, and thus embracing Craig before Carson.

Two further chapters look at the contemporary significance of militant politics within the nationalist and unionist traditions. As Joseph Ruane points out in chapter 8, the Good Friday Agreement led to renewed optimism among nationalists, notwithstanding continuing tensions between the communities and the remaining implementation problems. He identifies two particular causes for concern. First, he suggests that differences on core issues such as decommissioning may prove irreconcilable, halt the process and lead to a breakdown in the peace process. Second, while the agreement may be fully implemented, it may be on terms which will alienate previous supporters and drive them into the ranks of dissident groups. Dissident republicans already pose a serious threat to peace and stability, and although their political support appears to be limited, this could change. Ruane observes that it had been 'the best hope' of the Good Friday Agreement that all forms of political violence – and particularly the IRA campaign – would be brought to an end. This seems to have been substantially achieved, and Ruane takes the view that the IRA's 'currently depleted organisational state', and 'the ideological hostages to fortune' which its political leaders have given to the process, would impede any attempt by the movement to renew itself militarily. He concludes that the lessons of the past are not easily forgotten, even where population changes may reverse the current definitions of the majority and minority. Thus, although the agreement has set out the procedures to be followed in such circumstances, change would be 'unlikely to happen smoothly or consensually'. Another strand of public protest – armed loyalism – would appear, and with this another phase of political uncertainty.

It is precisely this other strand that Paul Dixon analyses in chapter 9. He argues that unionist activism developed between the extremes of consti-tutional and extra-constitutional politics, and that even major parties such as the Ulster Unionist Party and the Democratic Unionist Party may operate in a grey area between violent and non-violent politics. In a community which sometimes feels that the British government does not support it as energetically as Dublin supports nationalism, the sense of insecurity and the potential for its violent expression is high. This is reinforced by such develop-ments as Mrs Thatcher's perceived departure from the Tories' traditional attitude towards 'defence of the realm', which created a sense of vulnerability that was all the more marked because there was no other external force to defend the unionist position. But the forms of direct action that arise out of this sense of isolation may – even if they are violent – also serve conventional politics. Thus the campaigns of civil disobedience directed at the Anglo-Irish Agreement were condoned by unionist leaders as an attempt to assert political control over the anti-agreement campaign, and to face down paramilitary activists. Similarly, Dixon argues that Paisley's involvement in Ulster Resistance in 1986–7 acted as a moderating influence, putting a brake on a potential revolt. While violence was not condoned by unionist leaders, their retreat into the grey area of politics thus served both a tactical and a pragmatic purpose. The problem with this, of course, as Dixon concludes, 'lies in trying to distinguish shades of grey'.

Although our focus in this volume is on the past, and on the analysis of the circumstances that lay behind the decades-old link between paramilitary and conventional politics in Ireland, it is appropriate to conclude with a more pene-trating examination of the present and, perhaps, a glance into the future. In chapter 10, General John de Chastelain discusses another aspect of the interna-tional canvas of Northern Ireland: the involvement of the International Body, the International Chairmen, and the Independent International Commission on Decommissioning in dealing with the question of paramilitary arms in

Northern Ireland. He draws attention to the unionist perception that the decommissioning of paramilitary arms is fundamental to democratic government, with failure to complete this process acting as an impediment to the progress of the Good Friday Agreement. But he also reminds us that the nationalist and republican community regards it as of equal or greater importance to secure the installation of a police force which will be attractive to all elements of the community, and the removal of those military structures and installations which are offensive to nationalist feelings – and which in any case are seen as unnecessary while the guns of the main paramilitary groups remain silent. This chapter highlights the fundamental importance of a satisfactory resolution of these issues for the future of an inclusive government with devolved powers in Northern Ireland, with all which that implies for an end to violence and for participatory relations North and South, East and West.

A full decade after the ceasefires of 1994 that brought a quarter century of armed political conflict to an effective end, it is easy to forget the debilitating effects of the violence and its corrosive impact on political and social life. In chapter 11, however, John Coakley reminds us of the deep historical roots of political violence in Ireland and analyses the injuries suffered both in the long term and since the outbreak of civil unrest in 1969. This picture should allow some comfort to be drawn from the fact that, notwithstanding many difficulties since 1994, there has been no return to fully fledged military campaigns. The frightening potential of such campaigns emerges from that part of the chapter which discusses political violence from a comparative perspective. From this it may be seen that while the Irish experience may have been an unhappy one, it could have been much worse.

Conclusion

The chapters that follow in this book address, then, the ambiguous relationship between conventional politics and political violence that has been so characteristic a feature of the two main political traditions on the island of Ireland. While the story is not yet over, the rhetoric of the debate has at least been tempered. Although the colourful vocabulary of the 'fight for freedom' may have been transformed into a more politically correct dialogue about the application of the 'principle of consent', memory of the 'armed struggle' is fresh in many people's consciousness. The image of the 'armed struggle' is, of course, particularly associated with the republican tradition; but we should recall that the principle that it epitomises is not confined to just one tradition. Parnell may have helped to marginalise Captain Moonlight, and Hume encouraged P. O'Neill into retirement; but Captain William Johnston has not necessarily gone away.[5] Notwithstanding the current peace, then, the potential for destabilisation that is posed at present by nationalist and unionist dissidents and that might in future be offered by more mainstream forces should not be overlooked.

Since political leaders are normally committed not only to preventing matters from getting worse but to encouraging them to get better, it is, then, worth remembering the frail nature of the current peace. The lessons of Irish history, vividly illustrated in this book, are that violence may take a cyclical form, sidelined today but pushed to centre stage by a new generation. Furthermore, political violence or the threat of such violence has never been the monopoly of one political tradition; both nationalism and unionism have at least flirted with it, and there have been occasions when each has embraced it more fully. The challenge facing political leaders is not only to combat this strategy directly but to ensure that its preconditions are removed – not only to silence the guns, or even to put them beyond use, but also to remove the motivation for using them in the future.

Chapter 2

The invention and reinvention of public protest in Ireland, 1760–1900

Maurice J. Bric

Introduction

When rebellion broke out in Dublin on Easter Monday 1916, the British administration in Ireland was taken off guard. It is true that Dublin Castle expected some kind of militant unrest, that paramilitary-style volunteers – armed and unarmed – had been parading around the country for three years, that there had already been violent clashes in Dublin as well as in other parts of the country, and that the carnage of the Great War had numbed many to armed conflict and its effects. But in general Ireland was relatively peaceful, and, notwithstanding serious challenges to the authority of parliament over the issue of home rule, parliamentary politics seemed to enjoy a decisive edge over the alternatives. At one level, therefore, the violent events in Dublin which helped to launch a new era of paramilitary activism came as a surprise. However, there was another level at which the Easter rising was not altogether unpredictable. Rebellions had taken place before, and many of them had been glorified in popular culture. Paramilitary organisation had long-established roots, and voices calling for a more militant alternative to parliamentary politics were always to be heard, even if these were often politically marginal. The object of this chapter is to look at these subterranean forces in the period before overt paramilitary organisation moved into the mainstream of Irish politics in the early twentieth century.

Conventional politics and popular protest, 1760–1800

Before 1800, the Irish polity was an organic entity within which a supposed 'morally superior' group claimed to promote the welfare of the people as a whole. This was a notion which did not die easily, and even during the so-called age of democratic revolution, most accepted that it was better to reform than to abolish established conventions, and that the polity should be broadened to incorporate new members (Palmer, 1959–64).[1] When Daniel O'Connell was born in 1775, popular politics had a relatively limited agenda in contemporary Ireland: to seek the independence and reform of the Irish parliament and, more generally, to promote 'progress'. However, reform was not envisaged as being at the expense of established structures. This perspective was shared by the members of the Catholic Committee who led the other distinctive political campaign of the day: to repeal the penal laws which deprived Catholics, in particular, of their civil rights. While this committee had been prompted by a sense of injustice which had deep historical roots, it was also driven by a need for formal recognition within the existing establishment, rather than by an urge to displace it or to foster an alternative. One sign of this new attitude was the Test Oath of 1774, through which Catholics could establish their loyalty by denying the temporal authority of the papacy 'within this realm', while also 'utterly renouncing and abjuring' the Stuart Pretender, and promising to support the Hanoverian succession and the social and political structures which sustained it (Bric, 1987: 172). For the Catholic outsider and Protestant insider alike, the language of contemporary 'patriotism'[2] thus conveyed not only similar possibilities but also similar limits. For its part, Dublin Castle recognised that at a time of revolutionary agitation, and with the American Revolution still a fresh memory, the security of the state was best served by seeking to accommodate the leadership of a re-emerging Catholic Ireland.

Such a conventional approach to 'progress' did not appeal to everybody, not least because reform meant different things to different people. Patriotism may have offered opportunities to wrap the Catholic middle classes into the 'natural' leadership of a new Ireland. However, it did not have an obvious social or agrarian agenda, and between 1760 and 1790 these concerns were highlighted in another Ireland by popular protest movements such as the Whiteboys, Oakboys, Steelboys and Rightboys, which sought to counteract 'the wrongs done to the poor' (Froude, 1872–4, I: 26 n. 6; see appendix I for a note on these and similar movements). These movements were rooted in the countryside and published schedules of payment for various types of tithe, rent, cess, and dues, beyond which tenants and parishioners were instructed not to pay. In setting limits to their demands, these groups wanted landlords, and especially Church of Ireland ministers from whom most people derived no benefit for the onerous payment of tithe, to ask parishioners to pay only 'such as the house can afford'.[3] In reality, however, grievances of this kind could not be addressed as easily as those of the Catholic Committee, not least because they were perceived as an assault on property and, by extension, on the social and political hierarchy which maintained the contemporary polity. As one commentator put it, the established church was 'so essentially incorporated with the State . . . that the Subversion of one must necessarily overthrow the other'. Moreover, any assault on its position raised issues which, if recognised, would 'lead naturally to an equal change in the ranks or influence of the *religion itself* (Bric, 1986: 285). Thus, as the repeal of the penal laws promoted the more obvious leaders of Catholic Ireland within the walls of the establishment, parliament sought reassurance that 'the greatest grievance' of popular protest would not be 'the glorious revolution of 1688' itself which had led to the establishment of the Protestant ascendancy of eighteenth-century Ireland.[4]

Parliament responded to the development of agrarian protest not by inquiring into the grievances of the protesters but by passing measures which would strengthen the institutions of the state to deal with 'riotous and tumul-tuous assemblies' and activities (Crossman, 1996: 199–200; Bric, 1986: 287). However, the Catholic bishops announced in 1786 that they would investigate the extent to which parochial dues had become a burden on their particular communicants. As parliament steered clear of objective enquiry, the church thus sought to respond to the concerns of its flock and, by so doing, to renew its credibility with it. This was all the more important because it had been reported to Rome that 'the people [were] no longer following their pastors' (Bric, 1987: 173), while within a more secular world, the new middle-class leaders of Catholic Ireland could not automatically count on the deference which their aristocratic predecessors had received. In a society where the Catholic Church had traditionally provided a forum for articulating popular grievance, this enquiry was thus an important step in halting drift between priest and people.

As the Catholic Committee focused on the repeal of the penal laws rather than the redress of socio-economic grievance, the agrarian movements created a parallel structure of local Whiteboy captains which threatened the emergence of these newly respectable Catholic leaders. This challenge was all the more real because the 'Whiteboy oaths' bound parishioners together in a way which consolidated the popularity of these 'under-leaders'. Moreover, the organisation and *modus operandi* of popular protest had awakened the peasantry to its potential influence within the political process and enabled it to assert itself on its own terms. Catholic bishops may have urged agrarian movements not to draw on 'our holy religion, the odium of our mild government, and the gentle-men in power in our country', as the archbishop of Cashel put it (Bric, 1985: 161). However, such admonishments in favour of conventional politics, as well as occasional episcopal and clerical denunciations of the sporadic violence of the protesters, reflected not just a moral stance. They also had the political purpose of ensuring that the established structures of the polity, into which the Catholic middle classes and the clergy were now being received, would not unravel at a time when Catholics were being given an important role within them.

As the politics of accommodation incorporated a Catholic establishment into the polity, it also created an anti-establishment cadre of leaders within the reform movement. In 1791, these radicals formed the Society of United Irishmen to achieve 'a complete and radical reform of the representation of the people in Parliament' (Elliott, 1989: 140). Initially, the society was not separatist, although it slowly drifted in that direction, if only because it regarded English influence as a block to improvement in Ireland. It also promoted the ideals of the French revolution. Thus the society not only linked political reform and social justice with a particular type of culture, epitomised by the republicanism of contemporary France, but it also wove a more familiar nationalist theme into the vocabulary of public protest. It is difficult to assess the impact of republican ideas on the United Irish rank and file. When asked before a parliamentary enquiry in August 1798 how the mass of the people understood the society's commitment to reform, for example, one of its leaders, Thomas Addis Emmet, expressed the view that they were not particularly interested in parliamentary reform 'till it was explained to them as leading to other objects which they looked to, principally the abolition of tithes' (Emmet, 1915, II: 462). While Emmet may have over-simplified the influence of republican rhetoric, his comment is a reminder that while a French-supported rebellion was being plotted, and plans for a republic were being mooted, the United Irishmen had to consider the concerns of agrarian protest which had been ingrained in many parts of Ireland since the 1760s (Curtin, 1994; Quinn, 1998).

During the 1790s, these concerns were also articulated by two new organisations, the Defenders and the Orange Order. Though predominantly a Catholic movement, the Defenders also had a class-based interest in addressing agrarian grievances, especially tithes, rents and the renewal of leases. They drew on the organisational pattern of Whiteboyism, though it is clear that by the early 1790s they had developed a wider model of organisation and communication in some parts of Leinster and Ulster. In order to keep such a movement intact, Defenderism evolved a system of passwords and other types of mystical language, a feature that it shared with the United Irish lodges. While it is true that by the middle of the decade these two movements co-operated with one another and in some cases even overlapped, the continued existence of the Defenders highlighted the agrarian grievances of rural Ireland and ensured that the socio-economic concerns of Irish protest would not be overshadowed by the revolutionary aspirations of the United Irishmen (Bartlett, 1992; Curtin, 1994; Dickson, Keogh and Whelan, 1993). But when the United Irishmen – seen by the authorities as part of an international plot which had Britain as well as Ireland within its sights – were proscribed in May 1794, the Defenders were also tarred with the brush of conspiracy. The collapse of French efforts at invasion in 1796 and 1798 as well as the large-scale but unsuccessful United Irish-led rebellion of the latter year also undermined the potential impact of contemporary popular protest, as was reflected in the ineffectiveness of the rebellion of 1803. But this period left as its legacy a draconian Insurrection Act (1796), which was used in the 1820s and 1830s against popular movements that could be presented as threats to the state.

Given that the Defenders had originally been strongest in southern Ulster and northern Leinster, it was inevitable that some of their activities would focus on land which was either owned or being vacated by emigrating Protestants.[5] As a result, Defenderism in these places took on a sectarian character which was sometimes also 'infused with an almost millenarian zest' (Smith, 1992: 47–51). From this starting point, it was easy for Catholics to recall the circumstances in which the country had been 'planted' and 'cleared' in the first place, and thus for grievance to pile on grievance. Among Protestants, the repeal of the penal laws had already caused unease and insecurity. Reflecting these views, one pamphleteer wrote in 1793 that 'parochial meetings, county meetings, Catholic Committee, Societies of United Irishmen and Defenders were all jumbled together in one enormous mass of vice and wickedness' in a countryside which was also becoming increasingly violent (Smith, 1992: 66).

The Peep of Day Boys had been founded in the late 1770s partly to express these insecurities. By 1795, this movement had spawned the Orange Order as an organisation which, among Protestants, mirrored the agrarian concerns of the Catholic Defenders (Senior, 1966). Moreover, as mutual distrust grew into fear, and as the rebellion of 1798 unfolded amid prospects of a French invasion, Orangeism became as much a popular and armed instrument of the state as an outlet for agrarian grievance. For all intents and purposes, therefore, it was clear that the United Irish ideal that 'no reform is practicable, efficacious, or just, which did not include Irishmen of every *religious* persuasion' (Elliott, 1989: 140) could not be realised. Although some reformers, including many Catholics, kept a hopeless faith in Dublin Castle, Tone's ideal 'to unite the whole people of Ireland, to abolish the memory of all past dissensions, and to substitute the common name of Irishman in place of the denominations of Protestant, Catholic and Dissenter' (O'Brien, 1910, I: 51) was wrecked by the ways in which protest had been organised and led during the second half of the 1790s, by an increasing reliance on sectarian rhetoric to articulate the insecurities of the times, and by the ways in which the agencies of government confronted and dealt with unrest and rebellion. In this climate, many who would otherwise have remained aloof joined the Orange Order or the United Irishmen (McBride, 1998: 208–9).

The Act of Union helped to blunt the effects of this legacy: after 1800, reform would have to be discussed within the wider world of the United Kingdom. As a result, the union pulled most Irish Protestants from their erstwhile flirtation with late eighteenth-century radicalism and towards a clear loyalty to the new legislative framework. Catholics saw the union as giving them an opportunity to influence *domestic* Irish politics and culture, and their place within it. Thus, Irish Protestants and Catholics alike saw the union as a strategic asset – but for very different reasons. During the course of the nineteenth century, their respective approaches to the union would highlight all sorts of conundrums, among them the paradoxical conflict between loyalty to the union and loyalty to Westminster, the relationship between social and political agitation, and the manner in which each of these was pursued. They would also consider the cultural connotations of protest, the extent to which the affairs of Ireland were influenced by circumstances and personalities outside the island, and, as Ireland developed a more 'modern' culture, the extent to which change should be balanced with continuity.

New wine in new bottles, 1800–48

Shortly after the Act of Union was passed, the veto controversy indicated the extent to which Catholic Ireland had departed from the politics of accommodation of the later eighteenth century. The proposal that the government should be given a veto over Irish episcopal appointments, a practice common elsewhere in Europe, was rejected in 1808 by the Catholic hierarchy and its secular supporters, led by O'Connell. This signalled a new willingness to challenge the government, and over the coming decades there was to be confrontation on three fronts, each illustrating an interplay between parliamentary and militant strategies: the struggle for Catholic emancipation, the issue of tithes, and the question of repeal of the Act of Union.

This tension was evident even in O'Connell's personal career. Already during the 1820s, O'Connell's effectiveness as a barrister had challenged the home-made remedies of the Rockites and Ribbonmen, and encouraged the use of the established courts as a viable avenue of redress. O'Connell also turned his attention to the issue of Catholic emancipation – the right of Catholics to sit in parliament – and pioneered a new style of politics. In 1823 he founded the Catholic Association, a multi-tiered network of committees that culminated in a national organisation to which people of all classes could rally in the name of a common cause (Garvin, 1981: 47–8; O'Ferrall, 1985). The association drew on the support of the Catholic clergy whose established networks it used, and also relied on the structure and organisation of popular protest. However, its strength lay in O'Connell's capacity to bring together electoral politics (symbolised by his victory in the Clare by-election of 1828) and mass agitation, much of it at least implicitly encouraged by agrarian organisations. As a result, the government agreed to Catholic emancipation in 1829 (O'Ferrall, 1985). At first sight, O'Connell's success appeared to vindicate the belief that progress was best made through conventional channels. But this was only a partial victory. First, it was accompanied by a measure that raised the property qualification for the franchise five-fold, thus reducing the Irish electorate to a fraction of its former size. Second, the outcome was not particularly relevant to the peasantry. Nonetheless, it created an expectation that all sorts of grievances, over and above O'Connell's immediate concerns, would be resolved as part of this process, and in particular those which concerned the imposition and collection of tithe.

Tithe had long been central to Irish agitation. As early as 22 January 1786, the *Dublin Evening Post* observed that the issue had already 'kept Ireland in a state of civil war for years'. For a number of reasons, tithe was regarded as uneven in its application and unjust in its destination. Since 1735, pasture land had not been liable for tithe; as a result, while the upper echelons of the rural hierarchy were often tithe-free, those at the other end were rarely so. It was also intended for the Protestant established church, and was collected with great vigour by proctors who were often reinforced by police and the military. Resistance to tithe payments was co-ordinated at local level by the Ribbon movement which in the 1830s was organised around 'a sort of Parochial Tribunal, that adjudicate in all Cases of Complaint and Quarrel amongst the members of the Body, and also issue their Orders to the Ribandmen [*sic*] in their Parishes which they are bound to obey' (Garvin, 1981: 40). It also levied money to support resistance to tithe, and, usually under the guise of hurling matches, held huge public displays which later influenced the 'monster meetings' of the 1840s. Especially at local level, these popular movements thus helped to politicise and mobilise the masses even before O'Connell gave this process a greater degree of coherence, focus and self-confidence. The impact of the protests was clear: the 'tithe war' of the early 1830s effectively either halted or reduced the payment of tithe in those parts of Ireland where Ribbonism was strong.

O'Connell understood the challenge, and realised that if he failed to meet it, the Ribbon captains would provide an alternative to his leadership and organisation. He condemned Ribbon activities, which often involved murder and other types of violence, as being not only illegal, but a waste of energy. O'Connell urged the people to shun such activities and, indeed, his agents tried to diffuse local tensions. However, this was not an easy process, as one of the most publicised incidents of 1831, the so-called battle of Carrickshock, illustrated.[6] O'Connell led for the defence at the ensuing trial of those charged with attacking the police, and secured acquittals, consolidating his reputation as a leader of popular causes. But his objections to violence were never in doubt, and he had to remind his followers that in the midst of 'Ribbon justice', the institutions of the state could still be used, even to acquit men who had been charged with heinous crimes. Nonetheless, his successful defence was taken by some as indirect support for the protesters rather than as the outcome of a professional assignment.

O'Connell spent his parliamentary career confronting popular protest by suggesting that the petition to parliament was a more effective medium than a threatening letter from Captain Moonlight.[7] However, this approach called on O'Connell to be as effective a parliamentarian as he was a barrister. He urged the protesters to look to his new parliamentary presence and influence, to petition parliament, and to help get his candidates elected. He was able to demonstrate substantial political returns for this approach. The establishment of a number of parliamentary select committees to enquire into 'the condition of the poor' and into the tithe issue was quite revolutionary in its time, as were the reforms that were enacted by the parliaments of the 1830s, not just for what they put on the statute book, but because of the language in which they were discussed (McIntyre, 1965: 167–200). During the debates, suggestions that reform had moral as well as economic or constitutional aspects made some members of the contemporary establishment uncomfortable. However, although parliament's ultimate response showed an unwillingness to compromise on a system which was still intended 'to represent property rather than persons' (McCracken, 1971: 13), some significant gains were made. During the period of 'the Lichfield House compact' (1835–41), when the prime minister, Lord Melbourne, needed O'Connell's parliamentary support, O'Connell was in a particularly strong position to have parliament more effectively address a number issues of concern to Ireland. Tithe was substantially reformed in 1838 by its inclusion as part of the rent payable by tenants to their landlords; it was also to be paid directly by the landowner to the minister. The municipal reform act (1840) abolished the long-established monopolies of some 58 corporations and replaced them with elected councils. As a result, O'Connell's adherents could claim that their integrity and effectiveness as leaders of a new system of politics in contemporary Ireland had been vindicated. In 1841, O'Connell's own election as the first Catholic lord mayor of Dublin since 1690 made the point.

The third great issue was more intractable. This was the question of the union itself, a matter which O'Connell sought to address by the same means as those he had used in the case of Catholic emancipation. The blend of parliamentary agitation with peaceful popular protest took place under the umbrella of the Repeal Association, founded in 1841 on the model of the Catholic Association. However, the banning of a proposed 'monster meeting' at Clontarf in 1843 revealed the limits of O'Connell's methods. O'Connell had to choose between calling off the meeting, and thus, in effect, surrendering, or facing a serious risk of violence. He chose the latter course, ending the strategy of monster meetings, which one commentator had described as occasions 'where the ignorant and bigoted might be urged to insurrection' (Harrison, 1993: 47–8). O'Connell never intended these for such purposes, and after 1843 the militant challenge was taken up by a new, radical group known as 'Young Ireland' which did not feel confined by O'Connell's aversion to violence. As has already been suggested, O'Connell preferred to operate with due regard to the authority of parliament. His organisational skills and popular influence also had a lasting significance for the ways in which protest would be organised in Ireland and articulated in Westminster. However, the high expectations of success in 1843 led to a feeling of great pessimism which, after the Great Famine, would be channelled into an Anglophobia and a hardened separatism which helped to foster a narrow sense of Ireland (Davis, 1987). Thus, the second half of the nineteenth century began not only with an air of despondency but with an increasing air of detachment from Britain, and with the process of reinventing the Irish past as a way of defining its future.

Separatism and unionism, 1848–86

While some of the themes of the earlier part of the century would reappear after the famine, the expression of physical force, in particular, became more obvious and continuous. There was also a more dynamic interplay between nationalist sentiment and the issues of land and religion, a consolidation of the parliamentary tradition, and, ultimately, a marriage of convenience between these conflicting forces.

One of the less visible but more significant developments of the period was the foundation in 1858 of the Fenians, known in later years as the Irish Republican Brotherhood (IRB). The core Fenian belief was that Irish interests could be promoted effectively only by establishing an independent democratic republic (Moody, 1968: 17, 50). Towards this end, the Fenians rejected O'Connell's absolute faith in constitutional procedures. However, as R. V. Comerford has suggested, the leader of the Fenians in Ireland, James Stephens, also wished to control his followers and to keep them 'from being distracted by any alternative nationalist leadership' (Comerford, 2003: 12). Stephens failed in this respect, as O'Connell had before him. Even during the dispirited years after the famine, the nature of protest in Ireland was too complex to be managed in such an authoritarian manner, whether by con-stitutionalists or potential insurgents. However, by unequivocally committing itself to undo the union through a secretive, cell-based, physical force move-ment, the Fenians promoted a nationally organised armed insurrection and put the establishment of the republic before all other concerns, including agrarian grievances, however emotive these were. Moreover, although their rebellion of 1867 failed, the martyrdom of the Manchester Fenians,[8] together with a narrow image of a Gaelic Ireland, popularised the idea of total separation from Britain. Through many vicissitudes, this continued into the twentieth century to influence the character and attitudes of independent Ireland. In 1915, as he delivered the oration over the grave of the Fenian leader, Jeremiah O'Donovan Rossa, Patrick Pearse knew the power of this tradition when he said that 'Life springs from death; and from the graves of patriot men and women spring living nations . . . The Defenders of this Realm . . . have left us our Fenian dead, and while Ireland holds these graves, Ireland unfree shall never be at peace' (Edwards, 1977: 236).

As Alvin Jackson has pointed out, Fenianism also provided the means to 'shift away from the politics of deference . . . [and] towards a much more self-sufficient form of political expression' (Jackson, 1999: 95).[9] Thus, the often-repeated denunciation by Dr Daniel Moriarty, Catholic bishop of Kerry (1856–77), that 'eternity was not long enough and hell not hot enough for the Fenians'[10] reflected not only his worries about the perceived anti-clericalism and social radicalism of that movement, but also fears that episcopal authority might be challenged or even undermined. By this time, Moriarty and his fellow bishops had come to see themselves as at least a complement to the secular power, especially outside Ulster. In 1869, the disestablishment of the Church of Ireland reinforced this perception and the view that since O'Connell's time the parochial house could rival the 'big house'. The devotional revolution of this period also saw increased mass attendance and devotion to Mary, novenas, saints, and religious insignia, as well as the growth in parish missions which 'could reinvigorate the religious patterns and sense of identity of an entire locality' (Comerford, 1985: 31; Larkin, 1972). As a reflection of these new attitudes, 'the "Sunday suit" or the "Sunday shawl" became obligatory, for the rags that had sufficed in many of the pre-famine churches [now] seemed out of place' (Lee, 1973: 48). But the religiosity of the late nineteenth-century Irish church did not extinguish its secular equivalent in 'the Fenian idea'. The poor reception given to the papal decree of 1870 excommunicating those who remained Fenians made this point, not for the first or last time. Indeed, despite their increased authoritarianism, or perhaps as a *sine qua non* of maintaining it, many priests realised that they could not ignore contemporary Irish nationalism. The result was a type of 'Catholic nationalism' which, while not necessarily separatist, promoted what Cardinal Paul Cullen, Catholic archbishop of Dublin (1852–78), called an Ireland 'with its own distinctive life and institutions' (Comerford, 1985: 31).

What the tithe question had been to the episcopacy of JKL,[11] the land question was to those of Cullen and his contemporaries, even if it did not provoke the same level of violence, at least before 1878. In Connaught, most people lived on the margins of survival, and 'on the verge of starvation and eviction' (Townshend, 1983: 108); in other parts of the island, the 'modernisation' of post-Famine Ireland and the commercialisation of its agriculture created other imbalances within the rural economy which were only temporarily obscured. The consolidation of farms encouraged the appearance of a more aggressive middling farmer class, while the growth of grazing focused attention on the prices of grain and other cereals. In such volatile circumstances, the interests of all farmers, especially if they were tenants, had to be protected. It was in these circumstances that a number of farmers' clubs were founded and consolidated in 1850 into the Tenant League to campaign for better conditions for tenants. Although the league, with its support base among larger farmers, failed to generate popular support for the land question, agrarian issues were organised in a cogent manner for the first time since the debates on tithe, and, as during the campaigns of the 1830s, people now looked to parliament to provide practical solutions. However, as the 1850s progressed, the Tenant League was squeezed into impotence by the twin forces of Catholic clerical mobilisation and landlords' vested interests. It would also be overshadowed by the rejuvenation of home rule and by the emergence of Isaac Butt as founder of the Home Government Association in 1870.

Before 1870, Butt had had a long involvement in land issues. His pamphlet, *Irish people and Irish land: a letter to Lord Lifford* (1867) proposed an early version of the land reform package that became known as the 'three Fs'.[12] He also represented evicted tenants and landlords in ejectment cases and knew the land system intimately. Thus, although his reputation has been based conventionally on his defence of Fenian prisoners, his involvement with the land issue gave him an understanding of popular grievance which was not unlike that of O'Connell. Perhaps because of this, also like O'Connell, his Home Government Association began as a conservative movement, for which 'Home Rule would prevent rather than encourage radical excesses in Ireland . . . [which] would be Irish in sentiment and point of view, and thus respond to Irish opinion' (McCaffrey, 1968: 79). Its successor, the Home Rule League, was only slightly more radical in its approach, although the 900 delegates who brought it into being in 1873 did much to revive the cause of repeal and indeed, to move beyond it, and begin the process of popularising and organising home rule. However, as it slowly lost the support of Protestant landlords, many saw it as a 'Catholic party', albeit one which was led by a Protestant lawyer. The electoral success of the league – which returned 59 members in the 1874 election – owed much to the Ballot Act of 1872, which introduced secret voting and thus helped to reduce landlord influence at elections. New leadership also contributed to the vigour of the movement. Charles Stewart Parnell, who took over as leader in 1880, linked the parliamentary home rule movement with the two other outlets for protest in contemporary Ireland: the Fenian tradition and the reviving movement for land reform. Indeed, this interaction was to be one of Parnell's greatest strengths, as well as a potential weakness: the ability to build a movement of different interest groups for which he could act as the supreme arbiter and mediator between what were often contradicting tendencies (Jackson, 2003: 43).

Parallel to this development, by August 1879 a new agrarian movement had been born under the leadership of Michael Davitt – the Land League. A former Fenian, Davitt was in no doubt that reformers would have to focus aggressively on completely restructuring the land system rather than achieving the republic. Branches of the league were soon established in many parishes and advocated collective action, including the boycott of offending landlords as well as those who took over farms from evicted tenants. From its very beginnings, therefore, the league aggressively pursued its own recognisable agenda. But Davitt realised that he could advance only a limited distance without Parnell, while Parnell saw the league as a potential competitor which had to be brought inside his tent (O'Callaghan, 1994: 78). As a result, Parnell involved himself in the league's activities and addressed many of its meetings. His involvement in these events was not just a matter of political pragmatism. He also realised that the land question was 'the foundation . . . for the regeneration of our legislative independence' and that it could not be ignored or addressed in isolation from home rule (Lyons, 1977: 138). In October 1879, the practical politics of both Davitt and Parnell, as well as the multi-dimensional character of public agitation, was underlined when the league was reorganised with Parnell as its president.

For its part, the IRB realised that after the failure of the Fenian risings of 1867 it would not achieve its aims without casting a wider net into conventional and parliamentary politics. As Butt had defended the insurgents of 1848 and 1867, his stock was initially high with the IRB, while Parnell was reputed to have taken the Fenian oath in May 1882 (Maume, 1995). Parnell realised that Fenianism was an idea which still retained a powerful political hold and that it could contribute to a rejuvenated parliamentary party, and he courted the IRB accordingly (Hart, 2003: 24). At this time militant Irish separatism was being effectively led by John Devoy's Clan na Gael movement in America. Like its counterpart in Ireland, the IRB, with which it shared a directory after 1877, was reviewing its strategies. In general terms, despite disillusion with politics in contemporary Ireland, Irish Americans were willing to use every means to free their homeland from 'bondage', if only, as Thomas N. Brown has argued, to establish their own respectability in the United States (Brown, 1966). Now, Devoy became interested in the Land League as a vehicle that might create the conditions which would ultimately lead to the establishment of an autonomous, as opposed to a separate, parliament in Dublin. The league thus became for him a 'stalking-horse for revolution' (Miller, 1985: 441). A similar pragmatism led to the 'New Departure' of 1879, which brought Davitt and Parnell into an alliance with Devoy (Bew, 1978: 46–73).

Following Davitt's visit to the United States in 1877, Devoy agreed to provide financial support for anybody who was evicted and to fund a mass organisation to demand changes in the land system and create a peasant proprietary. For Devoy and Davitt, this initiative was a means to an end. It was no less so for Parnell, who saw it as a means of developing his popular standing in Ireland and softening crucial and lucrative support of Irish Americans in his favour. For all three, however, it was an uneasy and somewhat artificial convenience which could be discarded just as easily as it had been agreed. For the moment, if only because it was difficult to prevent collective protest from leading to 'illegal activities', it effectively led to the land war (1879–82) and to arson and destruction of property, as well as to assault and murder of landlords, their agents, and the constabulary. In 1881 alone, nearly 4,500 such 'agrarian outrages' were recorded (Townshend, 1983: 151). As the land war tainted all three leaders with the brush of violence, it was easy for the government, especially after the Land League was proscribed in 1881, to accuse them of being criminals and levellers rather than chivalrous advocates of land reform and home rule, and even to imprison Parnell (1881–2). This episode highlighted the tightrope which all Irish leaders had to walk, and in particular Parnell's difficulties in keeping together a coalition of interests and ensuring that it would not stray from a belief in conventional politics.

Like O'Connell, Parnell thought that violence could undermine the position of the landed elite, a group which he believed were the 'natural leaders' who would direct and manage self-government in Ireland. In Ennis in September 1880, he denounced violence in favour of 'a much better way . . . when a man takes a farm from which another has been evicted . . . you must shun him.. by putting him in a moral Coventry'.[13] But there were many who failed to recognise the subtleties of what Jackson has termed Parnell's 'popular militancy' and who thus did not see this speech as solely advocating moral pressure (Jackson, 1999: 117). Furthermore, Parnell criticised the Land Act of 1881, which had conceded significant rights to tenants, fearing that Gladstone's programme of 'justice for Ireland' could marginalise him and diminish the popularity of his own movement (Bew, 1991: 55). For similar reasons, he was suspicious of the attempts to criminalise the Land League, especially because, as he saw it, the League had tried to halt the spread of violence (O'Callaghan, 1994: 74). However, if Parnell had any worries on that score, his arrest, as well as the subsequent 'no rent manifesto',[14] put them to rest. The 'Kilmainham Treaty' of April 1882 saw Gladstone promise to end coercion in return for Parnell's release, and an end to popular disturbance. However, it also demonstrated Parnell's ability to influence the various elements of his coalition, including those who supported the land war more actively than he did. Four days after his release, the murder of the chief secretary and under-secretary for Ireland as they strolled through Phoenix Park drove the more militant nationalists underground. This also enabled Parnell to build on his political martyrdom in order to restructure his party and his movement as he saw fit. By the end of 1882, he was the 'uncrowned king of Ireland'.

Parnell used the suppression of the Land League as an excuse to establish the similarly organised Irish National League, primarily as an electoral vehicle for his party. This was dedicated to home rule rather than land reform and, although he did not regard the two issues as mutually exclusive, Parnell believed that progress would be made primarily by constitutional means by a disciplined, focused and properly funded parliamentary party, and not by MPs who either would be driven by personal interests or who would look over their shoulders at other organisations and pressures. However, Parnell did choose to accept the support of the Catholic bishops, most of whom were, like himself, socially conservative, and had mixed feelings on how to define and develop the home rule movement – now a mass movement after the electoral reform of 1885 almost quadrupled the electorate (Jackson, 2003: 48–9). Parnell thus managed to lead 86 Irish parliamentary party MPs into parliament in January 1886 – their base solidly in Ireland's Catholic constituencies – and to put Gladstone and his Liberals into power. The price of this support was Gladstone's open support for home rule, and the introduction of the first Home Rule Bill, eventually defeated in the House of Commons, in 1886. The Conservative response, and party leader Salisbury's parallel declaration of faith in the union, clearly parachuted the two general views on the Irish question into the formal policies of the two major parties in Parliament, thus bringing it into the mainstream of British politics, arguably for the first time. The persistence of Conservative government after 1886 did not alter this, although Parnell's hopes that Salisbury might inaugurate 'aristocratic home rule' and 'class conservative government in Ireland' (Jackson, 2003: 50) did suggest that his flirtation with Gladstone was not exclusive. The problem was that he could now become the victim, just as he had been the beneficiary, of being all things to all people.

The failure of the first Home Rule Bill and the collapse of Gladstone's government diminished the influence of the Irish parliamentary party within Westminster. These events also coincided with the renewal of violent agrarian protest and the introduction of further legislation directed against crime in Ireland (Crossman, 1996: 162–3). Leo XIII's Vatican had similar ideas to Salisbury's Westminster.[15] However, when in May 1888 the pope condemned a new collective action movement to force landlords to settle for a reduced level of rents (the 'plan of campaign'), Parnell's supporters in Ireland largely ignored the pope, as they did new papal diplomacy to conciliate Britain at the expense of the aspiration to Irish home rule. Despite Parnell's lack of enthusiasm for the 'plan of campaign', *The Times* tried to smear him with a charge that he had secretly encouraged agrarian violence in Ireland. Although Parnell was acquitted by a special commission, it was a pyrrhic victory for him; the other reality was that the charges had already damaged his movement by linking nationalism, crime and conspiracy:

> the constitutional achievement of the parliamentary party between 1882 and 1886 was effectively negated . . . By bringing every residual cattle hougher and informer to the same level as the parliamentary party, the sophisticated loose and undefined network that Parnell held together effectively collapsed. By recasting the debate [on home rule] in terms of defeating crime, which was, of course, synonymous with Parnellism, the vitality of the parliamentary party as a political force in Westminster was at an end . . . their [Irish parliamentary party] status as parliamentarians was treated as a manifest joke (O'Callaghan, 1994: 112, 119).

Cultural renewal, 1886–1900

The last years of the nineteenth century and the first years of the following century saw relatively few changes in the formal organisation of Irish politics. However, some significant qualitative changes were taking place. At this point, their political implications were largely unnoticed; they lay within the domain of culture, with sports and language issues to the fore. But these changes were to give a particularly acute character to later militant nationalism. Formal stability does not mean that the standing of the parliamentary party remained unchanged during this period. On the contrary, it had to confront major challenges. The split of 1890, ostensibly as a result of the mention of Parnell in a divorce suit, reflected the reality that the sum of the component parts of Parnell's movement no longer constituted a whole. Moreover, the history of the 20 years following his death in 1891 was to challenge once again the self-confidence of the main actors that they could promote their policies and aspirations effectively. Even after its reunification in 1900, the parliamentary party did not devote as much attention to agrarian and social concerns as Parnell had done. The various land acts that were passed between 1885 and 1909 effectively created the peasant proprietorship which had long been sought, and removed land as an issue of public agitation. In Britain, post-Gladstone Liberals began to backtrack on home rule and, with an eye to the rising Labour party, to promote social reform in Britain. As a result, the Irish parliamentary party became in the first instance a victim of its alliance with the Liberals (Jackson, 1999: 145), and in the second was compromised by the 'kindness' of Conservative reform. After 1900, this situation was not helped by John Redmond's personal reluctance to court popular affection, to address public meetings, or to heal the continuing and often acrimonious internal divisions of the Irish parliamentary party. However, the crucial card was the Land Act of 1903, of which John Dillon remarked that 'if . . . allowed to work,

there will be an end to the national movement before twelve months are over'
(Jackson, 1999: 153). While echoing Parnell's reaction to the Land Act of 1881,
Dillon's observation reflected the dilemma of a party which no longer had any
direct influence over government policy. What he did not recognise, however,
was that a new element would emerge within public protest in Ireland and
that this would reinvent old issues of public concern and pursue them in
a new way.

Against this background, the Gaelic Athletic Association (GAA) and the
Gaelic League, which were founded in 1884 and 1893 respectively, promoted
particular aspects of Irish culture. The former aimed to foster traditional Irish
games and the latter to revive and preserve the Irish language and to publish
its literature. These two organisations developed the romantic nationalism of
Young Ireland; in the words of Douglas Hyde, their agenda 'for de-anglicising
the Irish People . . . [was] the best claim which we have upon the world's
recognition of us as a *separate nationality*' (Grote, 1994: 19). They also
developed a vocabulary which drew on the symbols of the Gaelic past to
create a sense of cultural as well as geographical separation from Britain. The
GAA's ban on 'foreign games' which were, in the language of its patron, Dr
Thomas Croke, Catholic archbishop of Cashel (1875–1902), as 'alien . . . as
are, for the most part, the men and women who first imported and still
continue to patronise them', underlined the point (Boyce, 1992: 236). As the
two organisations grew, they helped to reinvigorate the more militant tradition
of Irish separatism, especially after 1900. However, what might have been
welcome for ideological reasons could prove troublesome in politics, especially if in this renewed world the agenda was being set by yet another cadre
of new leaders. Accordingly, many Catholic priests were worried about the
potential militancy of the two movements, and saw the evolution of a more
'Irish Ireland' as a rival to 'Catholic Ireland' (McCaffrey, 1968: 116), and as a
distraction from the wisdom of the pulpit. They need not have worried about
the Gaelic League, in which the Catholic clergy were prominently involved,
but the tensions between the traditions of Catholic and secular nationalism
were more marked within the GAA. From its establishment, the latter was
more obviously Anglophobic, and at least two of its seven founders, including
Joseph K. Bracken (father of Brendan, the later Conservative minister, and
close adviser to Winston Churchill), were members of the IRB; thereafter,
several other IRB activists joined, and many were elected as officers (de Búrca,
1980: 34; Murphy, 1985). The reality, as reflected in the police reports of the
time, was that the GAA was 'a political organisation of a particular caste, in
which athletics played only a minor role' (Mandle, 1977: 432).

Although Protestants and Unionists were members of the Gaelic League
during its earlier years, there were other and more agreeable places to express
their sense of identity. The Orange Order and the Protestant churches provided

such outlets, and although a mass Protestantism did not evolve to complement O'Connell's campaign, the evangelical revival of the 'second Reformation' of the pre-famine period had helped to sharpen a view that the 'blood-bought cherished rights' of Protestant Ireland were being 'imperilled by the audacious and savage outbursts of a Romish mob' (Miller, 1985: 379). The relationship between such domestic distinctions and a broader British culture remained unclear, and, in any event, it was defined in pragmatic terms rather than within those of a shared religion, history and kinship. However, in 1886, the reaction in Belfast to the first Home Rule Bill, when 30 were killed and over 400 were wounded, saw established Protestant leaders encourage their followers to channel their energies towards a more energetic defence of the Union and promote a sense of political organisation as well cultural connection. In this, Unionist leaders drew on the tactics of O'Connell, as Jackson suggests in chapter 7 of this volume. There are also parallels with Parnell, whom the Unionist leader Edward Saunderson echoed in 1885:

> at the present moment the political power had entirely drifted away from the class to which it belonged, and had been conveyed into the hands of the farmers and working men of the county . . . the industrial classes possessed the political power, but what they wanted was proper men to represent them (Jackson, 1995: 247)

Saunderson's task of re-establishing the new world of popular politics within the older regime of landed leadership was helped by his standing within the Church of Ireland and the upper echelons of the Orange Order. Moreover, although the relationship between the popular and parliamentary streams of Ulster unionism was not always comfortable, tensions were more class-based than the result of different constitutional outlooks. A renewed Orange Order attracted all classes to 'the cause of Ulster' and facilitated a certain sense of deference from popular elements towards the parliamentary leadership in the House of Commons. For most of his parliamentary career, Saunderson retained a special regard for Westminster. However, this was never absolute, and as home rule was repeatedly debated there, he began to justify 'active resistance' in Ulster, not only to home rule, but to the British connection itself (Jackson, 1995: 87–91, 116–17).

Conclusion

The tensions between the various strategies that have characterised recent political action are deeply embedded in the Irish past. Even before the union of 1800, the leaders of the politically excluded Catholic population were prepared to exploit constitutional methods in an effort to rectify their grievances. This tradition was developed by O'Connell in the early nineteenth century, with notable success during the period 1835–41, and also, with significant success, by Parnell and his successors from the 1880s onwards. But the major impact of these movements lay in the arena of social rather than constitutional grievance. Issues such as anti-Catholic discrimination, the poor laws, oppressive tithe payments, poor living conditions and agrarian insecurity were substantially addressed, and Irish parliamentarians could claim much of the credit for these reforms, even if on some of these issues they had not actively engaged. However, Ireland was even more firmly wedded to Britain at the end of the nineteenth century than it had been at the beginning.

An obvious response to the failure of constitutional nationalist leaders to win repeal of the union or even home rule was to argue for armed rebellion. Largest in scale was the 1798 rebellion, but the defeat of the rebels was so complete and brutal that the legacy of this period was ideological rather than organisational. Although Young Ireland in 1848 and the Fenians from 1867 onwards sought to revive this approach, their successes lay more in the creation and maintenance of an organisation that was to persist into the twentieth century than in any dramatic military victories. Concurrent with these organisations, local and more popular movements, normally with an agrarian motivation and sometimes with a sectarian flavour, made a particular impact on the Irish countryside. These movements sometimes brought political results, if only because the government wished to forestall further episodes of violence. In 1868 and 1869, for example, Gladstone silenced English opposition to disestablishment by representing it as a concession which was necessary to disarm the Irish sense of grievance that had been reflected in the rise of Fenianism. However, it was arguably the improbable marriage between militancy and parliamentarianism that brought the most fruitful outcome. The main offspring of this union was the phenomenon of peaceful (but not necessarily legal) civil protest. Governments yielded to pressures of these kinds in the 1820s, the 1830s and from the 1880s onwards, and far-seeing political leaders such as O'Connell and Parnell were content to go along with formal or unspoken alliances of these kinds.

On the unionist side, too, we can trace political violence back to old roots. Following the political polarisation of the 1880s, it was only a matter of time before unionism would be identified with Ulster, and that opposition to home rule would become associated not just with 'a people apart' but with 'a place apart'. However, the extent to which Ulster – and, indeed, Ireland as a whole – was ever part of a British paradigm is a continuing historiographical debate within which unionism has been discussed only peripherally (Pocock, 1975). E. P. Thompson is less interested in these issues than in the evolution of progress in terms of a 'moral economy' which might be related to the shifting structures of class and leadership (Thompson, 1971). The more successful of Ireland's parliamentary leaders recognised the pattern as well as the need to incorporate these changes, and those who espoused them, within the 'natural leadership' of contemporary Ireland, rather than have emerging new leaders 'invent a tradition' for themselves (Hobsbawm and Ranger, 1983). With the consolidation of the Catholic Church, 'natural leadership' itself became more vague, especially when it interacted with nationalist movements as part of exercising its new status. Deference to parliament and to the agencies of the state was also questioned and here, too, the relationship between the home-made solutions of popular protest and parliamentary procedures became increasingly grey. The main concern in this increasingly introspective world was what it had always been: who would 'speak for Ireland' at a time when, as W. B. Yeats observed, many were recognising 'the right of the individual mind to see the world in its own way, [and] to cherish the thoughts which separate men from one another . . . instead of those thoughts that had made man like another' (Kiberd, 1995: 161).

Chapter 3

The home rule crisis of 1912–14 and the failure of British democracy in Ireland

Ronan Fanning

Introduction

Although critics of the republican tradition indict militant nationalists for introducing the gun into Irish politics in 1916, the subversion of democracy in Ireland took root in 1912–14. It was Ulster Unionists and British Conservatives rather than Irish nationalists who first demonstrated how 'direct action' could paralyse the parliamentary process. The terms of the Parliament Act of 1911, which transformed the absolute veto of the House of Lords into a suspensive one, ironically had the effect of undermining the authority of the House of Commons by allowing the upper house to delay legislation for two years. By replacing a rarely used and constitutionally hazardous blunt instrument by a more deployable and politically safer surgical knife, it denied the government control of the parliamentary agenda, corroded parliamentary democracy by turning the 1912 and 1913 debates on the bill into a meaningless charade, and created a climate in which what happened in parliament was less important than what happened on the streets of Ulster. The Curragh crisis and the spate of gunrunning in 1914 reaffirmed the failure of parliamentary democracy and the primacy of extraparliamentary action. The conflict over the third Home Rule Bill of 1912–14, then, was Britain's Irish crisis. Never again did Ireland provoke such British passion, passion of an intensity that evoked the spectre of civil war. Never again is Ireland as important to Britain because it is never again so embedded in the fabric of British party politics.

Historians from the Irish nationalist tradition have found it difficult to reconcile an appreciation of the significance of the events which occurred between 1916 and 1921 for the future course of Irish history with an equal recognition of British indifference to what was then happening in Ireland. To many Irish nationalists it still seems almost incomprehensible that the

British government refused to attribute a significance to the events of 1916–21 comparable to the significance Asquith's government attached to the events of 1912–14. That the Great War engendered the collapse of party politics and utterly changed British attitudes is something of a commonplace. But the very scale of that climacteric has allowed historians to gloss over what should be another commonplace: that British parliamentary democracy first failed in Ireland not in 1916–21 but in 1912–14, and that the seeds encompassing the downfall of Ireland's democratic nationalists had taken root before the Great War began. The most honest and most eloquent acknowledgement of that failure comes not from any Irish nationalist historian but from Lord Blake – the doyen of historians of the British Conservative Party and biographer of party leader Bonar Law. The truth is, wrote Blake nearly 50 years ago,

> that Parliamentary democracy depends on certain conditions, which, because they have usually prevailed in England over the last two hundred and fifty years, tend to be taken by Englishmen for granted. In the last resort it depends upon a minority accepting majority decisions, and this acceptance in its turn depends upon the majority not taking decisions which the minority regards as genuinely intolerable. In England, the remarkable homogeneity of the population, the absence of violent disputes, the general agreement over the fundamentals of society, have made such conditions prevail. Minorities accept majority decisions, because they know that these decisions will not be insufferable and because they know that the majority of today will become the minority of tomorrow. As a result we have the swing of the electoral pendulum, the political neutrality of the Army and the Civil Service, the whole tradition of peaceful change which is England's greatest contribution to the science of government.
>
> But in Ireland these conditions did not apply. Ireland was – and is – a land of bitter, irreconcilable, racial and religious conflicts. The Protestant minority could never hope by any swing of the pendulum to become the majority. The two nations in Ireland were separated by the whole of their past history. They were divided by rivers of blood and bitterness. It was absurd to expect that the conventions which prevailed in placid England would be accepted by the Ulster Protestants with all this fear, suspicion and hatred in their hearts. For of all political disputes, nationalist disputes are the most bitter and recalcitrant. They are very seldom settled by peaceful means within the framework of a liberal constitution. On the contrary, they are usually resolved, as Bismarck observed, not by Parliamentary majorities but by blood and iron (Blake, 1955: 207–8).

The irony is that if one substitutes 'Catholic' for 'Protestant', Lord Blake's words serve as a prescient analysis of why the polity of Northern Ireland collapsed some 15 years after he wrote. Yet the Blake hypothesis offers a good starting-point for a re-examination of the larger significance of the home rule crisis: namely that, in 1912–14, 'it was absurd' to expect that the conventions of 'English' parliamentary democracy 'would be accepted by the Ulster Protestants' because Ireland 'was – and is – a land of bitter, irreconcilable, racial and religious conflict'. But before exploring this hypothesis, it is appropriate to recall the political events that provided the backdrop for this challenge to parliamentary democracy.

Gladstone's legacy

Bipartisanship had informed Britain's Irish policy since the enactment of the Act of Union of 1800 created the United Kingdom of Great Britain and Ireland. There were, of course, differences between Whigs and Tories, between Liberals and Conservatives, on Irish as on other policies. But consensus reigned on the core of the Irish issue: the immutability of that constitutional relationship between the two islands explicitly declared irrevocable and indissoluble under the terms of the Act of Union. All that changed when the leader of the Liberal Party, William Gladstone, introduced the first Irish Home Rule Bill in 1886; next morning he went to Westminster Abbey for the funeral service of 'Buckshot' Forster, his former Chief Secretary for Ireland – an occasion symbolic of the burial of the coercionary policies epitomised by the nickname of the deceased. Gladstone there remarked to Lord Rosebery, who was to succeed him as Liberal Prime Minister after the defeat of his second Home Rule Bill in 1893, that 'this Home Rule question will control and put aside all other political questions in England till it is settled' (Cooke and Vincent, 1974: 402). Gladstone's prophecy came to pass. In Ireland, the Union had been the great political divide even before Daniel O'Connell, the founding father of Irish constitutional nationalism, proposed its repeal to the House of Commons in 1834. But not until 1886 did the Union acquire the same status in British politics. Although home rule split Gladstone's party asunder when an alliance of Conservatives and Liberal Unionists threw out his 1886 bill on its second reading in the House of Commons, the next three decades saw the Irish question divide British political parties as it had not done before and as it has never done since. Until Gladstone broke the consensus, both great parties were unionist and neither, therefore, needed to be so described.

'Unionist' became a commonplace description of supporters of the Act of Union, in Britain and in Ireland, only after the Union was first imperilled in 1886. That the Tories swiftly rebaptised themselves 'the Conservative and Unionist Party' was a monument to its significance as the touchstone of party faith. It was also a monument to what they had gained and what the Liberals had lost by the abandonment of bipartisanship. Although Gladstone indelibly branded his party with the home rule stamp, many Liberals fled from the brand. The defection of Lord Hartington's Whig faction was unsurprising; they had already grown restive with Gladstone's leadership, particularly on Irish land reform. But the loss of the radical wing, led by the energetic and popular Joseph Chamberlain, was traumatic. Indeed it might be said, after Oscar Wilde, that to lose one wing of a party may be regarded as a misfortune, to lose both looks like carelessness.

Gladstone's messianic yearnings prompted him, moreover, to reject the Commons's verdict on home rule. Rather than resign, he dissolved parliament and carried his crusade to the people. Their decisive rejection of home rule in the 1886 election calcified the lines of the new party divide and ensured that the consequences would be cataclysmic. Only in 1914, when the Great War compelled Liberals and Conservatives alike to abandon partisan Irish policies in favour of the belated bipartisanship embodied in the coalition governments of 1915–22, was the shape of the great divide thrown up by the cataclysm of 1886 finally blurred.

The orange card

'I decided some time ago', Randolph Churchill wrote in mid-February 1886, 'that if the G[rand] O[ld] M[an] went for Home Rule, the Orange card would be the one to play. Please God it may turn out the ace of trumps and not the two' (Churchill, 1907: 474). The key to an understanding of how dramatically the 1886 crisis redirected the course of politics is to appreciate how prodigiously this Tory prayer was answered. In six of the seven general elections in the 30 years before 1886 the Liberals had won over 300 seats and formed the government. The Conservatives only once topped 300 seats in the same period, under Disraeli in 1874. After three of the four elections in the next 20 years (when it was the Conservatives who won at least 300 seats and formed the government) the number of Liberal MPs sank below 200 – an ignominy that had never befallen their opponents between 1857 and 1885. Even in 1892, when Gladstone formed his last government with the support of the Irish Parliamentary Party, the Liberals fell far short of 300 seats. The contrast wrought by 1886, painted in terms of the enjoyment of office, was correspondingly stark. The Liberals were in office for almost 20 of the 30 years before 1886 and they were out of office for all but three of the next 20 years.

Such, for the Liberals, were the stigmata of Gladstone's conversion. Such, for the Conservatives, were the blessings bestowed by the Orange card.

For the Conservatives, then, 1886 inaugurated those rare circumstances dear to all democratic politicians when the quest for electoral advantage dovetails with the celebration of party ideology. The Tory ideology, insofar as Tories had an ideology, was the ideology of empire. To urge the wisdom of cherishing imperial ties with more far-flung outposts of empire made little sense if Ireland (the country with which Britain had geographically the closest and historically the longest connection) broke the Union. 'On Tory principles', as Salisbury had written in 1872, 'the case presents much that is painful, but no perplexity whatever. Ireland must be kept, like India, at all hazards: by persuasion, if possible; if not, by force' (Curtis, 1963: 33).

The year 1886 also marked the birth of Ulster Unionism, albeit that its significance was obscured by the collapse of Gladstone's bill. Why? Because in 1886 Ulster Unionist implacability was redundant insofar as the defeat of the bill was so swiftly accomplished by the normal workings of the House of Commons. Gladstone's second Home Rule Bill, in 1893, was likewise defeated by conventional parliamentary procedures, this time in the House of Lords. In 1886 and 1893, concludes Alvin Jackson, the foremost historian of unionism,

> local agitation on behalf of the Union varied little from the types of pressure politics adopted in contemporary Britain: there was certainly much talk of an armed struggle, but no evidence has survived to suggest that such talk was ever seriously translated into action. Rather, the chief forum for Irish Unionist endeavour before 1911–12 was Britain and the British House of Commons (Jackson, 1989a: 322).

These circumstances created a conspiracy of silence about the fact that the ultimate fate of home rule would hinge on the demand of separate treatment for Unionist Ulster. All the major parties – Liberals and Conservatives, Irish Nationalists and Unionists – had a vested interest in preserving what was to become a 25-year silence. Silence suited the Liberals and Nationalists because it was the best climate for nourishing their always uneasy entente; they clung to the crutch of Ulster having returned 18 Nationalists as opposed to 17 Unionists in the 1885 election. Silence suited the Conservatives and Unionists because they wanted to defeat home rule not only for Ulster but for all of Ireland. So it was that the parliamentary defeat of both of Gladstone's home rule bills obscured a fundamental truth about the Irish question in British politics that became glaringly obvious in 1912–14: that it would be extraordinarily difficult – even, perhaps, impossible – to amend the Act of Union and devolve government to Ireland through the normal workings of parliamentary democracy.

By 1894 the consensus among Gladstone's cabinet colleagues was that he was no longer mentally or physically fit to continue in office and he formally resigned on 3 March 1894. The tragedy of Gladstone's Irish crusade was that it excited Irish nationalist appetites which neither he nor any other leader of a Liberal government could satisfy while at the same time turning a blind eye to

Ulster Unionist demands for separate treatment. The appointment of Lord Rosebery as his successor marked the end of the messianic phase of the Liberal Party's commitment to home rule.

Irish conflict and British prejudice

Rosebery was one of the earliest and most influential advocates of what Lord Blake described as the 'racial' dimension of British–Irish relations, and he laid bare the difference between his Irish policy and Gladstone's in his very first speech as Prime Minister in parliament when he endorsed Salisbury's statement

> that before Irish Home Rule is conceded by the Imperial Parliament, England as the predominant partner of the Three Kingdoms will have to be convinced of its justice and equity. That may seem to be a considerable adjustment to make, because . . . the majority of Members of Parliament elected from England proper are hostile to Home Rule (Blake, 1955: 337–8).

In other words, Irish, Scottish and Welsh votes should count for nothing when weighed in the democratic balance against English votes. Although Rosebery's doctrine may have been 'indiscreet' – he apologised for having 'blurted it out' (Ensor, 1936: 216; Morley, 1918, 11: 21) – it was not dishonest. He sought to turn back the clock and to recapture the bipartisan consensus on Ireland ruptured in 1886 and seemingly not re-established until the formation of the coalition governments of 1915 and 1916. Rosebery's 'predominant partner' thesis provided the ideological underpinning for that Liberal Imperialist retreat from Gladstonian home rule that characterised the Irish policies of the Liberal governments of 1906–14.

Asquith, Grey and Haldane were but three of the leading Liberal ministers in 1912–14 who had identified with Rosebery's Liberal Imperialism, although not with his aristocratic indifference to regaining office. 'Is it to be part of the policy and programme of our party that, if returned to power, it will introduce into the House of Commons a bill for Irish home rule', asked Asquith in a 1902 message to his constituents.

> The answer, in my judgement, is No. . . . Because the history of these years . . . has made it plain that the ends which we have always had, and still have, in view – the reconciliation of Ireland to the Empire and the relief of the Imperial Parliament (not as regards Ireland alone) from a load of unnecessary burdens – can only be attained by methods which will carry with them, step by step, the sanction and sympathy of British opinion (Jenkins, 1964: 132).

Relieved of dependence on the Irish Parliamentary Party by their overall majority in the 1906 election, the governments of 1906–10 could give full rein to the sentiments again voiced by Rosebery in October 1905 in a speech nicely calculated to tap the Nonconformist springs of anti-Catholicism which denounced 'any middle policy – that of placing home rule in the position of a reliquary, and only exhibiting it at great moments of public stress, as Roman Catholics are accustomed to exhibit relics of a saint' (James, 1963: 453–4).

Asquith's Liberal Imperialist instincts, his close ties with Grey, Haldane and Crewe, and his personal distaste for depending on the Irish, all contributed to his reluctance to co-operate with John Redmond, the leader of the Irish Parliamentary Party, after the first election of 1910. Asquith 'personally dislikes the Irish' wrote one minister's wife, in describing the 'anti-Irish prejudice' of his cabinet (Masterman, 1939: 159); Redmond 'hates Henry', fulminated Margot Asquith when the post-election crisis was at its height.[1]

The Tories' awareness of Asquith's contempt for his Irish allies was of long standing. It was evident, for example, in Arthur Balfour's reaction to George Bernard Shaw's *John Bull's other island* when it opened in London in 1904. The then Tory Prime Minister was so taken by the play that he saw it five times. On one occasion he brought Henry Campbell-Bannerman as his guest; on another he brought Henry Asquith. London audiences saw the play 'as a largely affectionate satire on the Liberal Party's attitude to Ireland, Balfour himself praised it for clearing away humbug at any cost'.[2] Who better to share Balfour's enjoyment at the character of Thomas Broadbent, Shaw's caricature of the well-meaning English Liberal in Ireland, than the two Liberal leaders who succeeded him in 10 Downing Street? That shared enjoyment nicely illustrates those unspoken prejudices about nationalist Ireland that privately united leading Liberals and Conservatives.

Opposition leaders were well informed about cabinet dissension on Ireland; this was due partly to information gleaned from friends at court (notably Lord Esher) and partly to ministerial indiscretion. Indeed it was as much a matter of indifference as indiscretion in a political culture that set small store on secrecy. Government and opposition frontbenchers mingled freely regardless of party affiliation, which was no barrier to friendship. Asquith's cabinet leaked like a sieve.

This point is fundamental to understanding Tory outrage about what they denounced as the corrupt bargain of 1910 between Asquith and Redmond. The Tory leaders knew that Asquith 'was probably one of the least enthusiastic Home Rulers in his party' (Ensor, 1936: 216), just as they knew of his personal dislike for Redmond and of ministerial repugnance at depending on the Irish. They knew that the government's commitment to home rule was, at most, lukewarm. They also knew that many Liberals shared the instinctive Anglo-Saxon aversion for all the works and pomps of Irish nationalism, especially in their Papist manifestations.

Let us move now from the racial to the religious dimension of the Blake hypothesis. 'I have always wished the Catholics in Ireland to govern themselves' wrote Lord Esher to Margot Asquith in April 1914.

> We have shown ourselves unfit to govern a community of Catholics; this, over centuries. But we are not half as unfit to govern Catholics as they are to govern the Protestant community. That is the whole ethical and political aspect of the situation (Esher, 1938: 165–6, 26 April 1914).

Although such anti-Catholic sentiments were but rarely committed to paper in the correspondence of the political elite, they coloured the mentality of government as well as opposition. Esher, as the King's liaison with ministers at moments of crisis would, moreover, scarcely have written in such terms to the Prime Minister's wife were he not satisfied that she was of like mind.

The Irish Parliamentary Party had inflamed the anti-Catholic susceptibilities of Liberal ministers by championing Catholic opposition in Britain to the Education Bill, embodying compulsory non-denominational teaching, which was thrown out by the House of Lords in December 1906. The plethora of thanks proffered John Redmond by English Catholics, including those of Francis Bourne, Cardinal Archbishop of Westminster, and the Duke of Norfolk (Gwynn, 1932: 130–2), fed the anti-Catholic sentiment found 'in any gathering of elderly English gentlemen', identified by Cooke and Vincent (1974: 66–7) as more characteristic of the Liberals than of the Conservatives. This was intensified by the 1907 papal decree *Ne temere*, enforcing Catholic upbringing of the children of marriages between Catholics and Protestants.

The depth of Asquith's anti-Catholicism was revealed only months after he became Prime Minister by his reaction to the Eucharistic Congress, held in London in September 1908. It attracted little attention until the announcement of a Eucharistic procession in the streets around Westminster Cathedral, planned for Sunday 13 September, roused certain Protestant societies to obtain counsel's opinion that carrying the host and wearing vestments in the streets was illegal under the 1829 Catholic Emancipation Act. An incensed King Edward bombarded his Prime Minister with telegrams to intervene but the Home Secretary, Herbert Gladstone, mindful of similar if smaller processions that had taken place without official interference in 1898 and 1901, declined to act. Asquith turned instead to the only Catholic in his cabinet, a humiliated Lord Ripon, whom he persuaded to make a last-minute appeal to the Cardinal Archbishop to abandon the ceremonial elements of the procession. Cardinal Bourne agreed, but only after he was authorised to say publicly that he was acting at the Prime Minister's behest (Jenkins, 1964: 189–93).[3]

The blandness of the prime ministerial telegraphic request revealed none of the venom of Asquith's private reaction. 'Such a procession appears to be clearly illegal', he had fumed to Lord Crewe, then bearing the brunt of royal wrath in a house party with the King; 'and there is a good deal of quite respectable Protestant sentiment which is offended by this gang of foreign Cardinals taking advantage of our hospitality to parade their idolatries through the streets of London: a thing without precedent since the days of Bloody Mary'.[4]

Asquith was again bland but unrelenting when asked in the Commons by William Redmond and Lord Edmund Talbot on 14 October whether he would introduce a bill repealing Catholic disabilities, saying only that his government 'cannot give facilities to any measure which is not of a wholly non-controversial character'.[5] He was also unrelenting when his Home Secretary, Herbert Gladstone, resisted ferocious royal pressure to resign and refused Asquith's first offer of a sinecure; but, a year later, Gladstone was exiled to South Africa as the first Governor-General – an apposite reminder that there was no place at Westminster for Gladstonian sentiment in the age of Asquith.

The anti-Catholicism of Lloyd George and Winston Churchill (apart from Asquith, the most important Liberal ministers in the home rule crises of 1912–14 and 1919–20) was more explicit, at least in private. In 1886, Lloyd George, according to Kenneth Morgan, had been 'one of that minority in the Welsh Liberal ranks who opposed Irish home rule, in large part on religious grounds' (Morgan, 1989: 84–6). John Grigg suggests that Lloyd George 'saw no good reason why what was good enough for Wales should not be good enough for Ireland' (Grigg, 1978: 109–10). Indeed Lloyd George argued that 'the case for national recognition was stronger for Wales', because its language and culture were 'more vigorous', because its industrial base prevented mass emigration, and, above all, because 'Wales had no Ulster'. That the few Irish migrants in Wales 'were regarded as virtual outcasts, socially isolated, technically unskilled and, of course, Papists in one of the most vehemently Protestant societies in Europe' was also significant. Lloyd George, in short, had no time for Papists: 'while not a religious man at all in the conventional sense – he veered between a deistic worship of nature and a stern rationalism worthy of his Unitarian father – he once told a Welsh friend, "I hate a priest, Daniel, whenever I find him"' (Morgan, 1973: 7). Churchill's hostility to Catholicism – unlike Lloyd George's – derived from his imperialist instincts. 'I know that . . . superstitious faith in nations rarely promotes their industry', he wrote from India in 1899:

> that, in a phrase, Catholicism – all religions, if you like, but particularly Catholicism – is a delicious narcotic. It may soothe our pains and chase our worries, but it checks our growth and saps our strength. And since the improvement of the British breed is my political aim in life, I would not permit too great

indulgence if I could prevent it without assailing another great principle – Liberty (Churchill, 1966: xxvii).

'The Catholic Church has ruined every country in wh[ich] it has been supreme & worked the downfall of every dynasty that ruled in its name', he scribbled in similar vein to his wife after the exiled King of Portugal had told him of his hopes to regain his throne with the help of his church.[6]

Home rule and Ulster unionism

Such anti-Catholic sentiments informed Liberal resentment when the results of the two elections of 1910 again reduced them to dependence on the Irish Party for their parliamentary majority, a resentment reflected in John Redmond's exclusion from the constitutional conference of 1910. 'The settlement of the Irish question would come up for consideration', pointed out Lloyd George in his revolutionary secret memorandum of 17 August 1910 proposing a coalition of the two major parties. 'The advantages of a non-party treatment of this vexed subject are obvious. Parties might deal with it without being subject to the embarrassing dictation of extreme partisans, whether from Nationalists or Orangemen'.[7] Asquith 'showed no resentment' at Lloyd George's initiative, 'although he was sceptical about the result it might produce', but then no one stood to gain more than the Prime Minister by the removal of the Irish issue from the arena of party conflict – especially after Lloyd George and Churchill had won over Edward Grey (Robbins, 1971: 219). It was, in Roy Jenkins's phrase, 'Balfour's caution and not Asquith's scepticism which wrecked the plan' (Jenkins, 1964: 216–17). The Tories refused to relinquish the electoral advantages of the orange card and the party leaders were forced back into the lists as the respective champions of the orange and the green. But where Asquith remained home rule's reluctant champion, Balfour and, still more, Bonar Law revelled in their orange armour.

Bipartisanship also found expression in the efforts of Lloyd George and Churchill to exclude Ulster from the first draft of the third Home Rule Bill. Their apprehensions about Ulster Unionist resistance must be placed in the context of a remarkable letter which the Chief Secretary for Ireland, Augustine Birrell, wrote to Churchill in August 1911 (and asked him to show Lloyd George); all three were members of the cabinet committee established in January 1911 to draft the bill (Jalland, 1976: 435). 'Personally, I had no more difficulty in comprehending the furious passion of the Protestants of Antrim and Down at the bare thought of being put under the heel of a predominantly Catholic Parliament in Dublin, than I had in understanding the equal passion of the rest of Ireland to stand up for themselves in the face of the world', wrote Birrell.

Great ferment and perturbation of spirit exists – mainly fed among the poor folk
by hatred of Roman Catholicism and amongst the better to do by the belief that
under a Home Rule regime Ireland will become a miserable, one-horsed, poverty
stricken, priest ridden, corrupt oligarchy. . . . Were the question referred to Ulster
county by county, it is probable that all Ulster save Antrim and Down would by
a majority support Home Rule and it might then be suggested and agreed to that
for the transitional period, say five years, Antrim and Down might stand out and
that at the end of that time there should be a fresh referendum to settle their fate.
If this was done, there could be no Civil War.[8]

The significance of the minister with cabinet responsibility for Irish policy
anticipating civil war unless at least part of Ulster was excluded, more than
seven months before the Home Rule Bill was introduced, can scarcely be
exaggerated. But equally significant was the yawning gulf between Birrell's
private fears and his self-appointed role as the Irish Party's cabinet spokes-
man. 'I had seen my own policy clearly from the first', he later explained in his
autobiography. 'It was to pave the way for Home Rule (on more or less
Gladstonian lines), and to do all that in me lay to make any other solution of
the problem *impossible*' (Jalland, 1980: 58–9). In other words, the political
expediency of keeping the Irish Party sweet demanded that Birrell conceal his
conviction that the exclusion of Ulster was imperative. So it was that the proceedings of the cabinet committee on Ireland dragged aimlessly on throughout
1911, so aimlessly that two successive drafts of the new bill, dated June and
August 1911, included schedules which failed to take account of Queen
Victoria's death! The cabinet's vacillation was more blatantly advertised by
the admission (in a confidential cabinet memorandum dated 29 January 1912,
twelve months after it set up its Irish committee; see Jalland, 1980: 435–6) that
it 'was not the result of serious consideration, but had been hurriedly thrown
together, and was not to be regarded as expressing the settled view of the
Cabinet'. Next day Lloyd George told two Liberal colleagues 'that Home
Rule could not be imposed upon Ulster by force and that if possible the
Protestant counties in Ulster should be exempted'.[9] Backed by Churchill, he
formally proposed Ulster's exclusion at a cabinet meeting on 6 February 1912.
The substance of their proposal was 'that every county should be given the
option of "contracting out" – really to apply to Ulster, but nominally for
every part', and they were backed by Haldane, Charles Hobhouse and –
according to Hobhouse – initially by Asquith (Jalland, 1980: 64–5).[10]

But Birrell objected, and the consequences of his refusing to support
Lloyd George and Churchill on the exclusion of Ulster – notwithstanding his
telling them privately of the need for exclusion to avoid civil war six months
before – were enduring. The cabinet did not again discuss Ulster exclusion
until 31 December 1912, and never after that until mid-October 1913.

Asquith reported next day (7 February 1912) to the King on the most significant cabinet discussion of Irish policy since 1886:

> . . . the Cabinet acquiesced in the conclusions . . .
>
> (a) that the Bill as introduced should apply to the whole of Ireland;
>
> (b) that the Irish leaders should from the first be given clearly to understand that the Government held themselves free to make such changes in the Bill as fresh evidence of facts, or the pressure of British opinion, may render expedient;
>
> (c) that if, in the light of such evidence or indication of public opinion, it becomes clear as the Bill proceeds that some special treatment must be provided for the Ulster counties, the Government will be ready to recognise the necessity either by amendment of the Bill, or by not pressing it on under the provisions of the Parliament Act. In the meantime, careful and confidential inquiry is to be made as to the real extent and character of the Ulster resistance (Jenkins, 1964: 276–7; Jalland, 1980: 63–4).

The cabinet would have been better informed if the 'careful and confidential inquiry . . . as to the real extent and character of the Ulster resistance' had been prosecuted before they met. In the event the inquiry was stillborn – largely due to Birrell's hostility, which dated back to August 1911 when he had refused Churchill's offer, in his capacity as Home Secretary, of 'his secret service machinery'. Although Birrell circulated to the cabinet 'conflicting and inadequate' reports on probable resistance to home rule and on drilling in Ulster (the Unionists were drilling in all Ulster counties except Donegal and Monaghan) on 14 and 28 February respectively, his senior officials at Dublin Castle disputed that 'platform speeches will materialise into deliberate and armed resistance to authority' (Jalland, 1980: 73–5). Neither the Royal Irish Constabulary (RIC) nor any other police or intelligence agency ever attempted 'to make a systematic appraisal of the opposition's strength, let alone to spy on or to penetrate its leadership'. Dublin Castle's determination to turn a blind eye to the Unionist threat to democracy has been persuasively explained by Eunan O'Halpin:

> no one in Irish government had anticipated that the forces of law and order would ever be in conflict with the Ulster Unionist establishment. . . . their attentions were normally confined to nationalist organisations and to the rougher elements of Protestant Ulster. The leadership of the Ulster opposition to the Home Rule Bill came from the professional and propertied classes who were normally the closest allies of the police and with whom many senior RIC officers mixed socially (O'Halpin, 1987: 101).

Nearly two years elapsed before Birrell began circulating statistics on 'the escalation in the importation of arms and ammunition' in November 1913 and he only did so then in response to ministerial complaints 'about the inadequacy of cabinet information on the "goings-on" in Ulster' (Jalland, 1980: 137).

Although Birrell may be blamed for defects in the cabinet's Irish intelligence, ultimate responsibility for Irish policy rested, as always, not in the Irish Office but in Downing Street. Yet again a Liberal government had decided nothing. Instead they had merely acquiesced (Asquith's own word) in the institutionalisation of the policy of 'wait and see'. For what were they waiting? To see 'fresh evidence' or 'indication of public opinion . . . that some special treatment must be provided for the Ulster counties'. It was tantamount to a tacit invitation to rebellion: the more seditious the Ulster Unionists became, the more persuasive the 'fresh evidence' and the more strident the 'public opinion' urging that they receive special treatment. The primary responsibility rested with the Prime Minister, who favoured exclusion but could not or would not decide on the timing or the manner of its implementation. 'I have always thought (and said) that, in the end, we should probably have to make some sort of bargain about Ulster as the price of Home Rule', he reminded Churchill – the most persistent cabinet advocate of Ulster's exclusion – in September 1913. 'But I have never doubted, that, as a matter of tactics and policy, we were right to launch our Bill on its present lines'.[11]

Home rule and Irish nationalism

In the meantime, the unique terms of the Parliament Act of 1911 continued to legitimise ministerial lethargy. Some days before the parliament of 1911–18 first met, Augustine Birrell remarked privately that 'it was almost inconceivable to him that Home Rule sh[oul]d be got through without another dissolution, that people did not realise what a "prickly hedge" was set up by the Parliament Bill with its two years delay and necessity for tripple [*sic*] passage of a Bill *substantially unaltered*'.[12] Historians have underestimated this aspect of the Parliament Act, because both its supporters and opponents preferred to ignore it. After the titanic constitutional conflict of 1910–11, ministers had a vested interest in protecting the currency of their victory against devaluation. This compounded the perennial tendency of legislators to exaggerate the benefits of their legislation which, in this instance, assumed particular significance because of the government's dependence on the Irish Party.

The blithe assumption that the Parliament Act smoothed the way for the passage of home rule cemented the Liberal–Irish alliance. Neither ally saw profit in dwelling on the unique features of the Act that corroded the cement.

The most corrosive and paradoxical feature was that, while it removed the largest obstruction to the resurrection of home rule, it effectively postponed the day of resurrection for at least three years. Although it destroyed the Lords' permanent veto, it legitimised their new, two-year veto. What this meant in practice was that, although a Home Rule Bill could be *introduced* in 1912, it could not be *enacted* before the high summer of 1914. Parliamentary politics were more than ever reduced to the level of charades since all the leading actors understood that, under the new rules, their performances could have no legislative effect in 1912 or in 1913. That the Home Rule Bill could not be enacted before 1914 not only diminished the authority of ministers in parliament but effectively surrendered interim control of the political agenda to the Ulster Unionists. That the Parliament Act also reduced the life of parliaments from seven to five years gave Unionists an added incentive to play the orange card in order to force an early general election.

The impact upon the conduct and the prestige of parliament was as devastating as the three-year window of opportunity to plot and to plan that was offered to the extra-parliamentary opponents of home rule was inviting. The Craigavon demonstration of 23 September 1911, when Carson addressed 50,000 representatives of Orange lodges and Unionist clubs from all over Ulster, was but the first example of their appetite for sedition. Although, in the words of Alvin Jackson, 'there can be no doubt . . . that the groundwork for civil war was being laid in the winter of 1910–11, with the first attempts at arming and drilling', the Craigavon rally was the moment when 'the movement for weapons was made public: even the menu cards at Craig's luncheon party on this occasion bore an illustration of crossed rifles and the motto – "The Arming of Ulster"' (Jackson, 1989a: 318–19).

Asquith had sedulously avoided discussing the Irish crisis with the King, but he was finally constrained to do so in a memorandum in September 1913 – just as Lord Loreburn's letter to *The Times* (calling for a conference 'to consider proposals for accommodation') dealt 'a staggering blow' to the Irish Party [13] because, as Birrell acknowledged, 'everyone thought it originated from the Cabinet' (Hobhouse, 1977: 147, 17 Oct. 1913). Asquith admitted to the King that, if the Home Rule Bill became law,

> there will undoubtedly be a serious danger of organised disorder in the four north-eastern counties of Ulster.
>
> . . . the genuine apprehensions of a large majority of the Protestants, the incitements of responsible leaders, and the hopes of British sympathy and support, are likely to encourage forcible resistance (wherever it can be tried); there is the certainty of tumult and riot, and more than the possibility of bloodshed.
>
> On the other hand, if the Bill is rejected or indefinitely postponed, or some inadequate and disappointing substitute put forward in its place, the prospect is,

in my opinion, much more grave. The attainment of Home Rule has for more than 30 years been the political (as distinguished from the agrarian) ideal of the Irish people. Whatever happens in other parts of the United Kingdom, at successive general elections, the Irish representation in Parliament never varies. . . . It is the confident expectation of the vast bulk of the Irish people that it will become law next year.

If the ship, after so many stormy voyages, were now to be wrecked in sight of port, it is difficult to overrate the shock, or its consequences. They would extend into every department of political, social, agrarian and domestic life. It is not too much to say that Ireland would become ungovernable – unless by the application of forces and methods which would offend the conscience of Great Britain, and arouse the deepest resentment in all the self-governing Dominions of the Crown.[14]

Asquith offered no solution, but his prediction was chillingly prophetic: nationalist Ireland took precisely this path between 1916 and 1921.

In December 1913 the government was finally spurred into action against gunrunning, not by the fact that the Unionists had armed but by the fear that the Nationalists might arm. The cabinet could persuade themselves that their decision to proclaim arms traffic was 'in the interests of *all* Ireland', but the contrast between their reaction to the reality of Unionist sedition and the prospect of Nationalist sedition was stark indeed. The Ulster Volunteers had been drilling and arming for over a year but the royal proclamation of 4 December 1913 prohibiting importation into Ireland of arms and ammunition was issued only days after the first Irish Volunteers were enrolled. Irish Nationalists, outraged at such blatant discrimination, would have been still more incensed had they known – as Redmond knew – that the government decision was made on the very day that the Irish Volunteers were inaugurated. To Redmond and his party the new development 'was a nightmare' and the government's reaction 'one of the many irretrievable blunders which were in the next few years to shake the constitutional movement to its foundations' (Gwynn, 1932: 245–6).[15] There followed the Curragh mutiny. 'No single officer or man in Ireland, or elsewhere, disobeyed a single order', the then Secretary of State for War later proclaimed about the events of March 1914. 'Harm had been done. But disaster had been averted' (Mottistone, 1930: 170). But at what cost to Irish nationalist perceptions of democracy was the fig leaf of military discipline held in place? The reality was that the government found itself in a position where it had to abandon its Irish policy and issue no military orders which Army officers might deem politically unacceptable.

'Strictly there was no mutiny', wrote R. C. K. Ensor in his magisterial volume of the *Oxford history of England* published more than 50 years ago, for the officers concerned disobeyed no order; they were offered an option to take a certain course, and took it. Yet if it be mutiny to conspire to paralyse from within the disciplined action of an army, unquestionably there was such a conspiracy, although the actual officers at the Curragh were not its authors. . . .

Asquith executed the heroic gesture of becoming war minister himself. His followers supposed that this betokened a drastic policy, such as only a prime minister could put through; in fact, it heralded a policy of surrender, such as only a prime minister could put over (Ensor, 1936: 478, n. 2, 479).

Conclusion

But let this chapter end as it began: with Lord Blake, who has written how, by 1914, 'the British Constitution and the conventions upon which it depends were strained to the uttermost limit; and, paradoxically, it was the outbreak of the First World War which, although it imperilled Britain's very existence, probably alone saved Britain's institutions from disaster' (Blake, 1955: 121).

That paradox explains the otherwise inexplicable sense of elation evoked in Asquith and his cabinet colleagues by the coming of war. 'The most dangerous situation of the last 40 years', mused Asquith on 26 July, 'may have incidentally the good effect of throwing into the background the lurid pictures of "civil war" in Ulster'. 'What you say a propos of the War cutting off one's head to get rid of a headache is very good', he enthused to Venetia Stanley; 'Winston on the other hand is all for this way of escape from Irish troubles, and when things looked rather better last night, he exclaimed moodily that it looked after all as if we were in for a "bloody peace!"' (Asquith, 1982: 126, 129). 'The one bright spot in this hateful war', remarked the Prime Minister to a cabinet colleague on 3 August, 'was the settlement of Irish civil strife. . . . God moves in mysterious ways his wonders to perform' (Asquith, 1982: 111; Jalland, 1980: 259). On St Patrick's Day 1915, when the deluded Redmond brought him 'bunches of shamrock', Asquith reflected on the first anniversary of 'that dismal Curragh business . . . now it is all dead and securely buried as Queen Anne'; a week earlier he had described his career to Venetia Stanley as 'almost a classical example of Luck. . . . above all (at a most critical and fateful moment . . .) in the sudden outburst of the Great War' (Asquith, 1982: 485, 471).

The essence of the compromise that shelved the Irish problem for the duration of the war was that Redmond agreed to the suspension of home rule in return for Asquith's agreeing to the suspension of partition as embodied in the government's proposed amending bill. On 18 September 1914 the third Home Rule Bill, accompanied by the Suspensory Bill, went through all its stages in the Commons 'on oiled castors in about 7 minutes' – I feel as if a great weight were off my chest', wrote Asquith (Asquith, 1982: 240, 15 Sept. 1914). The Suspensory Act provided that the Home Rule Act would not come into effect until an indefinite date 'not being later than the end of the present war'. It was also accompanied by an explicit assurance from Asquith to the Unionists that 'the employment of force, any kind of force, for . . . the coercion of Ulster, is an absolutely unthinkable thing . . . a thing which we would never countenance or consent to' (Mansergh, 1991: 85). The announcement of the Royal Assent to what was now the Government of Ireland Act, 1914, was greeted with wild enthusiasm in the Commons by Liberals and Nationalists and by the embittered absence of the Unionists who had walked out of the House *en bloc*. Unionist bitterness was as misplaced as nationalist enthusiasm, for the achievement of home rule was illusory.

For the Ulster Unionists, the Suspensory Act disguised what was in reality a victory. By the summer of 1914 ministers had gone too far down the path of partition to reverse their tracks. Lloyd George and Churchill had been committed to the exclusion of Ulster since February 1912, Grey since the summer of 1912; Asquith and the Liberal cabinet as a whole were publicly and irrevocably committed to partition once Asquith offered the exclusion of the six north-eastern counties of Ulster in the House of Commons on 9 March 1914.[16] The Suspensory Act disguised but did not reverse this commitment to the principle of partition. But Lord Blake's Bismarckian dictum that nationalist disputes are more usually resolved by blood and iron than by parliamentary majorities was not lost on those Irish nationalists who had already lost their faith in parliamentary democracy. The numbers of Irish Volunteers increased dramatically: from under 2,000 at the end of 1913 to 160,000 by July 1914 and, notwithstanding the split precipitated by the war, the instrument which enabled the revolutionary nationalists to oust democratic nationalists in Ireland after 1916 was already to hand.

Chapter 4

Republicanism in the revolutionary decade: the triumph and containment of militarism, 1913–23

Michael Laffan

Introduction

In the first quarter of the twentieth century Irish nationalists grew accustomed to being ignored, and they were forced to watch in frustration as their views were treated with polite or offensive indifference. British governments started the pattern of disregarding the views held by most Irish nationalists, and it was continued by Irish republicans or militarists. For several decades the democratic wishes of a large majority of the Irish people were either neglected or rejected by British parties and parliaments. No sooner did the Parliament Act of 1911 seem likely to provide a remedy for Irish demands than the forces of the British 'establishment' combined to challenge them in a new and undemocratic, even revolutionary manner.

In some respects the conduct of Irish republicans was strangely similar, and the years which spanned the First World War revealed some improbable parallels between British reactionaries and Irish revolutionaries. What had seemed to be virtually a 'predestined' moderate constitutional development, the creation of a subordinate, devolved parliament and government in Dublin, was thwarted by the actions of rival groups of extremists. One of these fed off the opportunities provided by the other; British Conservatives and Ulster unionists took the initiative, and Irish republican revolutionaries followed their example.

There was no 'pre-revolutionary situation' in Ireland during the First World War, and yet the actions of a small minority forced most nationalists to confront and then respond to a military insurrection which was carried out in their name. This rebellion was followed by a guerrilla war in the course of which, once again, the people were compelled to take sides in a conflict which few of them had sought. Moderate views were stifled in these struggles between rival extremes, between British soldiers and Irish rebels. Eventually most nationalists were radicalised, and they came to support policies which they would earlier have regarded as utopian. They were also marginalised by a self-appointed elite which distrusted the masses. Moderate politicians whose party and policies had dominated Irish public life for decades were swept aside, and new leaders whom the British denounced as 'gunmen' became the heroes of Irish nationalism. Their violence extracted concessions of the sort which could not have been secured by votes, speeches and negotiations. Nonetheless, the principle of majority rule triumphed in an indirect and improbable manner in the closing stages of the Irish revolution, and the majority was able to repudiate and to crush those extremists who continued to defy its wishes.

Despite the many failures of British-style democracy in Ireland, however, the Irish people had become thoroughly 'constitutionalised' long before the revolution began; the process went back as far as Daniel O'Connell's campaigns of the 1820s and 1840s. In consequence politicians as well as soldiers played a leading role in achieving independence for most of the island in 1922, and ultimately political methods and values triumphed over those elements who refused to abandon violence. If the Irish revolution went through a Jacobin phase in 1919–21, this was followed by a Thermidorian reaction in 1921–3. The methods used by those who defeated the uncompromising republicans may at times have been bloody, but their motives and the consequences of their actions ensured that Ireland experienced a 'democratic Thermidor'. A large majority of the people supported those soldiers who crushed – sometimes brutally – other soldiers who continued to defy the will of the majority; a decade of militarism and violence was followed by the consolidation of a stable, peaceful democracy.

The assaults on moderate nationalism

Ever since the mid-1880s, the great majority of Irish nationalists had voted massively and consistently for Home Rule, for a degree of devolution within the United Kingdom. They struck an enduring alliance with the Liberal Party, and on two separate occasions they held the balance of power in parliament. Much good it did them. Even after the House of Commons had voted in favour of home rule in 1893 the bill was thrown out by the Lords. Half-measures such as the Conservative proposals for devolution in 1904 were defeated by die-hard unionists.

When the Liberals returned to power in 1905 they did little to satisfy their Irish allies – although since home rule would undoubtedly have been vetoed by the upper house, there appeared to be little that they could do. And yet it was the House of Lords, an implacable enemy of Irish nationalism, which broke the deadlock; its rejection of the 'People's Budget' in 1909 precipitated a constitutional crisis, a struggle between the two houses of parliament, and two general elections in rapid succession. To the great joy of Irish nationalists these elections created a political balance which they could and did exploit. Only when the Liberals were once more dependent for office on Irish nationalist votes did they attempt to placate the Home Rule Party – although they did so with the utmost reluctance and distaste (Fanning, 1979: 281–91).

Winston Churchill might claim that the new, third Home Rule Bill was moderate and popular – 'never before has so little been asked and never before had so many people asked for it'[1] – and it was endorsed by more radical nationalists such as P. H. Pearse who saw it as a useful step towards a more distant goal (Edwards, 1977: 155, 159). But despite its modest nature the bill encountered ferocious opposition in both Ireland and Britain. Ulster unionists were determined to prevent any change to their status, and with the full support of the Conservative Party they threatened rebellion against the crown, formed a private army, and smuggled German guns into Ireland. Opposition to Irish nationalism reached an obsessive, almost fanatical level in some Conservative and unionist circles, and by 1914 there were widespread fears of civil war. Bonar Law, the opposition leader, was even prepared to risk the demobilisation of the whole British army in his efforts to undermine the government's authority and to block its measures. Asquith viewed the outbreak of the conflict with Germany as the most remarkable example of the good luck which had characterised his political career (Jenkins, 1964: 335). In the words of one historian, a small consolation for the horrors of the First World War was that 'England was at least spared a convulsion calculated to wreck the very foundations of her parliamentary system' (Blake, 1955: 218) – a point that emerges clearly in chapter 3.

In such circumstances, where the will of the Irish majority had been ignored for so long and where their enemies had resorted to military measures of the sort which they themselves had been urged to renounce, it is remarkable that so many Irish voters persevered with democratic procedures. Perhaps this can be explained by a fatalistic acceptance on the part of most nationalists that there was no alternative, and that other measures – such as violence – would be even more futile.

In important respects, British democracy failed the Irish electorate by ignoring its moderate demands for many decades. But in another sense, Irish democracy was no more than theoretical; the consensus for home rule (or against it, in the unionist-dominated north-east) was so thorough that parliamentary seats were rarely contested. Nationalist Ireland was a one-party nation, and to a lesser extent so were large areas of unionist Ulster. Only in a few evenly balanced and closely contested elections did seats change hands. In a two-year period in 1913–15, for example, eleven out of twelve candidates in Irish by-elections were returned unopposed (Walker, 1978: 183).

In these circumstances the contempt which the small number of militant republicans felt for democracy and majority opinion was perhaps understandable. They believed that parliamentarianism was a sham, and that – as Arthur Griffith argued – in the last resort British MPs would out-vote the Irish by six or seven to one (this duly happened during the conscription crisis in 1918). Radicals were determined to wait for a favourable opportunity, and they would then follow the example of the American colonists; they would fight for liberty. In Ernest Blythe's bloodthirsty words, 'the way to freedom is a sword-track through our enemies . . . let us train . . . our minds to the thought of war, that we may not shrink from slaughter . . . for to-morrow, or the next day, our opportunity will come'.[2] This seemed to be a logical conclusion – even though, in the past, violence had failed even more spectacularly than peaceful measures had done. Those who held such views knew that British governments, having for so long rejected the mild demand for home rule, would not concede full Irish independence unless the cost of denying it became unbearably high.

But for decades the world did not move along the lines which the revolutionaries had hoped for and predicted. Republicans assumed that sustained British oppression and coercion would provoke the Irish people into sustained and successful rebellion. This failed to happen, and from the 1880s onwards the land acts implemented a social revolution, thereby defusing the potential for any mass rising. Even moderate nationalists like John Dillon were wary of these reforms, and he warned that 'the land trouble is a weapon in nationalist hands, and that to settle it finally would be to risk Home Rule, which otherwise *must* come' (Lyons, 1968: 233). They feared that British kindness *might* work, and that Irish anger might be appeased. P. S. O'Hegarty, a member of the revolutionary Irish Republican Brotherhood (IRB), later complained that 'the bulk of the people were apathetic, and over the land hung the miasma of contentment' (O'Hegarty, 1952: 609). In 1911 the IRB newspaper *Irish Freedom* lamented that 'the Irish sense of national feeling has been largely dulled by so many years . . . of Unions of Hearts, of Conciliation, of all the other rottennesses that fester in the Irish body politic'.[3] The people's demands for a degree of self-government continued to be ignored, but as in other areas they had been partially bought off. Despite the widespread frustration and disappointment that there was still no Dublin parliament and government, Irish nationalists were in most respects more contented than ever before; above all, they were more prosperous and more mildly ruled.

A series of accidents enabled republicans to reverse this trend, to radicalise and militarise Irish society – in conjunction with and under the inspiration of their deadly enemies. The broad outlines are familiar, and they need not be discussed in detail here.

The Ulster unionists' resort to arms made possible the formation of a rival paramilitary force, the Irish Volunteers, and from its inception this body was infiltrated and manipulated by elements within the IRB. A series of provocations to Irish nationalists soon followed. The importation of arms into Ireland remained legal when only unionists might benefit, and was banned when a nationalist political army might receive them. It seemed as if different rules or principles were applied to the two Irish factions. The Curragh incident (or 'mutiny') seemed to indicate that large sections of the British army could not be relied upon to obey the government if it acted to prevent or to suppress a rebellion in Ulster. Soon afterwards the Larne gunrunning ensured that, in such an event, the unionist insurgents would be relatively well armed. And when a group of nationalists followed this example, on a much smaller scale, the aftermath of their Howth gunrunning included the shooting by British soldiers of civilians at Bachelor's Walk in Dublin. Irish nationalists were outraged. Throughout 1914 they joined in large numbers a political army which was regarded with deep suspicion and distaste by the established Irish political leaders. The IRB was no longer marginalised; for the first time since the land war 35 years earlier it had become, even if surreptitiously, a part of mainstream nationalism.

These were the first of a long series of what turned out to have been lucky breaks for the revolutionary minority. The Home Rule leader John Redmond retained the loyalty of the vast majority of Irish Volunteers when the movement split in September 1914, but the nature and duration of the First World War, combined with the unsympathetic treatment of Irish nationalists by the War Office, made him and his policies ever more unpopular at home. His support of the war effort – a policy which had appeared sensible to many nationalists at a time when the Home Rule Bill was at last about to be enacted – soon became an albatross hanging around the party's neck.

This pattern was consolidated by the Easter Rising. A small group of revolutionaries proclaimed an Irish republic and staged a rebellion in Dublin – even though they knew that in military terms their cause was hopeless. As it became clear that their insurrection had been a serious affair – rather than an embarrassing farce on the pattern of nineteenth-century insurrections – and as the Irish people realised that the rebels had fought bravely, early criticism of their actions was diluted by an often-reluctant admiration. The execution of the rebel leaders and of some of their followers aroused sympathy, while the widespread and apparently indiscriminate arrests which followed the Rising provoked a deep anger.

Even during Easter week it was clear to some observers that one target and likely victim of the violence was the constitutional Home Rule Party, and the

Rising's aftermath consolidated this trend. A new round of negotiations took place in summer 1916 with the aim of achieving an early settlement of the home rule question. There was a general recognition that constitutionalist politicians would not have been given this last opportunity to achieve their objectives had it not been for the shock provided by the rebellion. When the negotiations broke down amidst nationalist recriminations, their failure was ascribed solely to the British and to the gullible Irish politicians who believed them. Violence was no longer associated with ignominious failure. It was seen to have achieved results, while moderation, compromise and even the practice of politics were all discredited.

Soldiers and voters: the politics of militarism

For a decade before the Easter Rising Arthur Griffith's Sinn Féin party had provided a more radical alternative to the dominant Home Rule movement. Its policy was, oddly, that Irish independence should take the form of a dual monarchy linked with Britain only in the person of a common or shared monarch, and its model was that of the Austro-Hungarian Empire. In political terms it was a failure, although Griffith's writings ensured that he remained an influential figure after his party had declined. However, in the new circumstances of 1917, when the Rising had achieved a retrospective popularity and when the Redmondites had been discredited, a 'new model' Sinn Féin emerged which was very different from its earlier namesake. Its driving force was made up of members of the Irish Volunteers, some of them former rebels who had regarded politics and politicians with a soldierly disdain, and its policy was now the achievement of the fully independent republic which had been proclaimed in Easter Week. Griffith was replaced as president of the party by the rebel commander Eamon de Valera. This new mass republican movement managed to guide Irish nationalist sentiment in a more radical direction. It routed its constitutional, Home Rule Party, opponents in the general election which followed the ending of the Great War, winning 73 seats to a mere six gained by the latter. The implications of this triumph were ambiguous. Sinn Féin had been able to present itself as the 'peace party' which had saved many lives by sparing Ireland from conscription during the war, but its republican objectives could not be achieved without future violence.

In popularity and influence such a party was able to rival the Irish Volunteers – or the Irish Republican Army (IRA), as they were soon called. Militants viewed the party's role as being simply that of an auxiliary, but its energy and its successful record ensured that it would play a central role in the Irish revolution. It re-politicised Irish nationalism, ensuring that (relative) moderates would have somewhere to shelter within the new republican movement which was dominated by soldiers, and it also provided a means of organising or directing their energies. Crucially it secured the election of enough MPs in December 1918 to allow the summoning of an independent Irish parliament, the Dáil, and then a government which provided a 'democratic' political leadership. These were soon banned by the British authorities, and for most of the next few years they operated in secret, 'on the run'.

Between 1919 and 1921 the party and the army co-operated with one another, and both of them accepted the nominal supremacy of the Dáil and its government. This nominally civilian authority, which was dominated by serving or former soldiers, was tolerated by the army – provided that it did not interfere unduly with military activities. The Dáil even decreed that IRA units should swear allegiance to it, and most of them appear to have done this. In general the cabinet kept its distance from military activities, although on rare occasions it imposed its will. Sometimes this had unfortunate consequences – as in de Valera's insistence that the Dublin brigade carry out its disastrous attack on the Custom House, the centre of local government in Ireland. The building was destroyed, but the capture of many IRA members was a devastating blow which lessened the soldiers' respect for civilian authority.

In general, however, the military continued to view civilians with a condescension which sometimes amounted to contempt. In Robert Barton's view, for example, 'the strength of the national demand resembled the strength of an egg . . . The army and political leaders were the shell, the people the fluid contents'.[4] Clearly the people needed wise and firm leaders – and they needed the army – to provide them with coherence and an identity; the mass of the population could not be let out on their own.

Such views were enhanced by the pattern of the Anglo-Irish War, when society became polarised between the forces of the crown and the small number of active IRA units. Politicians kept their heads down, and when people were forced to choose between rival extremes the vast majority seem to have overcome their reservations and responded atavistically with the slogan 'up the rebels!' Everyone knew well that when the time for negotiations came in 1921, and the British government was prepared to make an offer which extended far beyond mere home rule, much or most of the credit for this change lay with those republican militarists who had weakened the centuries-old British determination to hold on to Ireland at all costs. In Mary MacSwiney's words, 'it was the minority in 1916 that made 1918 possible; it was that minority all along that made it possible to have this offer [of the Treaty] today'.[5] Violence worked.

But Irish leaders were acutely aware that in several important respects they did not represent their followers. Moderate home rulers had been discredited, and men of violence were lionised, but the mass of the people did not feel outraged by Britain's reluctance to surrender unconditionally. With the important exception of partition – which had been accepted in principle by nationalists before and during the First World War, and which was by now an established fact – the British were prepared to concede far more than most nationalists had hoped to achieve a decade earlier.

In the 1921 negotiations the Dublin cabinet and the Irish negotiators in London were concerned primarily with questions which were at least in part symbolic – crown and republic, dominion status and external association – but they realised that these priorities were not widely shared by their followers. If the discussions should break down and war should be resumed, the break should come on the question of Ulster; here was an emotive issue which might rally a tired and peace-loving people for yet another military effort. But it was not the issue closest to the heart of the Irish leadership – as was shown, famously, by the paucity of references to partition in the Treaty debates (Wall, 1966: 87; Laffan, 1999: 232).

Of course the demand for a republic did have a certain emotive appeal, and in a perfect world where great powers ignored their own interests and were concerned only with the 'rights' or wishes of their 'colonial subjects', it would have been conceded by the British. But – as later election results soon proved – the vast majority of the Irish electorate was prepared to endorse a compromise settlement in which the achievement of an Irish republic would either be abandoned or postponed. Peace was the main priority, and many hard-headed, unromantic nationalists would have agreed with Pope's lines

> O'er forms of government let fools contest;
> Whate'er is best administered, is best.

The Treaty settlement would at least ensure the establishment of an independent Irish administration; a governor-general might still represent the king in Dublin, in place of a viceroy, but at least there would be no more chief secretaries or under secretaries. The British army would depart, and in almost all respects the Irish people would be able to govern themselves in congenial 'Irish' ways.

Towards a democratic thermidor: implementing the treaty

The Anglo-Irish Treaty split the Dáil and its cabinet, but in both bodies there were small majorities in favour of the settlement. From January 1922 onwards Michael Collins, the chairman of the new provisional government, began taking over the powers which had been exercised by the British. He also struggled to consolidate his authority without allowing the divisions over the treaty to escalate into civil war. But an irreconcilable minority among his opponents would not compromise on symbols. Many of those in the army who had fought for a republic did not abandon their objective, and they refused to accept the insertion of the British monarch into the Treaty or the proposed new Irish constitution. In some cases they were disconcerted by the prospect of normality, of an end to fighting, and of their return to the ranks of the civilian population. Even before the truce came into effect in July 1921 one IRA internee in Ballykinlar wrote that 'we are about to be faced with the prospect of peace, peace, ruthless, relentless and remorseless peace. What a prospect! How are we to find precedents to guide us?'[6] Some opponents of the Treaty were motivated by habit and self-interest as well as by principle.

They were supported, reluctantly, by the more moderate de Valera whose miscalculations had allowed or encouraged him to drift into the radicals' camp. It is appropriate that one of the chapters on the civil war in Lord Longford and Thomas P. O'Neill's uncritical biography of de Valera should be entitled 'The darkest hour' (Longford and O'Neill, 1970: 215–23). It was the nadir of his career, when he was in hiding from the forces of a government which he could have headed, and when he was dependent on anti-political soldiers who despised his political skills. In later years he would be careful to avoid repeating the mistakes which he had made in 1921 and 1922.

Until the Treaty, the militaristic, republican element had predominated within the nationalist leadership. Now it split. Collins and others took the view that the British terms were the best which were likely to be got, at that time; more could be acquired later. There was a limit beyond which the British could not be forced into humiliating concessions, so the Irish would have to swallow their pride, take their winnings, and wait. After all, militant republicans had much experience in waiting. In effect Collins and those who shared his views changed sides and sought public support. They joined the moderate, 'democratic', 'constitutional' elements whose beliefs and habits they had often belittled in the past. The former Home Rule Party leader John Dillon noted with scornful amusement how 'Collins & Co.' appealed for perfect freedom of election meetings, 'laying down the law as to the right of a minority to revolt against the elected representatives of the people'.[7] It now suited rebels to become democrats, and the war-weary electorate welcomed these new converts.

Unlike his former colleagues, and unlike some later commentators, Collins did not take the view that British governments had no right to intervene in Irish affairs once the Treaty had been signed; ultimately, if reluctantly, he accepted that they were entitled to insist on the Treaty's implementation and to defend what they perceived to be British national interests. He was acutely aware that the British retained troops in Ireland, and that he depended on British goodwill (at least in the short term) if he were to exploit the opportunities which the Treaty provided: the freedom to achieve freedom.

In consolidating his position Collins played for time, trying to convert or isolate the radicals, and building on the popular support which would legitimise his government. For a while his devious manoeuvres were successful. The republicans' efforts to block the 1922 elections met with some success, and at least in geographical terms the results were an incomplete expression of the national will. Nonetheless the results were a massive (if tragically futile) repudiation of violence. However grateful the people might have felt towards the rebels of 1916–21, and however happy they might have been to enjoy the wider degree of independence which had been secured for them by the violent actions of the IRA between 1919 and 1921, they had had enough. The republic, or external association, or a kingless constitution, were not worth the blood-shed and destruction which would accompany any effort to achieve them. The electorate voted by 78 per cent to 22 per cent for candidates who supported the Treaty – even if some of them displayed little enthusiasm for it and (like Collins himself) regarded it as the lesser of two evils. Heroes of the war against the British, such as Dan Breen, were rejected by voters who were more concerned to prevent violence in the future than to honour it (and its practitioners) in the past. 'Normalcy', a term which was associated with the American president of the time, Warren Harding, was an objective also cherished by most Irish people.

Far from bringing peace the elections may have helped precipitate civil war. The government, having secured an endorsement of the Treaty, had now less reason than in the past to show restraint towards its republican critics, and it was more willing to enforce its authority. The republicans showed their usual logic and consistency in dismissing or glossing over the voters' wishes. As had been the pattern in earlier years public support was seen as a welcome but unnecessary luxury, and the radicals were once more prepared to follow their own preferences or beliefs rather than those of a fickle and short-sighted majority. After the elections both sides seemed to lose patience and to assume that their differences could be resolved only by force. Within two weeks the killing was resumed.

Throughout the bloody civil war which followed, the republicans were sustained by their reading of recent Irish history. They were convinced that if they could provoke the government into repression they could bring about a transformation of public opinion similar to that which had followed the Easter Rising and accompanied the Anglo-Irish War. They succeeded in the first of these aims. Like the British before them – and like most armies faced with the provocations of guerrillas – the government forces often hit out blindly and brutally. Notoriously, more prisoners were executed by the Free State in 1922–3 than by the British between 1916 and 1921.

But ultimately a large majority of the people were prepared to acquiesce in atrocities carried out by an *Irish* government, of the sort which they would not have accepted from the British. The republicans' contempt for the views of the masses had long been apparent, and now in many cases it was returned in full. Accounts from both sides concur in describing widespread resentment at the republicans' conduct. Uncompromising nationalists might believe that they represented an abstract Ireland, but they had no illusions that they represented the Irish people. In the course of the civil war the democrats (some of them converts of very recent vintage) resorted to extremist and militaristic methods in order to consolidate majority rule. Their actions were often harsh and sometimes shocking – like those of their republican opponents – but they did not provoke a revulsion against the government comparable to the change of nationalist opinion which followed the British repressions of 1916 and 1919–20.

One indisputable consequence of the war was the ultimate triumph of the moderate, 'political' majority, and the containment of those extremists who were unwilling to compromise: the marginalisation of a faction among the militants who had been the principal players in the upheavals of the decade between 1913 and 1923, and whose intransigence now brought about their downfall. In the beginning of the period, before the outbreak of the Great War, the wishes of Irish nationalists had been ignored or overruled by British Conservatives and Ulster unionists; at the end, in what became the Irish Free State, they were defied by Irish republicans. In between, of course, the unionists had achieved virtually all their objectives through the creation of a Northern Irish statelet which, they believed, they would control in perpetuity. No longer could they stand in the way of southern nationalists, but they could ensure that they ruled the largest possible (by which was meant the largest 'safe' or 'manageable') number of Irish nationalists remaining under their control.

In this the unionists were aided – if only marginally – by the priorities of the republican political and military leaders who were concerned with status rather than with unity. Since the mid-twentieth century, since republicans have 'discovered' or 're-discovered' Northern Ireland, this priority has been a source of some embarrassment. In some cases they have tried to ignore the copious evidence that in 1921–3 most of them saw the North and partition as minor problems. But it would be very hard to imagine the end result being significantly different, even if Irish nationalists had not been mesmerised by the republican mirage.

For decades to come, Irish militarists lapsed even further into futility. For nearly 30 years they virtually ignored their 'real' enemies (the British and the Ulster unionists) and launched a series of attack on 'false friends' – on governments in Dublin, moderate nationalists who aided and shared the people's demand for normality. Democracy worked – famously in 1932 when it facilitated a peaceful transfer of power from victor to vanquished. Republicans who had been defeated in a war fought to achieve 'the republic' took power, and then postponed indefinitely the achievement of the republic. Those who carried out attacks against a democratic *Irish* government – as some of their predecessors had done against a less democratic *British* government – were treated firmly by their former colleagues. Republicans in power were prepared to imprison and even kill republicans who did not share their sense of 'realism'. De Valera, who in 1922 had joined those rebels fighting against an Irish government which was supported by the Dáil and by the electorate, executed other republicans when he too felt obliged to maintain the authority of the democratic state.

Conclusion

Ever since the radicals' defeat in the civil war the militarist tradition has appealed only to a tiny minority in what is now the Republic of Ireland, although understandably it has attracted wider support in Northern Ireland where old grievances and frustrations persisted, and where the nationalist population experienced discrimination over many decades. It has enjoyed intermittent phases of wider support, provoked – as in the period of the Irish revolution – by the errors of Ulster unionists and of British governments and their armed forces. It was sustained by memory, or folk-memory, or imagery. In some respects this 'memory' is one which every student of modern Irish history must endorse. In particular there can be no doubt that British and unionist actions undermined moderate nationalists and stimulated their radical rivals. There *was* widespread nationalist support for a republican programme in 1918 – and hostility towards the British during the war of 1919–21. Most historians believe that in many respects violence did work – even if, as Paul Bew argues in chapter 5, it had 'made its point' by May 1920. At the very least it hastened full independence, and it can also be argued that it expanded considerably the nature and potential of that independence.

But other aspects of the Irish revolution deserve more attention than they have often received. It witnessed a latent, inherent conflict between militant republicanism – an elitist movement committed to an abstract objective – and the mass of the Irish people which, as in all democracies, was sometimes muddled, selfish and short-sighted. The relatively harmonious co-operation between the elite and the masses survived as long as the fighting continued, and as long as unity appeared necessary in the face of a common enemy. Negotiations allowed for (or imposed) alternatives, and republicans were forced to prioritise their objectives. The Treaty which resulted from these negotiations split the coalition between the intransigents or 'extremists' on the one hand, and moderates or 'realists' on the other. This latter group was supported enthusiastically by most Sinn Féin party members when individual branches throughout the country voted on the agreement, and later by voters in the general election of June 1922. The long-silent majority decided, firmly and massively, that the revolution was over, and it supported those in power who showed themselves ruthless in enforcing this decision. 'The new Irish Free State forcibly imposed democracy on the rebellious republicans and on a large minority section of the population' (Garvin, 1996: 3).

After this democratic Thermidor the 'unreconstructed' radicals (or Jacobins) were marginalised – although throughout the rest of the twentieth century defectors from their ranks, who were converted to majority rule, were welcomed warily or enthusiastically into political life. On occasion they were voted to parliament and even to power. They had come to accept that it was no longer enough to advance the interests of an abstract 'Ireland'; the interests of the Irish people would come first.

In the closing years of the twentieth century and in the early years of the twenty-first a similar pattern can be observed within the republican movement in general, and within the Sinn Féin party in particular. In some respects Irish history can appear to follow a cyclical path.

Chapter 5

Moderate nationalism, 1918–23: perspectives on politics and revolution

Paul Bew

Introduction

The home rule issue dominated Irish nationalist politics from 1874 to 1916. Home rule was the policy of seeking the creation of an autonomous Irish parliament, subordinate to Britain, through the maintenance at Westminster of an independent Irish Parliamentary Party, led with considerable flair by C. S. Parnell in the 1880s and by John Redmond after 1900. After the Easter Rising of 1916 both the policy and its principal instrument, the Parliamentary Party, were destroyed by the rise of the separatist Sinn Féin movement. As an unfulfilled possibility, home rule has provoked much historical debate. More dismissive interpretations stress the cynical element in Liberal support for home rule; the cultural, religious and economic differences between Britain and Ireland; the errors and confusions of the home rule leadership; the ambiguity of the concept, which could be interpreted as anything from a modest form of devolution to a stepping stone to separation; and the failure of virtually all home rule leaders to recognise, until too late, the reasons for Ulster Protestant hostility. Nevertheless, both in Britain and Ireland, there has always been a strong intellectual tradition which asserts that home rule was the obvious basis for a peaceful settlement of the Anglo-Irish conflict, but that it was frustrated by selfish opportunism, physical force and romantic nationalism.

This chapter reconstructs the constitutional nationalist critique of the Irish revolution.[1] It employs the writings of prominent constitutional nationalists to illustrate the views of those Irish parliamentarians who were marginalised by the emergence of Sinn Féin as the dominant force in Irish political life after 1918. Stephen Gwynn, in particular, claimed that republican violence only exacerbated the damage done by the failure of constitutional nationalists to grasp the need to compromise over Ulster. Indeed, Gwynn argued that the violence of the Collins era – which has been justified on counter intelligence and broader political grounds – played a major role in shaping the sectarian institutions of the Northern Irish state. His reflections on the self-defeating aspects of the Collins strategy are linked to a wider consideration of the role of the British government. This chapter also attempts to qualify a scholarly orthodoxy: that British policy in 1920–2, undoubtedly subject to fluctuations, was incoherent and essentially reactive. Instead, it argues that from the spring of 1920, Britain evolved a strategy, dependent on a considerable degree of intelligence success, involving the application of a carrot and stick policy designed to lead precisely to the Treaty compromise of 1921, but available much earlier to any Sinn Féin leadership willing to take it.

The struggle between nationalism and republicanism

Five years to the day after the death of the Irish Parliamentary Party leader John Redmond, J. L. Garvin, a former Parnellite turned social imperialist, lamented in an *Observer* editorial the subsequent transformation of Irish nationalism:

> The Ireland of the new Gaelic extremists was a pure myth. It could not be. Even the dream of it has brought to the country division, turmoil and tyranny. [The Redmonds] believed in Irish self-government and the purposes of our wider commonwealth . . . They died serving a bigger, broader and bolder ideal than that of the exclusionist Gaelic anachronism, not shirking Ireland's response to the modern world looking forward and not back to the golden age.[2]

On the tenth anniversary of the 1916 Easter Rising in Dublin, *The Observer*, on Easter weekend, carried an article, 'A decade of Ireland', by Stephen L. Gwynn, its regular Ireland correspondent and formerly a Redmondite MP for Galway from 1906 to 1918 (Hogan, 1996: 509–10): 'Ten Easters ago, Ireland, full of war-time prosperity, stood heartily behind the Irish divisions in France, with twice as many Irishmen scattered throughout the services'.[3] Gwynn continued: 'The right of self-government had been conceded in principle . . . and 19/20th of the people were with John Redmond and his willingness to wait till the end of the war before putting it into operation'. In early 1916 – contrary to his later image as politician 'let down by everyone' – Redmond was in highly optimistic mood (Bew, 1996: 30). But there was, of course, the nagging problem of the other one twentieth – the tiny elite of Irish separatist revolutionaries who launched the insurrection that was to become known as the Easter Rising.

It is possible to have grave doubts about Gwynn's estimation of the balance of forces within Irish nationalism: it is clear that in early 1916 Redmond retained the support of a majority, but it was not an overwhelming majority. Redmondites had won the five contested by-elections since the start of the war (three of them against candidates with separatist associations), but none of the victories were resounding ones (Bew, 1994: 43–150; see also Maume, 1993, ch. 7). The rural results tended to be more positive for the party than the urban ones, but even in rural areas the declining salience of the land question – and the prospect of wartime profits – reduced the enthusiasm of some in the farming community for the Irish party's role at Westminster. As Gwynn put it in his book *The Irish crisis*, published in 1921:

> Moreover, the farming community, immensely the most important element in Ireland, saw for the first time a prospect of large profits in their own industry. Disaffection for the once dominant party grew, and they no longer attributed their prosperity in any sense to Redmond and his colleagues in the parliamentary movement (Gwynn, 1921: 38).

Redmond became emotionally committed to the allied cause. A man who, in 1881, had apparently been suspended from King's Inns for refusing to drink the Queen's health, now initiated the singing of the national anthem at Westminster social gatherings, and at Aughavanagh, his country retreat, flew the Union Jack beside the Green Flag (Gwynn, 1919: 189; Barton, 1933: 13–14).

In a poignant passage, dated February 1916, in his preface to Michael MacDonagh's *The Irish at the front*, Redmond wrote:

> I have given my lifetime, such as it has been, to the service of Ireland in a deep faith in the essential nobility and wisdom of the Irish people. I should be untrue to that faith if for a moment I had any doubt on this matter – if I could harbour for a moment the idea that the young men of Ireland could think unmoved of the wistful bewildered faces of their noble brothers while they held back, could watch the ranks of the Irish armies thinning, and the glorious regiments, brigades and divisions gradually filling up with others than Irish soldiers until their character as Irish armies finally vanished and ceased to exist – and something, I fear, would go with their character that Ireland might never get back (Redmond, 1916: 13–14).

But Redmond's view of the matter was not, in fact, shared by the young men who remained in Ireland, and who were prepared to take part in public displays of strength. In Cork City, for example, a few hundred Redmondite Volunteers formed the municipal St Patrick's Day procession. Carrying a banner declaring that 400 comrades had joined the colours, they were vastly outnumbered by 1,000 Irish Volunteers.[4] As Gwynn admitted five years earlier in *The Irish crisis*, there were in Ireland: 'thousands of young men who, in time of general war, desired their adventure of war but would not have it on England's terms' (Gwynn, 1921: 46; Hepburn, 1998: 114–46).

But even if all of Redmond's sources of weakness are admitted, the Easter Rising did not claim the united support of the majority of the nationalist 'family'. Gwynn, in the *Observer* article of 26 April 1926, felt sure that the British decision (supported by Redmond, at least in the four most prominent cases) to execute the leadership had played a key role in changing the sympathy of the populace. Referring to the Irish premier, W. T. Cosgrave, he noted:

> Everyone of the men who were in that rising, Mr Cosgrave not least of them, admits that if the rank and file – many of whom had no idea for what purpose they had been mobilised on Easter Sunday – had been dismissed contemptuously to their homes and the leaders treated as lunatics the whole thing would have been over.[5]

This begs the question of whether such a mild governmental response was ever likely to be the response to a rising launched in association with imperial Germany, one which had cost at least 450 lives. But Gwynn, bearing in mind perhaps some of his own pre-war writing on the subject, was determined not to lay all the blame simply at the door of the British government (Gwynn, 1911: 109–15). In 1919 he published his major work, *John Redmond's last years*; ignored by the revolutionaries, it dismayed the parliamentary nationalists who reviewed it.

Nationalists and the Ulster question

Gwynn's work was peppered with criticisms of British Tory and Ulster unionist ideology and practice, but it is clear that some reviewers – notably Henry Harrison, the Parnellite ex-MP, and the *Freeman's Journal*, the principal organ of constitutional nationalism – felt somewhat uneasily that Gwynn had sold the pass. Gwynn made it clear that he thought that Redmond should, in effect, have accepted Carson's offer of a compromise in March 1914: an open-ended exclusion of the six counties, leaving the way open for Irish unity on the basis of consent. The *Freeman* noted that in his closing chapters Gwynn argued that the difficulties which obstructed Redmond were set in his way not so much by those with a different end, but by those who desired 'the same end'. Unhappily, the reviewer protested, Gwynn's conclusion 'is in conflict not only with the facts but with the facts laid down by Captain Gwynn'.[6] Gwynn was undeterred by these critics. Ten years after the Rising, speaking as one who had been a senior figure in Irish nationalism from 1908 to 1916, he insisted: 'The fault was partly our own . . . We would not consent to let Ulster take her way and her own time. After ten years we have learnt the lesson but have probably added ten years to the period of waiting. It will last forever if Ireland is to be joined to the republican aim set out by that handful in 1916.'

Ulster unionists undoubtedly saw Redmond's Irish Volunteer movement as an attempt to 'coerce a province under the yoke of home rule'. Yet, by September 1914, in an impressive parliamentary speech, Redmond indicated this opposition to the coercion of unionist areas – a belief his friends knew he had held in private for some considerable time.[7]

By 1918 democratic nationalism in Ireland had clearly, though belatedly, embraced the principle of consent; the most prominent members of the Irish Parliamentary Party – which had dominated Irish public life since 1885 – believed that it was wrong to argue that the predominantly unionist north-eastern area of the island should be coerced to accept the principle of Irish political unity (Bew, 1994: 114). John Dillon told Tim Healy in 1914: 'How can we coerce Ulster with our own record against coercion? And we can not face civil war as a beginning of home rule' (Healy, 1928, II: 538). Somewhat belatedly Joe Devlin, the key figure of northern nationalism, who had from 1900 to 1914 acted as a force preventing the expression of such opinions in public, agreed in June 1916: 'Ulster unionists may be conciliated, who says they should be coerced? Does anyone lightheartedly propose to provoke another rebellion in the North, and if such were provoked, what hope would there be for many a long year in wiping out the fatal legacy it would leave behind?' (Bew, 1994: 138).

It may be argued that such a collective public wisdom was too slow to form, especially when it is noted that it came only after the generation of much inter-communal polarisation during the third Home Rule Bill crisis of 1912–14. After all, William O'Brien and his small group of All for Ireland League MPs, on the fringe of the party and then outside it, had been arguing the case for a more conciliatory attitude towards unionists since at least 1903. But it is not possible to deny that by the time of the 1918 general election, which destroyed the old party and elevated the new Sinn Féin movement into a position of national leadership, the party had embraced the principle of consent, while Sinn Féin – in most cases – appeared to oppose it. The party leadership treated with disdain the claims of Sinn Féin on the northern question. 'God help the Orangemen of Ulster if de Valera and Griffith come to deal with them', Dillon commented sarcastically.[8] It is worth noting that from the point of view of northern nationalism in 1914 there was one key advantage in a constitutionalist approach. The legislation for the 'excluded' area in the north-east clearly envisaged continued direct rule by London, but with a decidedly green tinge through the pressures exerted both by an Irish parliament within the United Kingdom and those Irish MPs staying at Westminster. In Redmond's view, this Irish representation could, in principle, after the implementation of home rule, provide United Kingdom cabinet members. These arrangements, on the face of it, constituted a strong potential defence of the interests of the Catholic and nationalist minority in the north-east; they were certainly perceived at the time to be superior (from a nationalist point of view) to later proposals for a local Protestant state, which gained ground after Easter 1916.[9] This was a point understandably harped upon in later years in provincial newspapers owned by Redmond's close supporters, for example William O'Malley's *Galway Observer* and J. P. Hayden's *Roscommon Messenger*. It was the latter which pointed out in August 1921: 'The policy of optional exclusion was quite different to that which gives to the cut-off area all the machinery of legislation'.[10]

Republicans and the Ulster question

On the surface at least Sinn Féin rejected any compromise on Irish unity. In early 1916 Michael Collins wrote to a friend: 'Just at present I'm in good form over the smashing of home rule proposals. Anything but a divided Ireland – you understand, of course, that I mean geographically divided' (Coogan, 1991: 52). In early September 1917, at Cootehill, County Cavan, Eamon de Valera declared: 'We say to those planters . . . If you continue to be a garrison for the enemy . . . we will have to kick you out'.[11] In the same month Arthur Griffith, in a Belfast speech, gave the Orangemen some six months to change allegiance, otherwise Sinn Féin would deal with them (Bew, 1987: 218).

In the summer of 1920 a British intermediary, the American journalist Carl Ackerman, later dean of journalism at Columbia University, made contact with Desmond Fitzgerald to find out Sinn Féin's negotiating position. The first point was unambiguous: 'That any settlement would have to include Ulster'.[12] As late as March 1921 de Valera insisted:

> The difficulty of the problem was not the attitude of Ulster but the attitude of England. It is to the interest of no section of Irishmen to keep their differences alive, but it is to the interest of certain English politicians and statesmen who desire these differences as a cloak to screen their own imperial greed.[13]

De Valera was the president of Sinn Féin; his vice-president was, however, a charismatic nationalist priest, Father Michael O'Flanagan. But O'Flanagan was a heretic on the partition issue: 'If we reject home rule rather than agree to the exclusion of the unionist part of Ulster, what case have we to put before the world? . . . The island of Ireland and the national unit of Ireland simply do not coincide'.[14]

He rejected the notion of coercing the Ulster unionists:

> Now, is there any other method we could try on the Orangemen? I confess I don't like the word coercion, whether it be applied in Ireland or in Belgium or in any

other part of the world. Forty million of [British] people have tried to coerce four million [Irish] people, and they have failed. The relative proportion of the forces was ten to one, and the ten failed to coerce the one – so also, I believe if the three million tried to coerce one million, they would fail, too.[15]

Given these publicly stated differences of opinion, it is impossible to argue that Sinn Féin had a unified line on the Ulster question. Indeed, it also appears that the issue was not of such a salience that a unified line was required.

Good, but not spectacular, results in by-election contests against the Redmondite party were achieved by Sinn Féin in 1917 – one key by-election, South Longford, was only won when the returning officer had a recount of Sinn Féin votes, perhaps encouraged at pistol point.[16] Despite three Nationalist Party by-election successes, the momentum moved much more radically in Sinn Féin's direction in 1918, especially after the so-called 'German plot', an intelligence fiasco which led to mass arrests of leading Sinn Féin members.[17]

Within nationalism, Sinn Féin achieved a dramatic victory in the 1918 general election; the party received a popular vote of 485,105, and won nearly all (73 against 6) of the old Irish Party seats. In terms of actual votes, on the other hand, the result was less impressive. The Irish Party retained the loyalty of 237,393 electors; the 'total anti-republican vote', including unionists, was 557,435 (Kee, 1989: 53). Against this, it has to be said that some 25 seats out of 105 seats were not fought, and most of these would probably have registered handsome Sinn Féin victories. Was this a vote for a 32-county republic achieved by force, whether Ulster unionists consented or not? Given the position of the unionists, the pro-consent positions of the Irish party, and even of some in the Sinn Féin leadership, it seems hard to argue this. Was it a vote for a 26-county republic? This is a considerably more serious argument; while some argue that the Sinn Féin vote should not be seen as a pro-republican vote because other contingent factors – such as fear of conscription – played a role in generating it, it is difficult to deny that a majority of the electorate in the 26 counties supported an explicitly republican separatism. After all, Sir Edward Carson, no less, declared: 'As regards Ireland, the elections have cleared the air. The issue is between an independent republic or government under the parliament of the United Kingdom. Every other alternative has proved to be a sham.'[18] The republican *Mayo News* commented approvingly: 'We would have thought that such a pillar of coalition would have been more considerate for the feelings of his chief or tool – Mr Lloyd George – not to so bluntly raise the issue . . . but with Sir Edward Carson the Irish people always know where they are'.[19]

It does not, however, follow that there was a mandate for violence; no such mandate was explicitly sought by Sinn Féin candidates, who stressed the primacy of peaceful means. One outspoken product of a celebrated parliamentary nationalist family, Serjeant A. M. Sullivan, made the point forcefully: 'Many murderers were elected, but they had not stood as murderers' (Sullivan, 1927: 237). As *The Irish Times* put it: 'Sinn Féin has swept the board, but we do not know – does Sinn Féin itself know what it intends to do with the victory?'[20]

The *Freeman's Journal* claimed that 'whatever democratic nationalists may think of the result, they had accepted it'.[21] In fact, such acceptance was decidedly grudging: John Dillon, who had succeeded to the leadership of the Irish Party after Redmond's death, never accepted that the election was a 'free' decision of the Irish people.[22]

Serjeant A. M. Sullivan, moreover, was the most vigorous exponent of the notion that Sinn Féin had not actually received a mandate to speak for Ireland. Sullivan noted that 443,000 voters had abstained from voting in contested seats (the percentage turnout in Dublin was low – only 79,984 voters out of 124,428 bothered to vote). He argued that this implied a total anti-Sinn Féin majority within Ireland of at least half a million.[23] In a letter to *The Times* Sullivan argued that under a system of PR voting, the result of the election would have been: Anti-Catholic Orangemen 10 per cent; Anti-Protestant Hibernians 14 per cent; Rational Unionists 16 per cent; Rational Nationalists 27 per cent; Sinn Féin (anti-England) 33 per cent; giving a combination of rational unionists and rational nationalists a decided majority over Sinn Féin.[24] But few could take much comfort from Sullivan's interesting but essentially speculative attempts at political analysis. Many worried about an impending confrontation between the government and Sinn Féin. The *Freeman* noted: 'The republicans have already achieved as great a preponderance in the representation of Ireland as the reactionaries in the representation of Great Britain'.[25]

In January 1919 the Sinn Féin members met in Dublin and proclaimed themselves Dáil Éireann (the parliament of the Irish Republic), reaffirmed the Easter Rising declaration of 1916, adopted a provisional constitution, and appointed delegates to attend the peace conference of the Allied Powers in Paris. It was widely and correctly assumed that this strategy would in itself be ineffective, but what would then follow? The constitutionalist *Cork County Eagle* noted: 'Attempting to create Irish republics is no child's play. There is a world of difference between using a vote and using a gun. Sinn Féin will very soon, if it lives up to its declarations, become a very serious business for many.'[26]

But there was still good reason to believe that 'moderates' had influence within Sinn Féin. In the aftermath of the electoral triumph, Father O'Flanagan spoke of not being in a state of 'hysterical impatience'[27] to achieve a republic; Eoin MacNeill spoke of the republic becoming a reality in, perhaps, 'ten years' (Mitchell, 1994: 8), and Thomas Kelly, recently elected for St Stephen's Green, seemed more keen to launch some new cultural struggle against allegedly pro-unionist intellectual institutions in Dublin than any military struggle against the state (Jones, 1997: 55). In the general election campaign Lloyd George had indicated that any settlement short of a republic and the 'coercion of Ulster' might be discussed. Perhaps there was room for compromise?

The British government and Irish republicans

In fact, in early 1919 it appeared that the British government, rather than Sinn Féin, was girding its loins for battle. Lloyd George, responding to pressure from Lord French, the lord lieutenant, appointed Ian Macpherson, a Liberal MP, as Chief Secretary for Ireland in place of Edward Shortt (McBride, 1991: 259–60). *The Nation* summed up: 'Ireland is given over completely to militarism and reactionism. Mr Shortt, who opposed Lord French and would have released the Sinn Féin leaders and other MPs imprisoned without trial, is himself removed.'[28] Stephen Gwynn publicly implied that unionists were hoping that Sinn Féin would act in a provocative manner in order to encourage a crackdown.[29] If Irish unionists were, indeed, thinking along such lines, Sinn Féin soon provided the provocation. On 21 January, Seamus Robinson, Sean Treacy, Dan Breen and six other Irish Volunteers ambushed a cart carrying gelignite at Soloheadbeg, County Tipperary, killing two policemen, whilst a group of quarry workers, who had been warned beforehand to stay silent, watched in horror. Breen later made it clear that for him the purpose of the operation was to kill the policemen rather than to get the gelignite.[30]

In the most complete condemnation to appear in print, Serjeant A. M. Sullivan declared in a letter to the press: 'The episode itself was the natural development of the brutalising and pagan creed that for the past three years has been proclaimed as "patriotism" in Ireland, while those who should have refuted it have sat in cowardly silence' (Sullivan, 1927: 25; see also Callanan, 1996: 477 and Foster, 1995: 7–12, 30).

The *Cork County Eagle* agreed fully with Sullivan: 'The distinguished Irishman takes the present cowardice and shrinking of responsible people in Ireland, before the prevailing anarchy, by the throat, so to speak, and shakes the wretched thing in our shameful faces'.[31] Speaking at the first funeral mass in Tipperary, Monsignor Arthur Ryan described the victims as 'martyrs to their duty'. In Ryan's view the murderers had acted as if the victims had no immortal souls in their bodies, as if there was no judgement to follow, as if they 'were dogs, not men. The fair name of Tipperary and of Catholic Ireland were involved. It used to be said that "where Tipperary leads, Ireland follows". God help poor Ireland if she follows that lead of blood.'[32]

But other condemnations were more ambiguous in their effect. The Reverend William Keogh, speaking at the second funeral mass at Soloheadbeg, noted: 'They read with horror of the crimes of the Bolsheviks, but nothing they had done was worse than this frightful outrage which had been committed at our own doors.' But he added words which would have been music to the ears of the Sinn Féin leadership:

> Ireland's enemies would try to lay this crime against the new popular movement striving for her independence, but they were wrong. The leaders of that movement were far too logical and God-fearing to countenance such crimes. No party in the country would be more pained by the crime or condemn it more strongly than the leaders of that movement.

Even more significant was the reaction of the *Tipperary Star*. On the same page as it printed these sermons, in a comment on Serjeant Sullivan's letter, the *Star* noted critically: '"The Sullivans were always cowards", said Parnell, "He was right."' Over the next two years Sullivan became a figure of hate, and a frequent target of violence. One prominent voice in the provincial press, John Murphy (former MP for East Kerry, 1900–10), took a different tack from the *Star*, but with the same denunciatory effect – Sullivan was betraying the proud tradition of his patriotic and politically prominent family: 'He has unlearnt every lesson ever his own father taught.'[33] A close reading of the local debate, provoked by the Tipperary murders, suggests that condemnation was far from unequivocal. Sullivan, a crown prosecutor, soon found that his courage was put to the test: the kinsman of Tim Healy and a product of one of nationalist Ireland's most celebrated families, he became the target of serious assassination attempts.[34]

But all did not appear to be lost: Soloheadbeg did not, in itself, signal an irreversible break with the past. It seems clear that the Volunteer leadership, including Michael Collins, gave serious consideration to a plan which would have removed the attackers to a safe haven in the United States. This reaction harked back to the strategy of secret society assassins of the Land League era; but the militants involved refused to participate (Mitchell, 1994: 734; Augusteijn, 1996: 88).

The Sinn Féin leadership clearly did not seek an escalation at this moment. Lord French struck on a surprisingly conciliatory course; it is clear that by February 1919 he had decided to release the remaining Sinn Féin prisoners. In March, even more reassuringly, Harry Boland repudiated any suggestion that a recent interview by Mr de Valera with an American journalist was offering any support for violence.[35] Less reassuringly, later in the month, a young medical student, M. Farrell, appeared in court in possession of a pamphlet entitled *Ruthless warfare*, which argued against 'passive resistance' and advocated, instead, a fight with utter ruthlessness and ferocity.[36]

At first the build-up of military activity was relatively slow. All operations of the Dublin Volunteers combined led to 12 casualties among the crown forces prior to 1920. By the end of 1919 only 18 policemen had been killed throughout the country (Kostick, 1996: 88). In 1920 the Volunteer executive finally endorsed a policy of open attacks on crown forces. Collins, two years later, presented these actions as a necessary defence against an omniscient British intelligence service. Collins later told a gullible American journalist: 'Every street in every city was an open book to the English agents' (Talbot, 1923: 76), but it is unlikely that he really believed this. Before 1916, Dublin Castle, on the orders of Augustine Birrell, had radically reduced its expenditure on intelligence gathering operations. Even so, Birrell received adequate warning of the Easter Rising, but did not utilise it (Winter, 1955: 290). At the time of the Easter Rising, the Dublin Castle system itself was already penetrated up to the highest level by the revolutionaries.[37] Collins's own obituary acknowledged:

> Even in 1918 the British knew little of him, for when they had him in custody in Sligo jail on a charge of having made a seditious speech in Co Longford, they allowed him to escape from the net. Later, when they learned what an active brain they had let loose, they must have felt the weakness of their Intelligence Department.[38]

There was, therefore, no strong purely 'intelligence case' for political violence – so why the slide into inevitably 'dirty' war? All the most recent studies of the most forceful and extreme of the Irish leaders who emerged in 1917, Michael Collins, sidestep this crucial issue (Coogan, 1991; Mackay, 1996; Costello, 1997). The precise nature of the calculations which underpinned the slide into violence is not clear. More recently, however, Ronan Fanning has argued that it was the methods of Collins that alone had permitted a remarkable victory for nationalism, one which was unattainable by other means.[39] This has at least the merit of facing up to the key question – how did Collins justify to himself the slaughter of fellow Irishmen?

As Peter Hart has shown, two thirds of the IRA's victims in 1921 in Cork, a highly active county, were not actually killed in combat (Hart, 1997: 187; but see also Murphy, 1998). Rather more typical were the large-scale executions of so-called spies and other 'enemies of the people'. As early as 24 January 1920 the *Western News* bitterly noted: 'It is now perfectly clear that any species of grudge is called spy as a justification for murder'.[40] British intelligence sources insist that 'few of those who were assassinated had ever given information'.[41]

Hart has also demonstrated the existence of a distinctly sectarian and anti-Protestant tinge to the IRA's activity in Cork (Hart, 1996, ch. 5; Hart, 2002). But such sectarianism was certainly not confined to Cork. Protestant farmers were also shot in Fermanagh, Louth, Leitrim, Longford and Tipperary; and in Cavan the 80-year-old Protestant clergyman, Dean Finlay, was murdered at Bawnboy.[42] The pattern was set: by 20 October 1920, 23 British soldiers had been killed, but this was to be set against 117 policemen (and it should be noted that the RIC was an 80 per cent Catholic force) and 32 civilians (Hart, 1996, ch. 5; Hart, 2002). Some of the police victims were inevitably connected to the old parliamentary tradition. District Inspector D. J. Brady, who was killed by the IRA in County Sligo in October 1920, was the nephew of former Redmondite MP P. J. Brady,[43] who had been defeated by Sinn Féin dove Thomas Kelly for the St Stephen's Green seat in 1918. When the son of a well-known Macroom doctor, District Inspector Philip Kelleher, MC and Irish rugby star, was killed at the bar of the hotel owned by the family of Kitty Kiernan, Collins's fiancée, in Granard, while chatting to the local Sinn Féin executive, Tim Healy could not bring himself to believe that the IRA could have done it – though, of course, they had.[44] John Dillon had a row in one of his business establishments with an edgy Constable J. Gallagher, a Strabane man, but was shaken when, within a few days, Gallagher was murdered by the IRA.[45]

The net of supposedly legitimate targets was cast remarkably wide. William Kennedy refused to close his chemists' shop as a mark of respect for Terence MacSwiney; he was supported in this by his close friend T. J. O'Dempsey, who took an action for intimidation in the Dublin courts. Both men were immediately shot dead. Both had been loyal Redmondites; O'Dempsey, an old Clongownian like Redmond himself, had been the founder with Tom Kettle of the Young Ireland branch of the United Irish League and later became the secretary of the Wexford United Irish League.[46]

But if, as has been stated above, the precise nature of the calculations which underpinned the slide into violence is not clear, there can be no doubt about the polarising impact of the decision to reintroduce terror. Even at the end of 1918, a substantial constituency still supported moderate nationalism, but it was this constituency, alongside southern unionism, which was to be pulverised by the incoming cycle of provocation and repression. The fear that, as de Valera put it to Harry Boland in February 1921, the British government would be able to 'force an Irish party into existence' haunted Sinn Féin (Street, 1922: 113–14). But moderate nationalists, initially inclined to condemn republican violence, fell silent when confronted with British reprisals. Even though not infrequently – either through design or more frequently by accident – they fell victim to the conflict, they could not bring themselves to side with London against the IRA, unless it was clear that continued conflict would simply mean a descent into anarchy.

Once it was clear that Sinn Féin had mobilised a critical mass (not necessarily the majority) of the Irish people behind the 'War of Independence', British policy developed a grim and ultimately successful logic. It was not directed towards 'reconquest' or vindicating the union – to the dismay of Irish unionists like Sir Henry Wilson, chief of the imperial general staff from 1918 to 1922 – but rather to forcing Sinn Féin to negotiate on a compromise agenda.

   The British were well aware of the existence of a form of dual power in the
countryside which made it difficult to envisage the restoration of any form of
Dublin Castle rule. As early as May 1920 the prominent Protestant supporter
of a dominion settlement, Horace Plunkett, told an American journalist: 'You
have now in Ireland two governments, a de jure government repressing a de
facto government, which has the greater force of the people's will at its back'
(Ackerman, 1922a: 633). The emergence of a parallel judicial system – the Dáil
courts – was of particular significance here. The historian Alice Stopford
Green, whose ascendancy house in Dublin was, in fact, a key element of Sinn
Féin's underground railway, naturally praised the Dáil courts:

> In them was seen the unique spectacle of a revolutionary party protecting
> property. Landlords asked for their arbitration in cases where thousands of cases
> and many thousands of pounds were in question. Great and small landowners,
> Protestant and Catholic citizens of Ireland, policemen and Sinn Feiners, all
> found equal justice, rapid and economical, and manifestly carrying with it the
> consent of the people in the settlement of these problems of the gravest danger to
> the state.[47]

But the fact remains that a surprisingly wide variety of sources testified to
their effectiveness. In 'Tales of the RIC', the powerful anti-Sinn Féin series of
articles published by *Blackwood's Magazine*, it was acknowledged: 'The
summer of 1920 saw the greater part of the south and west in the hands of the
Republic, who not only boasted an army in the field, but ran their own police,
law courts and local government board.'[48] The liberal *Nation* agreed: 'The
British administrative system is being laid to waste and there is a general
assumption of power through the country by Dáil Éireann'.[49] But so did *The
Times*: 'The Sinn Féin courts are impressing the minds of all thinking men'.[50]
Some key figures of the old Irish Parliamentary Party had to bend the knee.
W. J. Duffy, MP, who had, in the 1880s, humiliated others before the
National League 'courts',[51] now found himself having to attend the Dáil
courts on an agrarian matter.

   But who were to be the instruments of a new policy that would take
account of such unpalatable realities? Following the assassination of Alan Bell
in March 1920, and the departure of Sir John Taylor[52] in April – both men
had successful 'counter terrorist' experience which went back to the 1880s –
the power of the old hands in Dublin Castle was destroyed.[53] Any remaining
officials who expressed sympathy for the ancien régime were marginalised
(Headlam, 1947: 216), and a new clique was created which governed policy.[54]
A network was instituted, involving 'flexible' Irish officials like W. E. Wylie,
the crown prosecutor, G. C. Duggan of Dublin Castle and, above all, new
English officials like Sir John Anderson, Mark Sturgis and Andy Cope, now

the driving force in Dublin Castle. This group worked closely with Philip Kerr in the prime minister's office, Sir Basil Thomson at Scotland Yard, and C. J. Philips, chief assistant to the foreign secretary, Lord Curzon.

In recent years scholars have largely agreed in their treatment of British policy. Eunan O'Halpin concluded his fine study: 'The incoherence of British government policy influenced the kind of state that emerged in southern Ireland in 1922' (O'Halpin, 1987: 217). A similar emphasis on incoherence and vacillation can be found in the important work of Sheila Lawlor (1983: 74) and Charles Townshend (1983: 348), whose influence on Nicholas Mansergh should be noted (see Mansergh, 1991: 145–57). All these historians see the significance of the Anderson group but do not quite grasp the way in which it drove policy, refusing to get knocked off course, or be deflected by setbacks such as the British government's demand in late 1920, later dropped, for IRA decommissioning. In fact, this group had a clear picture of the settlement from the outset and a confidence in their ability ultimately to deliver the prime minister. Friendly journalists were told to disregard all superficially hardline statements from the government and concentrate on the effort to bring about a negotiated outcome. In May 1920 C. J. Philips told a journalist: 'Within three years Ireland would be a republic in everything but name and in less time than that all the British troops would be out of Ireland' (Ackerman, 1922b: 812). Echoing his aide's views, Curzon told the cabinet on 23 July 1920: 'You must negotiate with Sinn Féin. We shall be driven to dominion home rule sooner or later'.[55] Balfour replied: 'That won't solve the question. They will ask for a Republic'.

Herein lay the greatest difficulty of all: did Balfour have a point? Was there any possibility of compromise with a movement whose ideologues expressed themselves in purist terms? Aodh de Blacam was a celebrated exponent of Sinn Féin's worldview:

> They should realise the beautiful Ireland upon which they should set their hearts. They should see that the evil forces of England were not brought into this country, such as industrial capitalism, the modern state system and militarism. Under dominion status, Ireland would have the institutions at present . . . the same parliamentary system and the same permanent officials to run the country.[56]

In a direct engagement with a classic Redmondite theme, de Blacam declared: ' They did not want to bind up the wounds at the Empire's heart'. Aodh de Blacam was one of nature's purists, but were all Sinn Féin executive members so unbending? One such, Father Patrick Gaynor, insisted:

> They said they wanted to be clear of the Empire and they would never be content to give the deliberate sanction of their votes to any measure that left Ireland

within that Empire. They would not have colonial home rule . . . They stood for a principle and until the crack of doom they would stand by that principle.[57]

But Gaynor – at least according to his later recollection – knew quite well that he had little chance of winning a Republic of Ireland. Were there others like Father Gaynor? This was the nub of the problem. The 'Anderson group' employed Carl Ackerman, an American writer, who made contact with Collins in the summer of 1920 to find out, in effect, if Balfour's contention had substance. Ackerman reported that it had not:

> He [Sir Basil Thomson] asked whether I thought Mr Collins really desired and expected a Republic and whether the Republic were merely a slogan and that he would compromise if the British government accepted this fundamental proposal. I told Sir Basil . . . that an Irishman always asked £100 for a horse if he expected to get £25 (Ackerman, 1922a: 441).

The turning point came on the Sinn Féin side – Ackerman called it 'the American education' of Michael Collins (for more detail see Bew, 1997). It was the gradual awareness on the part of Collins and others that the United States of America was not going to throw its weight behind their case. Those who had argued that this would happen – Eamon de Valera and Harry Boland in particular – were discredited among the fighting men on the ground.[58]

There were, of course, other pressures on Collins. Given his obsessive interest in the importance of intelligence operations, he was well aware that the British had regained the initiative in this field: indeed, dozens of new agents were in place and working effectively. One intelligence report sarcastically reported: 'If it is possible to extend sympathy to those who have been particularly devoid of it, then the seizure of a leader's entire office correspondence each successive month, is possibly a worthy subject for it.'[59] Indeed, by March 1921 British intelligence penetration in Dublin, if not the country, was advanced – even to the extent of being counterproductive, as, for example, where the interception of de Valera's warlike communications (signed suggestively 'Godfather') with Irish-American militants temporarily inclined Lloyd George to the view that a compromise was possible (Ackerman, 1922b: 811). On 31 March 1921 the Sinn Féin propagandist Erskine Childers called on Anderson 'very much shaken, as he thought that evidence against him had almost certainly been discovered at the offices of the [Irish] *Bulletin*, which was raided a day or two ago. He asked if he might sleep that night in Anderson's study and he, of course, accepted'.[60]

But of course – as this incident clearly shows – these intelligence operations were designed principally to soften up the Sinn Féin leadership, and make it more amenable. One of Andy Cope's colleagues noted: 'He had an agreeable, but complex, personality, and was certainly an able supporter of Lloyd George whose attempts at settling the Irish problem appeared to consist of hitting the insurrection on the head by means of Tudor and MacCready, and offering its leader a bouquet by the underground method of Cope' (Winter, 1955: 309).

As Tim Healy told his brother: 'Cope continually meets the Sinn Féin leaders, including Michael Collins. The military desire trouble, for to crush is their job.'[61] Collins reported to de Valera the message of another British intermediary ('not Cope', he specified) on 18 June 1921: 'He is in a veritable panic and anxious to avert the awful times'.[62] The message had been a simple one – if there was no compromise, the British were prepared to triple the number of soldiers in Ireland and back this up with a policy of martial law, heavy investment of troubled areas, and internment. When the document cache – of which this letter formed a key part – was seized by British forces a few days later, the diehard Colonel Martin Archer-Shee MP, a Catholic with strong unionist views (as well as well-known personal ties to Edward Carson), demanded their publication in the House of Commons; it is not difficult to see why he was unsuccessful, and he was, in fact, shouted down amidst cries of 'peace'.[63]

In June–July 1921 the *Review of Reviews* published a remarkable article, alleging that the government concealed many Black and Tan casualties. Sinn Féin claimed to have killed 3,000 Black and Tans, RIC members and soldiers in Cork alone in the past six months, whilst Dublin Castle's official weekly summary gave a total of less than 300 for the whole of Ireland. IRA active service units, it was said, had already succeeded in clearing a wide area of west Cork from the occupation of the crown forces.[64] Some republicans revelled in this account – which was, of course, denied by the British authorities – but Michael Collins later offered a considerably more sober assessment of the state of play in April 1921: 'In July last there were many parts of Ireland where the British forces could operate without the slightest interference. There were some parts where they could operate with difficulty. There were no parts where they could not operate even by a small concentration of numbers.'[65] Collins is, of course, here justifying his decision to compromise with Britain. There is no doubt that the measure of self-government granted to the 26 counties in 1922 was significantly greater than that achieved by Redmond; indeed, that it precisely fulfilled the Sinn Féin programme as it existed during the home rule crisis. Nevertheless, there was an obvious weakness in the Treaty settlement from a nationalist point of view. The editorial in *Sinn Féin* on 8 April 1911, for example, complains that Redmondite home rule would 'leave to the imperial parliament the management of all imperial affairs – the army, navy, foreign relations, customs, imperial taxation and matters pertaining to

Crown and colonies'.[66] On this basis, Sinn Féin had fulfilled its agenda – but what about unity and the Republic? One writer, C. H. Bretherton, put his finger on the sore point: 'The two things at which the Catholic Irish were supposed to balk at were partition and the King. By the Treaty they accepted both. Had they accepted them in 1914, they could have had all the self-determination they are now getting'.[67] This was an overstated argument from a staunch unionist who enjoyed stirring up trouble.

Conclusion

As they reflected on the events that had been associated with their political marginalisation, the survivors of the old party believed that Bretherton's analysis had some force. In 1923 William O'Brien published his *Irish revolution and how it came about*; despite his later leanings towards an idealistic republicanism, his work could also be interpreted as a defence of certain types of parliamentary moderation. One old parliamentary colleague, Jasper Tully, a former MP for Leitrim South, summarised his own 'reading' of O'Brien: 'In fact, more than was got under the Treaty could have been got if 'partition' was swallowed then, as it has been swallowed now'.[68] In similar vein, John Dillon wrote to an old colleague, Mr P. Jaguers of the Australian United Irish League, on 27 December 1922:

> We left in 1918, when control passed from the hands of the old party, an Ireland in possession of all the reforms mentioned in the programme of the Land League . . . with a settlement of the national demand on the statute book, which, had it been allowed to stand, would undoubtedly have united Ireland and which was unquestionably in all essential particulars a much better settlement than that acquired under the Treaty signed on 6 December 1921.[69]

W. J. Duffy, former MP for Galway South, 1900–18, wrote immediately to praise the Jaguers letter, which had provoked 'great discussion' in the country – 'an age had passed since they were told the truth'.[70]

John Dillon appears to have acquired a taste for this sort of intellectual provocation. At the beginning of 1925 he told a meeting at the National Club in Dublin: 'When we look back on the days when we were oppressed by England, it would look like paradise if we could get the same sort of oppression now' (Lyons, 1968: 477). Dillon's biographer, F. S. L. Lyons, comments: 'This was an extraordinary conclusion to have reached at the end of a lifetime spent in opposing British rule in Ireland, and there can be little doubt that the speech embarrassed some of his friends' (Lyons, 1968: 477–8). Nevertheless, Horace Plunkett, who had advocated dominion settlement for a united

Ireland throughout the crisis, and had his life threatened by Sinn Féin on that account, offered Dillon his support for a 'remarkable speech'. He added:

> In my field, I have serious complaints to make. I had something to do with building up a system of practical [technical] education and you can imagine my feelings at the treatment of the College of Science and of the whole system of vocational education at which I was the head. Yesterday I heard of a county council which had voted £1,400 for the teaching of Irish and £200 for technical education. I give it up.[71]

At the beginning of February 1923 Stephen Gwynn's house at Kimmage Road was blown up in his absence. The stated reason was 'the lack of sympathy' for the republican ideal exhibited in his articles. Gwynn's public reaction was restrained. He described one of the terrorists – who had helped his daughter remove some items of sentimental interest from the house – as a 'probably decent little boy who is ordered out to do dirty jobs'.[72] Gwynn took the loss of his library in his stride: 'Books suffer very little'. But it is unlikely that the event had no effect on his political attitudes; having been a stern critic of the Craig regime in Northern Ireland in the early days, he became a defender.[73] Replying to criticism of the regime's allegedly partisan security policy, Gwynn noted that there were, indeed, no Protestant internees, but 'There is, however, no danger of Protestant conspiracy to overthrow the government and therefore no need to arrest Protestants on suspicion . . . there are plenty of Protestant gunmen doing time and some with marks of the cat.'[74] He added: 'For my part I refuse to condemn the action of a government which has established peace, and is giving at all events rough fair play.'

As for allegations of sectarian employment in government service, Gwynn was equally resolute: 'Sinn Féin honeycombed the British service in Ireland with persons who thought it honest to conspire actively against the government which paid them. One cannot expect Sir James Craig and his ministers to have forgotten that nor blame them for acting on the memory.'[75] Stephen Gwynn had travelled a very long way, indeed – other parliamentary nationalists could not go so far. Nevertheless, it remains the case that the eventual resolution of the Anglo-Irish conflict represented not a triumph of the middle ground (see Garvin, 1996), but rather its radical displacement.

Defeated and marginalised though it was in the aftermath of the settlement, the Redmondite tradition did not lack allies in London journalism. In September 1922, J. L. Garvin, the editor of *The Observer*, wrote privately to Stephen Gwynn: 'The atavistic chinoiserie of the Gaelic Revolution can never unite any part of Ireland, but can only organise the real and lasting partition in a way that is going on now.'[76] But until recently such considerations had little impact on the writing of the history of the Irish revolution. This has had its unfortunate side if it is true, as Reinhard Koselleck has claimed: 'In the short run history is made by the victors. In the long run the gains in historical understanding have come from the defeated' (quoted in Hobsbawm, 1997). The historiographical neglect of the parliamentary nationalist critique of the impact of violence of the Irish revolution of 1916–23 has had a remarkable effect: the writing out of mainstream Irish history of any serious consideration of the role of that violence in exacerbating the Ulster problem, traditionally the most challenging aspect of even the moderate constitutionalist nationalist project (see, for example, Hopkinson, 2002; Augusteijn, 2002).

Similarly, those who have perceived British policy as being purely a matter of crisis management have ignored the degree to which, from spring 1920, official British policy – that is, the policy of the key officials, as opposed to public rhetoric – was always based on the necessity of making a pragmatic deal with Sinn Féin, but that objective was frequently complicated by upsurges in republican violence. There is a remarkable similarity with the 'peace process' of the 1990s. It was Sir John Anderson who said that 'he had never agreed with the government policy of singling Collins out as a murderer', because it was 'evident' that the British would have to talk peace with him (Moloney, 2002; but for a sceptical comment, see Trimble, 2002). It would be a mistake to see this as simply a cynical *Realpolitik*, for there was also a moral or ideological dimension. Stephen Gwynn saw this clearly: 'They [the British] had fought a great war cleanly, and their terrible losses had left them little but their pride. It lessened their pride and satisfaction to find themselves using force in Ireland to deny self-government to a small nation when they had regarded themselves as champions of self-government' (Gwynn, 1925: 303).

Chapter 6

The geopolitics of republican diplomacy in the twentieth century

Eunan O'Halpin

Introduction

This chapter explores the nature of the republican movement in post-independence Ireland with particular reference to its external links and their possible geopolitical consequences. In looking at aspects of the external relations of the Irish republican movement since the foundation of independent Ireland, it reflects on the ways in which republicanism's various alliances have been analysed by the British and American states, and the impact of such analyses on policies and actions in terms both of Irish republicanism and of Anglo-Irish relations. The chapter takes account of two recent dramatic developments which have occurred in the international security environment as these affect Irish republicanism – the discovery in August 2001 of apparent links between the Colombian narco-terrorist movement FARC and the IRA, and the attacks in the United States of 11 September 2001 (referred to hereafter as '9/11'). These events have occasioned sustained analysis and criticism of Irish republicanism's external relationships, and they have clear implications for American government support for Sinn Féin's role in the Irish peace process.

The discussion which follows is based on the premise that the best single motif for Irish republicanism's external relationships remains 'England's difficulty is Ireland's opportunity'. That hoary maxim, rather than a shared sense of suffering amongst oppressed peoples, or attachment to some vaguely transnational political ideology – Bolshevism in the 1920s, Stalinism and Nazism in the 1930s and 1940s, anticolonialism and revolutionary socialism in the 1950s, 1960s and beyond – best explains militant republicanism's eclectic range of political bedfellows. It has been precisely Irish republicanism's ideological promiscuity which prevented all but the chilliest or most eccentric of Cold War warriors from arguing that Irish republican violence after 1969 could be explained largely in terms of Soviet manipulation.[1]

Much recent debate on the Northern Ireland crisis has, nevertheless, centred on the ending of the Cold War as a defining moment, in terms of the internationalisation of the search for an end to conflict and in particular of the involvement of the United States in the peace process. Such arguments rely largely on the assumption that geopolitical change has resulted in local change through facilitating the involvement of the world's remaining superpower, no longer preoccupied by the spectre of a powerful, insecure and unpredictable military and ideological foe in the Soviet Union. However, no one has argued that the collapse of state communism and of the Soviet threat to the West has changed American government assessments of the nature of militant Irish republicanism. Even during the height of the Cold War, American policy-makers, while they rightly pointed to interconnections between terrorist movements including the IRA, and to evidence of a degree of Eastern bloc support, did not portray the mainstream IRA as a Soviet puppet, still less as a potential Soviet military partner in the event of an East–West conflict.[2]

Nor, it appears, did the United States hold back from sticking its oar into the Irish question because of the strategic salience of a British controlled Northern Ireland in a possible East–West conflict, an argument which frequently appeared in Irish republican analysis in its most anti-Western phase in the 1970s and early 1980s. How, then, can we explain American engagement with the Irish peace process in the last decade? Did it reflect a gradual dilution, in post-Cold War circumstances, of the Anglo-American 'special relationship'. There were occasional hints from inside the American foreign policy and intelligence systems that this relationship was indeed undergoing a graceful attenuation as the global interests and preoccupations of the two unequal partners diverged and as Blair's Britain moved towards accommodating itself within a distinct European Union security structure. But developments since 9/11, and in particular the campaign against the Taliban in Afghanistan in 2002 and the invasion of Iraq in 2003, indicate that the two states are still remarkably close in security matters.

There remains an even simpler explanation for America's lack of inde-pendent interest in the Irish problem: continuity of American policy on Ireland since the First World War. The Northern Ireland crisis was, at least in the State Department's anglophile eyes, if not simply an exclusively British problem, then one in which the United States had no positive role to play beyond limited action against Irish republican fundraising and arms procure-ment in America, and mild encouragement for Irish government moderation. President Carter's 1977 statement on Northern Ireland accords with that approach; his vague offer of general help amounted to support for any settle-ment which the parties to the conflict would reach, rather than suggesting an independent peace-forming or honest broker role for the United States (Dumbrell, 2000: 215).

Two final questions meriting exploration relate to republicanism's world-view. First, to what extent has the abandonment of republican absolutism and acceptance of a compromise settlement within Northern Ireland been accompanied by any reorientation towards an ideological position on international affairs generally broadly acceptable to mainstream American opinion? Second, was that spectacular shift at all influenced in the 1990s by the disintegration of the eastern bloc and of most Marxist states, resulting in the loss both of role models and of quiet sponsors for armed action? Or was it, as recent commentary maintains, the result primarily of the Provisional leadership's reassessment of Britain's underlying interests and willingness to meet republicanism half way (Moloney, 2002)? Using a handful of historical examples, I propose briefly to discuss a number of related questions. What have been the consequences arising from Irish republicanism's eclectic variety of alliances and understandings with foreign states and movements? How have these been analysed by the British, Irish and latterly the American governments? How has such analysis influenced states' perception of and policy towards militant republicanism? Does mainstream Irish republicanism have residual external ties, allegiances or obligations which would have alarming resonances for the troika of countries at the heart of the current peace process – Ireland, the United Kingdom, and the United States – or perhaps for some of Ireland's EU partners or other friendly states? Can Irish republican IOUs offered during the long war of the 1970s and 1980s now be honoured – perhaps a quid pro quo for ETA, back on the battlefield after an uneasy ceasefire, or for some Palestinian guerrilla group who gave a hand with training, weapons or operations – without antagonising the very governments which Sinn Féin now courts so relentlessly? Or is the newly respectable republicanism of Gerry Adams's Sinn Féin – pursuing inward investment from the United States and sporting the shamrock in the White House every March – now open to a variety of the charge which was levelled against de Valera in 1932 at a Fianna Fáil ard-fheis (shortly after he took office and declined to purge the public service), of forgiving foreign enemies and forgetting foreign friends (Andrews, 1982: 120)?

This chapter thus considers three broad sets of questions. The first has to do with the reality of the continued existence of the republican movement after 1922 as a factor in domestic Irish politics: waxing and waning in strength, sometimes prominent in the public consciousness and at other times entirely subterranean, it nevertheless formed part of a permanent backdrop to the pursuit of conventional politics in independent Ireland and in its neighbours to the North and to the East. Second, it was an enduring characteristic of this movement that, notwithstanding the implication of self-reliance embodied in the name of its political arm, Sinn Féin, it sought to maximise its own effectiveness by pursuing external allies in its struggle against British influence in

Ireland; these links are assessed below. Third, it is important to assess the significance of these external links; although a number of perspectives are considered, that of the IRA's principal enemy, the British government and its agencies, is accorded particular attention.

Irish republicanism: the internal dimension

As will be clear from chapter 4, the roots of the contemporary Irish republican movement lie in the split within the independence movement in 1922 over the Anglo-Irish Treaty of December 1921 which established the Irish Free State within the British Commonwealth and which left the six counties of Northern Ireland as part of the United Kingdom. This split resulted in civil war and in the decisive defeat of the anti-Treaty republican forces. Republican critiques of the Treaty at the time focused mainly on the fact that the Irish negotiators had achieved not a republic, but rather a new British dominion within the empire; it was only after the civil war that the problem of partition, and the difficult position of the nationalist minority in Northern Ireland, became the major focus of republican concern. The majority of those republicans who had opposed the Treaty fairly quickly recognised the practical legitimacy of the new state. In 1927 Eamon de Valera, who had led the political opposition to the treaty in 1922–3, abandoned the republican policy of abstention from state institutions and led his newly created Fianna Fáil – 'the Republican Party' as it claimed – into Dáil Éireann. Within five years he was in power.

A minority of anti-Treatyites clung to a purer republicanism, embodied in political terms by the abstentionist party Sinn Féin and in military terms by the IRA. The IRA recognised no authority save its own, and the tiny and eccentric Sinn Féin exercised no control over it (for an authoritative account of the IRA in this era see Hanley, 2002). In Northern Ireland the IRA faced severe repression after 1922, enjoyed little active support within the nationalist community, and was very weak structurally. In the early 1930s republicanism was distracted by internal disagreements, with left-wingers urging the adoption of a revolutionary socialist programme. These disputes resulted in 1934 in a left-wing breakaway organisation, the Republican Congress, which greatly reduced the influence of the left within the mainstream IRA (Hanley, 2002: 105–9). For some years after 1926 the IRA leadership thought that a deal acceptable to republicans could be made with their former comrades, now in Fianna Fáil. This calculation, together with sporadic state repression and considerable organisational problems, meant that a widespread military campaign against the state was deferred again and again, although occasional operations were carried out.

It was only in the mid-1930s that hopes of a *rappochement* were finally abandoned. By then, however, the Irish state was too strong for the IRA to contemplate armed action against it, while the continued abstentionist tactics of Sinn Féin rendered the party politically meaningless. In Northern Ireland the position was even worse, with the IRA reduced to a small and ineffectual organisation which survived only by inactivity. It was in these circumstances that republicans sought to use the international climate to their advantage, making overtures to a number of states regarded as hostile to Britain. In the late 1920s and early 1930s the Soviet Union appeared the most suitable foreign friend, reflecting the strength of the left within the republican movement; in the event, the most significant links established were with Nazi Germany (these are discussed below).

During the Second World War the IRA was reduced almost to extinction by vigorous repression once its Nazi links were uncovered. The years which followed were about survival rather than about a military campaign or a revival of political action. The former IRA chief of staff Sean MacBride did establish a radical republican party, Clann na Poblachta, but this sucked away support and talent from anti-state republicanism. Yet the republican movement survived, and by the mid-1950s it was sufficiently organised to plan a new military campaign. Launched in December 1956 as 'Operation Harvest', this 'border campaign' focused on the core republican grievance of partition. Despite its emotional appeal in both parts of the island, the campaign was a damp squib. It resulted in the introduction of internment on both sides of the border, severely limiting the IRA's ability to mount further operations, and it shook neither the southern nor the northern states, although Sinn Féin abstentionist candidates won four seats in the 1957 general election in the Republic (O'Halpin, 1999: 300).

The 'Border campaign' was formally ended early in 1962. Its abject failure led to major debate within the republican movement. Many argued that what republicanism needed if it were to rally public support was a coherent political agenda which addressed the wider social and economic ills of Ireland. In this rerun of the debates of the early 1930s, a new IRA leadership emerged under Cathal Goulding which adopted a broadly Marxist analysis of Irish politics, taking inspiration from left-wing liberation movements elsewhere in the world and arguing for a socialist revolution which would unite the Irish working classes north and south. This gave an intellectual coherence to republican doctrine, but problems remained. It exposed the IRA to accusations of external communist influence, a charge which had much resonance amongst traditionalists within the republican movement who saw partition, not capitalism, as the source of Ireland's woes. On the other hand, the new emphasis on social and economic factors enabled the republican movement to relate to emerging themes in politics abroad, particularly in respect of civil and human rights.

The republican movement supported, if it did not partly foment, the civil rights agitation in Northern Ireland which began in 1964. That campaign, with its emphasis on debate and on limited and peaceful protest, posed an acute dilemma for the Northern Ireland government and unionist majority. Attempts to acknowledge and to address unarguable minority grievances were halting and half-hearted, as Prime Minister O'Neill sought to juggle limited reform with the need to placate his own supporters. The outbreak of serious rioting and sectarian street fighting in the autumn of 1969 proved the catalyst not only for O'Neill's resignation but for a major split within the republican movement. In December 1969 an IRA Convention carefully stage managed by Goulding saw a defining split: a large majority of delegates supported the leadership, but a dozen walked out. A new coalition was formed, linking traditionalist southerners with northerners who were frustrated by the failures of Dublin-based theorisers. The latter allegedly did not understand conditions in Northern Ireland, and particularly in Belfast, and had provided neither leadership nor security to nationalists during the street violence in the latter half of 1969. This coalition immediately established new military and political organisations, the Provisional IRA and Provisional Sinn Féin (Moloney, 2002: 70–3).

Within three years the Goulding-led 'Official IRA' had declared a ceasefire in the armed campaign that had begun in 1970, leaving the field to the Provisionals, who had become the dominant force in militant republican politics and military action. By 1974 republicanism had two militant paramilitary groups and attendant political wings: the Provisional IRA with Provisional Sinn Féin, and the small, fractious Irish National Liberation Army (INLA) and the Irish Republican Socialist Party, founded by former supporters of the 'Official' movement and adopting a broadly Trotskyite analysis of the Irish conflict. The latter groups were never more than fringe players in republican politics. The people who mattered, militarily and as time went on politically, were the Provisionals.

Irish republicanism: the external dimension up to 1945

It is useful briefly to take stock of Irish republicanism's various external alliances in the first half of the twentieth century, and the interpretations placed on these in London and Washington. The Easter rising of 1916 was, after all, largely inspired and financed by Germany. That these 'gallant allies in Europe' of the 1916 proclamation were themselves imperialists with scant respect for the independence of other states was an incongruity with which the Irish revolutionaries could live, just as a later generation could accommodate themselves to alliances with more hideous tyrannies. The arrangements for the rising were made through contacts in the United States between the German embassy and the Irish-American secret society Clan na Gael, while the Germans also attempted to harness the Irish diaspora on the East Coast for sabotage operations against munitions shipments bound for Britain and France. Germany's modest investment of money and captured weapons for Irish separatists proved a remarkably good one in terms of strategic diversion, albeit one which she signally failed to exploit either militarily or politically in the succeeding years. Strangely, however, it was the British rather than the Germans who sought to capitalise on this investment. In London in May 1918 politicised intelligence officers concocted a 'German plot' out of what the cabinet secretary described as 'evidence of the most flimsy and ancient description' in order to provide an excuse for cracking down on Sinn Féin in the wake of the Irish conscription crisis.[3] Significantly, when approached by the British the American government made clear that it would neither publish the relevant documents as though they had been discovered in the United States, 'nor give public sanction to their publication in England'.[4] Washington was reluctant to be publicly associated with action against the Irish separatist movement. For instance, no action was taken against the American-based Irish instigators of the 1916 rising, nor was any effort made to play up Irish involvement in Germany's shipping sabotage schemes. By contrast, Indian nationalists based in the United States were harassed vigorously for conspiring against British rule in India, most strikingly in the 'Hindoo-German conspiracy' trial in San Francisco in 1915 which centred on plans to ship arms from California (Popplewell, 1987: 49–76). American unwillingness to take similar action against Irish–German conspiracy and sabotage was most likely attributable to the perceived power of the Irish–American diaspora in domestic politics.

From 1919, Irish separatism sought support from the new Bolshevik regime in Russia. This essay in revolutionary diplomacy prompted the British government in 1921 into a half-hearted attempt publicly to demonstrate a meaningful link between Sinn Feinism and Bolshevism and thereby to imply that in essence they were part and parcel of a single revolutionary wave which threatened the established civilised order. The reality, however, was that while some in the Irish labour movement were undoubtedly inspired by the Russian revolution, the interest of the Dáil government in the new Russia was limited to securing mutual recognition of their respective claims to independent statehood. Bolshevik interest in separatist Ireland also proved minimal, as the Dáil government's emissary, Dr Patrick McCartan, reported from Russia in a perceptive undated memorandum in 1921: 'I am not so sure . . . that self-determination for Ireland would raise much enthusiasm in official circles. Anything they are likely to do for Ireland will be done in the hope of helping to break up the British Empire and thus further the world revolution' (Fanning et al., 1998: 156–8).

Subsequent efforts to obtain weapons and money from Russia during the Irish civil war of 1922–3 got nowhere, while the only concrete outcome of a visit by a republican delegation to the Soviet Union in 1925 was a confused and short-lived understanding whereby the IRA was to collect military intelligence in Britain. The arrangement, maintained through a contact in Berlin, did not last for long. The British later became aware of this limited exercise in IRA–Soviet collaboration, and it was adduced two decades later by the Irish director of intelligence as proof of how a foreign power could harness Irish extremism for its own strategic interests, threatening Anglo–Irish relations in the process (O'Halpin, 1999: 275). In 1927 the IRA, by then under considerable left-wing influence, committed the republican movement to side with Russia in any future Anglo–Soviet conflict. It seems unlikely that this second coming of the *Skibbereen Eagle* weighed much in the scales for Stalin, but it indicated at least an ambition on some republicans' part to link their struggle to a wider revolutionary cause (O'Halpin, 1999: 72–4). Whether this resolution was ever rescinded is unknown, but too much weight should not be put on such pronouncements.

Bolshevism was regarded in British and American defence and security circles in the 1920s as the greatest single threat to the international order and, to quote an MI5 document, for almost the entire interwar period Soviet Russia was viewed, with Germany, as 'one of the two real threats to British security . . . Russia as a powerful military State controlling the Comintern organisation and utilising the national communist parties all over the world.'[5] On the face of it, consequently, one might expect to find evidence of British unease at Irish republican and communist links with the Soviet Union. In fact, concern that the IRA might become a tool of the Soviets is conspicuous by its absence in the available diplomatic and security records. Red scares had their day in independent Ireland, most significantly as a result of ill-judged government propaganda during the fevered 1932 election campaign which resulted in de Valera's first coming to power. Even at the time, however, no one outside Ireland appeared to take the charge remotely seriously. The British government, transfixed with worry at the prospect of having to deal with de Valera if he won power, saw him not as the Bolshevik stooge depicted by his Cumann na nGaedheal opponents, but rather as an irresponsible and unpredictable republican demagogue who would do all he could to wreck the Treaty and who might be an irritant in wider dominion relations. They hopelessly misjudged his probable tactics, if not his long-term aims, but they at least avoided the trap of labelling him as Moscow's puppet (O'Halpin, 2000c: 65–7).

Nor, it appears, did the British worry much about good evidence of actual exchanges between republicans and communists in Ireland and the Soviet Union in the 1920s and 1930s. In fact, in defiance of isolationist caricature, the

American State Department was more inclined to fret about the slightest signs of communist influence in the new European states. This was despite visible growth in left-wing influence within the Irish republican movement after 1927, as well as increased contacts between the Irish left and the Soviet Union through the work of the Communist International (Comintern) and associated Soviet controlled groups. In building up links with the IRA, the Comintern sometimes 'bypassed the Irish communists' altogether, instead dealing with individual members of the IRA leadership (Hanley, 2002: 179). Occasional scraps of intelligence on such links, some fantastic and some credible, continued to surface in London well into the 1930s. For example, the British Secret Intelligence Service (SIS, also known as MI6) received reports of a complex agreement signed in Bergen in Norway between 14 and 20 April 1933 between representatives of the IRA and of 'the Military Section of the Executive Committee of the Communist International', under which the Soviets would

> help in camouflaging .. . purchases of arms in Germany. The IRA buys arms directly from Messrs. SPIRO (Berlin and Hamburg). Up till now the firm camouflaged the Irish orders as if they had been received from the Chinese and Paraguayan governments. As this camouflage is no longer practicable they want a new one. The Soviets have agreed to arrange such a camouflage . . .
>
> The deliveries of arms and munitions to the IRA began in the end of May last. Up till the end of June 6000 rifles with considerable quantity of rounds of ammunition, 60 bomb-throwers and 120 heavy and light machine-guns have been delivered. According to the convention altogether not less than 80,000 rifles and considerable number of machine-guns must be smuggled into Ireland . . . during the summer months of this year.[6]

If only a fraction of this weaponry had reached Ireland, the IRA's history might have been very different. In fact, by the early 1930s the organisation had switched its arms buying energies from Europe to the United States (Hanley, 2002: 28–35). Perhaps chastened by a false alarm in 1932, when reports of major Soviet arms shipments from Hamburg had been taken very seriously by a cabinet committee, this report of an IRA–Soviet concordat was dismissed because it came from an unreliable Russian émigré source.[7]

The equanimity with which the ramifications of communism in Ireland were regarded contrasts with Britain's acute nervousness about such matters elsewhere in the empire, particularly in India. There it was an article of faith amongst security officials – at least until June 1941 – that the Indian separatist movement was under the indirect control, through the Communist Party of India, of the Soviet Union. The government of India expended enormous energy on the detection of communist wrongdoing throughout the interwar decades. Indeed, mention of the Meerut conspiracy case of 1929–32 still has resonance for old British India hands.[8] Yet it was clear even then that there was more to Indian nationalism than sly Soviet manipulation; as readers of Kipling well know, the great game of British–Russian competition and intrigue in the region long predated the Bolshevik revolution.

If the British overestimated the significance of covert communist activity and Soviet intrigue in India, they made no such mistake where Ireland was concerned. The new state was, its republican faction notwithstanding, manifestly rural, conservative and Catholic. If the British were at all concerned about the possibility of communist influence, they were presumably reassured through their interception and decoding of secret Comintern radio traffic in the mid-1930s. This indicated that Moscow, far from seeking to stir the Irish pot for wider ends, did not even bother to deal with the handful of Irish comrades bilaterally. Instead the Soviets replicated the power relationships of the British empire which in principle they sought to destroy, leaving it to Harry Pollitt, the general secretary of the Communist Party of Great Britain (CPGB), to give the Irish their orders. Pollitt also passed on a monthly subsidy pitifully small even by Comintern standards. The decrypted traffic which has survived in British records suggests that no-one in Moscow had the least understanding of actual political conditions in Ireland, or any sympathy for the travails of the perennially indebted and misfortunate Irish communists.[9] Although these mid-1930s decrypts and other evidence indicated vague ambitions for combined action on economic and social issues with the republican movement within Ireland, there was no hint that the Comintern or any other Soviet agency planned to harness the Irish left for a wider subversive, sabotage or intelligence gathering agenda of the kind feared elsewhere in Europe and the empire. In this connection it is notable that, when war came in 1939, Whitehall's not entirely fanciful fears about CPGB-orchestrated anti-war activities in the United Kingdom (until June 1941, when Germany attacked the Soviet Union) were not accompanied, then or later, by any stated worries about Soviet manipulation of the Irish left against British interests in Northern Ireland. It is also significant that the lengthy in-house wartime history of MI5's Irish section did not even mention either communist influence within the republican movement, or known pre-war links between some Irish republicans and the Soviet Union. This was despite the fact that as a pan-island body the Irish communist network operated in both jurisdictions and thus would have appeared as a natural vehicle for subversive action against the war effort.[10]

In the 1930s republican diplomacy switched targets, with senior IRA figures such as Sean MacBride, Sean Russell, Tom Barry and Seamus O'Donovan in turn focusing on Hitler's resurgent Germany as a power with which business might be done at Britain's expense. There is also fragmentary evidence – decoded telegrams from Dublin from 1935 and 1936 – in which an Italian diplomat spoke of his contacts with the IRA, 'the only Irish party that by fighting against' Britain 'fights against sanctions' and 'might be useful to us for propaganda work' and possibly 'other kind of force'. He reported that he had interviewed IRA leaders and had agreed with them on a plan for action in the United States; the IRA contact in New York would be John T. Ryan.[11]

Mention of John T. Ryan in this cable does suggest that genuine contact had been made with elements of the republican movement. Ryan was an experienced gunrunner and a significant figure in Clan na Gael, although it is hard to understand what propaganda help the Italians could have secured from Irish–Americans. In Ireland the IRA newspaper *An Phoblacht* consistently condemned Italy's actions in Abyssinia (Hanley, 2002: 174). But the Italian–IRA contacts, even if only with an unrepresentative faction within the IRA leadership, underlined the ideological heterogeneity of republican diplomacy.

This is also reflected in the fact that the key external link forged by the IRA in the late 1930s was with Hitler's Germany. For a miscellany of reasons – ranging from straightforward anti-British feeling to the memory of Germany as a former ally to the affinity with aspects of Nazi ideology felt by some republicans – serious contact was established between the republican movement and Germany in 1939 with a view to co-ordinated action against Britain. The Germans showed some interest in the IRA's potential for disruption, sabotage and intelligence gathering in the United Kingdom, and these contacts facilitated the development of propaganda and espionage links when the Second World War broke out. The German–IRA relationship was almost entirely pragmatic, as reflected in the involvement in Berlin in the planning of German schemes of the former International Brigade officer and IRA left-winger Frank Ryan. On the other hand, at least one Irishman centrally involved was regarded not only by the Irish authorities but by his friends to be ideologically attracted to Nazism and to see himself as the future 'Irish Quisling', while the IRA's illicit newspaper *War News* was at times rabidly anti-Semitic as well as violently pro-German (O'Halpin, 1999: 149; Hanley, 2002: 184–5).

It would be mischievous to argue a continuity with contemporary republicanism's support for the Palestinian cause, although that position is not without its embarrassments and inconsistencies. Germany also sought to strengthen and exploit links between the republican movement and ethnic nationalists in France, Belgium, The Netherlands, Wales and Scotland before and during the war. This had no tangible results, but in the years after 1945 Ireland became a haven for a handful of Breton and Flemish activists fleeing prosecution for their wartime collaboration with Germany. These were warmly welcomed in republican and radical circles, where they were viewed not as Nazi collaborators but as fellow nationalists and refugees from political persecution.

The very existence of the German–IRA link, which had first come to British notice through an intelligence report from Berlin of July 1939, provided both Britain and independent Ireland with acute problems throughout the war period, and was a major and at times almost decisive element in British policy making. British military planners took it for granted that the IRA would operate in support of a German attack, and in the fraught weeks after the German assaults on The Netherlands and Belgium in May 1940, the British fully expected a German paratroop assault on Ireland in concert with action by the IRA 'fifth column' as a prelude to, or as part of, an attempted invasion of Britain (Churchill to Roosevelt, 15 May 1940, quoted in O'Halpin, 1999: 174). On 29 May 1940 Prime Minister Winston Churchill was informed by his closest intelligence aide that such an attack was almost certain, and that even if it did not soon materialise the IRA was sufficiently well organised, equipped and prepared to overwhelm the almost 'derisory' Irish army on its own.[12] A day later, British diplomats informed the Department of External Affairs that a German attack, to be supported by concerted IRA action, was not merely expected but was 'imminent'.

These calculations formed an important backdrop to the frenzied British search for ways to get Ireland into the war, short of invading her before the Germans acted. These included such esoteric ideas as the promotion of a Franco-Irish alliance on the basis of a shared revolutionary heritage. That suggestion was superseded by the better-known proposal of eventual Irish unity in return for Irish participation. British fears about the IRA's military potential to aid a German assault on any part of the island of Ireland gradually lessened in the face of energetic Irish government action and of better intelligence on Irish affairs, resulting in more sober assessments of IRA capacities, intentions and links with Germany. After Pearl Harbor, the dispatch of American troops to Northern Ireland gave the United States government a direct interest in the threat posed by the republican movement's haphazard efforts to collect intelligence of use to Germany. The problem of German intelligence gathering, to an extent assisted by republicans, continued to create acute difficulties in Anglo–Irish and in Irish–American relations for almost the whole of the Second World War and in early 1944 seemed likely to jeopardise the maintenance of neutrality (O'Halpin, 2000a: 71–83).

For our purposes, what is most significant about the IRA–Nazi nexus between 1939 and 1945 is not its particular potential, achievements and failures, but the speed and ease with which the republican movement was able to shed the memory of this odious alliance. They were helped in this by a number of domestic factors, including widespread Irish resentment at Churchill's intemperate attack on Irish neutrality in his VE ('Victory in Europe') day broadcast, and perhaps a quiet awareness that pro-German and even Nazi sympathies had not been confined to any one Irish party or movement.[13]

What is more surprising is that the British were not inclined to dwell on the IRA's perfidy in courting Hitler. In the latter part of the war and in the years which followed, it was mainstream Irish neutrality and the Irish government's supposed sneaking regard for the Nazis which were the main targets for British public criticism and reproach.

Republicanism's external links after 1945: official interpretations

The most striking aspect of republicanism's links with anti-western groups and states is not their demonstrable existence, but the very limited impact which their discovery appears to have had on western analysis of what might be termed the republican movement's geopolitical significance and potential in terms of East–West conflict. This was despite evidence of Moscow gold and of East German succour for republican splinter groups, and despite the belated discovery of Libya's crucial quartermastering and financing of the Provisional IRA in the 1970s and the 1980s. There was also a clear ideological shift within Sinn Féin, which in the 1980s adopted at least a patina of Marxist terminology – in 1984 a leading Sinn Féin theoretician took umbrage when questioned about his claim that he was 'a socialist first, and a republican only second'.[14] But there has been a dearth of what might be termed Cold War centred analyses of modern Irish republicanism.

As the Cold War began in the late 1940s, the intermittent foreign inter-actions of anti-state republicanism and of Irish left-wingers evinced some British and American security interest. However, the evidence suggests that the security services of Ireland's nearest neighbours to the east and west were disinclined to worry much about Irish republicanism as a potential fifth column in a time of tension with the Eastern bloc. They sought Irish information on the communist movement, but there was seldom more to talk about with Irish intelligence officers than could be dealt with by a few 'good lunches' a year.[15] The fact that Irish republican activities were excluded from the Anglo-Irish security dialogue perhaps contributed to the British tendency to see these as a local problem quite unrelated to the Cold War. The RAF's Sir John Slessor wrote in 1952 that there was 'a pretty nasty gap in NATO to which no-one has paid any attention recently, namely the completely defenceless position of EIRE, and the inability of NATO to make any use of IRISH bases', but what was absent, then and later, was any concomitant fear that Irish republicanism could successfully be courted by the Soviets as a strategic ally, as previous generations of separatists had been encouraged by imperial Germany and by the Nazis.[16]

Considerable evidence was available in the 1950s and 1960s of some intermingling of republicanism and Marxism, and also clear indications that this development was supported, though certainly not initiated, by the Soviet Union as part of its general anti-western strategy (Patterson, 1997: 96–110; Goren, 1984: 171–2). But British analysis of the Irish republican threat remained determinedly parochial. Even when Northern Ireland was plunged into crisis following the Derry riots in August 1969, British intelligence organisations construed events almost entirely in local terms. In a sombre review of 'the past week', which 'has seen the most serious disturbances in Northern Ireland since the 1920s', the Joint Intelligence Committee's (JIC) Ulster Working Group adduced no evidence of external manipulation. Under 'International Links' it reported only that 'Extremists in London have established links with Northern Ireland Civil Rights leaders. Known London Trotskyites are trying to gain international support for demonstrations; some foreign students were seen to be active in Londonderry.'[17]

In the early 1970s both the Provisional IRA and the Marxist-oriented Official IRA broadened and deepened their links with Eastern bloc countries and with some Middle Eastern states which were close to the Soviet Union. They also developed quite extensive contacts with a variety of anti-Western terrorist organisations in the Middle East and in Europe. Eastern bloc material published since the end of the Cold War, for example in the contested but probably authentic *Mitrovkhin Archives* and in Boris Yeltsin's memoirs, confirm the impression of a pattern of somewhat lukewarm and bemused Soviet and Eastern bloc support for the republican movement, and particularly its Marxist wing in the 1970s and 1980s, with Moscow's help being sought through the tiny Irish communist movement (Andrew and Mitrovkhin, 2000: 492, 501–3; Yeltsin, 1994: 311–16). Irish republicanism's Middle Eastern links were, however, probably of more practical significance despite their ideological incongruity. Libya was particularly generous for some years in the 1970s and 1980s, providing weapons and financial support without, apparently, demanding any reciprocal actions. It was enough that the IRA was fighting Britain, which ranked below only the United States and Israel in Colonel Gadhafi's demonology (Moloney, 2002: 3–32).

The arrest of three Irishmen travelling on false passports in Colombia in August 2001, one of them a convicted IRA bomb maker, led to charges by the Colombian authorities that the IRA had for years been providing the Colombian terrorist organisation FARC with technical expertise on explosives and mortars in return for large amounts of money. One of those arrested was the Sinn Féin representative in Cuba, a connection initially denied by the party. The eventual forced admission of this link compounded republican embarrassment because it highlighted Irish republican engagement with what the United States regards as largely Cuban-inspired South American subversive movements. These developments occasioned strong statements from the American government; for example in May 2002 Ambassador Richard Haass,

President Bush's Northern Ireland envoy, said there were 'obviously links' between the IRA and FARC which would have to be abandoned, while a Congressional committee drew broadly similar conclusions.[18]

Whatever the case against the 'Colombia Three' on trial in Bogota, the Bush administration maintained that evidence had emerged of a lengthy commercial relationship between FARC and the IRA in which Irish terrorist expertise has been traded for money. There is a certain irony in the possibility that such arrangements, besides producing cash for the mainstream republican movement as it converts to a mainly political path, in recent years have provided a continuing professional outlet for some of the IRA's most experienced operatives and may thus have contributed to the stability of the peace process by keeping some of its veterans doing what they know best well away from Ireland.

Put simply, few academic observers or even professional analysts appear ever to have believed that mainstream Irish republicanism was either the willing tool or unwitting cat's paw of outside forces. Rather, in the 1970s and 1980s even the most resolute Cold War warriors continued to analyse the IRA in terms of its parochial anti-British and anti-partition agenda, and to note the relative insignificance of the more overtly Marxist Official IRA and IRSP/INLA. The fact of militant Irish republicanism's alignment with anti-Western regimes and movements – particularly important for the arms, explosives, training, and money necessary to keep the long war going – seemed to count for very little in either Britain or the United States (where Provisional propaganda naturally eschewed left-wing rhetoric and stuck to old-style denunciations of British rule). Aside from an occasional piece in the *Daily Telegraph*, and the idiosyncratic fulminations of the eccentric one-time deputy head of MI6, George Kennedy Young, even those who were most vehement in exposing and denouncing Eastern Bloc support for the IRA stopped short of arguing that the Provisional IRA were simply Moscow's puppets (Young, [1985?]: 72, 80–1).

This might appear to be no more than common sense. It does, however, contrast markedly with the difficult experience of Latin America since the 1960s, where even the most moderate and pacific advocates of land redistribution or greater social equity could expect to be branded as Eastern Bloc stooges by influential American policy makers. It also contrasts with the parallel debate over the tide of events in South Africa during the struggle for majority rule. In that case, the argument was forcibly and repeatedly heard in Britain, not simply on the right wing of the Tory party but from academics and commentators of some standing with links to the foreign policy and defence establishments, that whatever the failings of the apartheid regime, the popular movement against it had been hijacked by the Soviet Union and its local proxies. Such arguments are neatly encapsulated in a study by the

Institute for the Study of Terrorism resonantly titled *ANC: a Soviet task force?*, but they were also accommodated within conventional academic discourse on terrorism and the Cold War (Campbell, 1986).

So why was mainstream Irish republicanism not daubed with the red brush, when movements and even elected governments in other parts of the world with greater commitment to democratic values, far greater popular legitimacy, and far less violent methods were? Is it perhaps because Eastern Bloc assistance to Irish republicanism since the late 1960s, while vaguely intended to produce diversionary dividends, was evidently not linked to any wider strategy or future plans, and was provided entirely without strings? Is it simply that no one who knew anything about the mainstream republican movement could seriously regard it as authentically revolutionary in an international context? Or is it the case that a movement which commanded support within elements of the traditionally conservative, anti-communist and Catholic Irish–American diaspora could not possibly be construed as Marxist inspired or controlled?

There may be merit in all of those arguments, but a further possibility can be advanced. Despite the German–IRA nexus during the Second World War, the British policy system has long been conditioned to look at Irish problems as something apart from the normal run of international business, neither deriving from nor relying on wider political trends, and not to be confused with larger geopolitical challenges. In addition, even when the IRA's subversive and espionage potential was a major British security preoccupation during the Second World War, and despite other security problems posed by the permeability of the Irish border, MI5 had not been allowed to operate in Northern Ireland because of the RUC's sensitivities. After the war, furthermore, it appears that the study of Irish republicanism was left almost entirely to the RUC and to the Scotland Yard Special Branch (O'Halpin, 2000b: 149–50).

This hypothesis is supported by the fact that as late as St Patrick's Day in 1966, when there was considerable concern at the political level in London and Belfast about the possibility of IRA violence to mark the fiftieth anniversary of the 1916 rising, MI5 remained so preoccupied with the reality of Eastern Bloc espionage, and with the phantom of domestic ideological subversion, that it loftily declined responsibility for studying anything so local, familiar and idiosyncratic as Irish republicanism: that was a criminal matter for the Special Branch to handle (O'Halpin, 1999: 291).[19] We might also note statements at the Bloody Sunday inquiry, which, if true, indicate that when MI5 finally did take a direct interest in Northern Ireland in 1969, initially without the knowledge of the RUC Special Branch, the main job of the first officers in the field was the study neither of republicanism nor of Ulster loyalism but of local offshoots of British far-right fringe parties.[20] In November 1997 a very senior Whitehall source, answering questions about the changing role of MI5 in the post-Cold War world, was asked to identify what he regarded as the organisation's biggest mistake of the previous 30 years. He unhesitatingly replied 'not taking the IRA seriously enough early enough'.[21]

Anecdotal evidence also bears out the argument that in the late 1960s the British machinery of intelligence analysis and assessment was so preoccupied with the Cold War that nothing else mattered. In the summer of 1968, as the Northern Ireland lid began to rattle, the Cabinet Office's Joint Intelligence Committee (JIC) was solemnly pondering an accumulation of evidence of a Warsaw Pact military build-up close to Czechoslovakia – 'we knew the call sign of every field ambulance unit' – before cheerfully discarding as implausible, just before the Russian tanks began to clank towards Prague, the straight-forward explanation that the Soviets were preparing to invade a fellow Warsaw Pact country in order to put a stop to Dubček's dangerous experiment in liberalisation.[22]

Analysis of the threat from Irish republicanism was not excessively coloured by Cold War perceptions and concerns. On the contrary, there appears to have been too great a division between the apparently local and sporadic Northern Ireland problem and the obviously geopolitical challenges of the Cold War, with the energies of the policy system and of intelligence collection agencies going into the latter – not, as the Czechoslovak example indicates, always to great effect – while within the United Kingdom catastrophic trouble brewed unstudied by the state's intelligence machine. The collection agencies, by this argument, were simply not interested in the local question of Northern Ireland because the problem of republican terrorism had always been treated as *sui generis*, had never been seen in a Cold War light, and was consequently not sufficiently important in geopolitical terms to merit their attention.[23] Events in Northern Ireland soon forced a revaluation of these priorities, as the establishment of the JIC's 'Ulster Working Group' indicates.[24] In the following years the JIC and the Cabinet Office's co-ordinator of intelligence, Sir Dick White, who while a senior MI5 officer had managed Anglo-Irish security liaison during the 1940s and 1950s, were to spend considerable time attempting to bring coherence to the British intelligence effort against Irish terrorism.[25]

American assessments of contemporary republicanism's external links have, similarly, treated them as incidental relationships rather than as long-term affairs or as evidence of instrumental external control. The Bush admin-istration signalled its irritation at Colombia. That embarrassment, Sinn Féin's enthusiasm for Cuba and the party's vehement opposition to war against Iraq notwithstanding, Gerry Adams met President Bush at the St Patrick's Day celebrations in Washington in 2003.[26]

Conclusion

The post-Cold War spectres which haunt the imaginations of intelligence officials – rogue states acquiring weapons of mass destruction, environmental terrorism, Islamic fundamentalism – have no obvious Irish ideological resonances, although we should recall the dramatic military benefits to the Provisional IRA of their links with Libya in the 1970s and 1980s. Furthermore, Sinn Féin's dialogue with successive American administrations since 1994 has been paralleled by the quiet setting aside of Marxist rhetoric in favour of the language of political pluralism, of human rights and of economically justified investment. In any case, revolutionary socialism is out of fashion: the Soviet Union and the peoples' republics of central and eastern Europe are no more, and Cuba and North Korea are scarcely inspiring political role models. On the other hand, Irish republicanism has identified itself increasingly closely with the Palestinian cause against Israel. This makes some sense in terms of Sinn Féin's pursuit of both domestic and international standing as a radical political party, although it also recalls the awkward memory of the IRA's past association with Nazi Germany.

In a period when it has commanded the unprecedented attention of the United States, a combination of geopolitical and domestic factors has ensured that mainstream Irish republicanism has shed most of the broadly anti-western trappings it had acquired since the early 1960s. It would, however, be wrong to infer a causal link between this ideological reorientation and the growing respectability of ceasefire republicanism in the post-Cold War world. Despite its various external alliances and its record of co-operation with Britain's enemies in both world wars, the reality is that the republican movement was never analysed primarily in Cold War terms by either the British or American governments. This is reflected in the fact that the monitoring of Irish republicanism in the post-war era was seen in Britain primarily as a police task. In short, in spite of its history Irish republicanism was never seriously regarded as part of a broader threat to Western defence interests. Consequently its close links with anti-Western states and movements during the last three decades proved neither an embarrassment nor an obstacle as it sought to build on its new-found acceptability in America's corridors of power. Notwithstanding the shocks of Colombia, of 9/11, and of republican involvement in an Irish anti-war movement in 2003 that was associated with pronouncedly anti-American rhetoric, the evidence is that the United States administration remains unwilling seriously to sanction Irish republicanism for its foreign friendships. In its international alignments, Sinn Féin can still have its cake and eat it.

Chapter 7

Modern unionism and the cult of 1912–14

Alvin Jackson

Introduction

Like other major political movements that aspire to develop a mass support base, or that have succeeded in doing so, contemporary unionism needs an origin myth. To the extent that internal structural divisions, disputes over policy priorities and disagreements over tactics intensify, so too does pressure for the generation of a potentially unifying image of the movement's past. Irish nationalism has possessed a powerful mythology of this kind, one seen as rooting the 'Irish nation' in the mists of prehistory and describing its struggle for survival over the centuries. The purpose of this chapter is to examine a parallel development in the case of the unionist community: the packaging of a vivid account of a formative period in modern unionist history, that associated with the campaign of resistance that temporarily thwarted Irish home rule and that contributed directly to the birth of Northern Ireland.[1]

The events of 1912–14 in Ireland have served as a creation myth for unionism in the twentieth century – as a kind of Orange Genesis. Shaped and strengthened by the patriarchs Edward Carson and James Craig,[2] unionism survived political challenge from a serpentine H. H. Asquith and reappeared, with the steeples of Tyrone and Fermanagh, from the deluge of the Great War. The unionist rulers of Northern Ireland saw in the issues and personalities of 1912–14 an important moral prop in the same way as varieties of nationalist have sought to cultivate the legacies of Wolfe Tone or Padraig Pearse, and varieties of English commentator have sought retroactive definitions of the Glorious Revolution.[3]

Carson has emerged as an Orange icon, a fact recognised in a literal sense in the diptych painted by Joseph McWilliams; he has emerged as an Orange Daniel O'Connell, 'the saviour of his tribe' – protecting the least of his people from British betrayal, unifying and mobilising his community in a uniquely thorough manner.[4] The emotional bond between this latter-day Counsellor and his following, a bond well captured in Gerald Dawe's poem 'A question of covenants', was of a peculiarly intense quality: mill-women kissed his hand; country squires treated him with an exaggerated reverence (Dawe, 1985: 13). The emotional charge of Ulster Day, 28 September 1912, when thousands gathered at Belfast City Hall to oppose home rule, long persisted in the northern folk memory. It is an ironic testimony to the potency of this image that contemporary unionists, in organising their first major demonstration against the Anglo-Irish Agreement, should have chosen precisely the same location as their forefathers, opposing an earlier act of ministerial 'treachery', did in 1912. Photographs taken from the dome of the City Hall in 1985 consciously mimic the sepia images of 1912.[5] Ian Paisley plays Carson to James Molyneaux's Craig: both invoke the men of 1912 in legitimising their creed. The mythology of 1912–14 is therefore a central feature of latter-day unionism, with memories of Edwardian derring-do remaining alive and relevant, and with the actions of the Edwardian leadership generating a still complete respect and reverence.

Nevertheless, just as the reputation of O'Connell was illuminated in different ways, depending on the needs of nineteenth-century Irish nationalism (McCartney, 1984), so Carson and the men of 1912 have been examined from different perspectives, and exploited in different forms. Successive generations of unionist, and successive forms of unionism, embrace different aspects of the myth, even if all tacitly agree in looking back to 1912–14 for whatever form of legitimisation they seek. Unionist chroniclers and propagandists, beginning with Ronald McNeill in 1922, accepted that this was a period of unique internal unity within northern unionism, a period when the cohesion of unionism and between unionism and its allies was pretty well complete (McNeill, 1922; Jackson, 1989b, 1990a). The Protestant clergy, women and children were politicised, and were bound into organised or active unionism as never before: the young C. S. Lewis, cocooned in suburban loyalism, was writing essays on the home rule question from the age of ten, on the eve of the constitutional crisis.[6] An Ulster Women's Unionist Council was first formed in 1911, and was quickly followed by local offspring (Kinghan, 1975: 9–95; Urquhart, 2001). Generally the numbers of men and women responding to their leaders were unprecedented: just under 500,000 signed the Ulster Covenant; some 100,000 were (nominally) recruited to the paramilitary Ulster Volunteer Force (UVF).

English Conservative sanction was as apparently thorough as it was astonishing. When Andrew Bonar Law made his fiery Blenheim pledge in July 1912 (declaring that 'I can imagine no length of resistance to which Ulster can go in which I should not be prepared to support them'; Blake, 1955: 130), Craig was as startled as English commentators with a rather more vigorous sense of political morality (Ervine, 1949: 219). English Conservatives of the second rank, like Sir William Bull, actively promoted Ulster unionist gun-running; first-rank Tories such as Walter Long, even possibly Bonar Law himself, approved the mass importation of weapons into Larne, County Antrim, at a preliminary stage.[7]

Here, then, was a period apparently characterised by organisational and strategic success – a period when the unionist leadership was as unequivocal as its following. There was no perception of moral greyness, no reprehensible ambiguity. Moreover unionists did not, ultimately, have to follow through the implications of their own behaviour: in August 1914, with the outbreak of the Great War, they could back away from the precipice in a more credible fashion than marked their later retreats from vulgar bluster. The chasm was reached only with the first battle of the Somme, when fears of annihilation, of race death, came close to fulfilment – though in circumstances very different from those envisioned before the war. Set against the carnage of the Great War, and against the more modest brutalities of the Troubles, the struggle against home rule appeared as heroic without being bloody. And, in retrospect, the combination of threatened militancy at Larne, and the actual immolation at the Somme, had served to prepare the way for partition and for a unionist *Heimat*: the Government of Ireland Act, the foundation of Northern Ireland, could be credibly interpreted as a tangible reward for their political investment before and during the Great War. Kenneth Pyper, the protagonist of Frank McGuinness's *Observe the sons of Ulster* (1986: passim), was not alone in seeing, even in his despair, a logical progression between the UVF, their role on the Somme and the later struggles of unionism (the success of the play indeed indicates the resonance of the issues).

This chapter explores the historical perspectives of modern unionism, and the bond between this vision of the past and contemporary unionist action. The argument is divided into three principal sections. First, the resonance of unionist actions in 1912–14 is charted: the ways in which the popular memory of 1912–14 was cultivated and the importance of unionist imagery from the period are both examined. Secondly, one episode in the period – the gun-running coup of April 1914 – is isolated in order both to illustrate some of the broader themes of the chapter, and to compare popular and official memories with available historical evidence. The chapter closes with a variety of reflections on the interrelationship between the loyalist past and the loyalist present, and on the ways in which contemporary unionism is illuminated through an exploration of its historical consciousness.

Perceptions of 1912–14

It was little wonder that unionists should have returned to 1912 in piety, and with a sense of nostalgia for what, for them, was a more vital and coherent political faith. The increasingly confident governors of Northern Ireland saw

Carson and Craig as state-builders, and perceived themselves as the sole legatees of these men. Their reputations were bitterly guarded. Carson chose a judicial career in England rather than office in Northern Ireland, but his contribution to unionism, and to the North, did not go unattested.[8] His occasional visits won lavish press coverage. A reverential literature was consolidated, culminating in Edward Marjoribanks and Ian Colvin's triple-decker 'life' of 1932–6. Carson was actively involved in the manufacture of his own mythology, supplying forewords to unionist publications and co-operating in the Marjoribanks and Colvin project: indeed he was so pleased with this biography that he was prepared to distribute inscribed copies of the first two volumes to his intimates (Marjoribanks and Colvin, 1932–6). When he died in 1935 there were a state funeral in Belfast and an ornate memorial in St Anne's Church of Ireland cathedral (McIntosh, 1999). He was given a statue, cast in an appropriately defiant pose and placed in front of the Stormont parliament building. He was in competition with Queen Elizabeth II when the Belfast city fathers were considering how to name their new bridge across the Lagan in 1965 (Bruce, 1986: 77–8). Craig gained lapidary immortality in the form of a bridge – in this case over the Foyle in Derry – and through the name of the new town linking Portadown and Lurgan in North Armagh. He, too, had successive literary apologists: Hugh Shearman (1942) and St John Ervine (1949).

Generations of unionist politicians have vindicated themselves through genuflecting to the men of 1912. In the later 1960s this became less a matter of celebrating the Northern Irish state through celebrating its founders and more thoroughly a matter of seeking legitimacy within unionism. With the movement threatening to disintegrate, to revert to its constituent parts, rival unionist sects sought to annex the Carson mystique and thereby to consolidate their claims over the tradition as a whole. This is partly why Terence O'Neill's experimental unionism in the 1960s was marketed as much by reference to the perceived legacy of the men of 1912 as by reference to any more universal principle: in arguing for a progressive unionism in 1965 O'Neill warned that 'no one anywhere [should] make the mistake of thinking that because there is talk of a new Ulster that the Ulster of Carson and Craig is dead' (O'Neill, 1969: 50–1; Gordon, 1989: 79).

Yet, surprising as it seems, and despite O'Neill's repeated references to the unionist patriarchs, this mistake was made. It was precisely because O'Neill deviated from the familiar in other respects that Ian Paisley could appeal with increasing persuasiveness to fundamentalist unionism, and could credibly invoke the achievement of Carson. Paisley courted Carson's son, the bewildered Edward Carson Junior, deploying him in election campaigns in February 1965 (Gordon, 1989: 64). When Paisley opened his Free Presbyterian cathedral, the Martyrs' Memorial Church in east Belfast, a monument to Carson was erected in a conspicuous position at the front of the building. In a nicely symbolic incident in 1967 Paisley used the cover of Carson's statue at Stormont to snowball the car of the Taoiseach, Jack Lynch, then paying a courtesy visit to O'Neill (O'Neill, 1972: 74). In November 1985 Paisley, opposing the Anglo-Irish Agreement, concluded his peroration at Belfast City Hall with Carson's view of the rights of citizenship.[9]

From his magpie passion for Carson memorabilia, through to more overt acts of identification (such as the Carson Trail campaign tour of 1981), Paisley exhibits an absolute loyalty to this perceived political forebear. It is partly a particularly devout form of ancestor worship – but it is also, as Steve Bruce has pointed out, an exercise in political legitimisation (Bruce, 1986: 212). For Paisley, the most successful critic of mainstream unionism, the most thoroughly *arriviste* of unionist leaders, the men of 1912 have been used both as a touchstone of orthodoxy and as an amulet to ward off the suggestion of novelty or of radicalism. Yet, enthralled as he is by the past, Paisley is as much a victim of myth-making as he is an exploiter and perpetuator of myths. His image of 1912–14 is certainly, in part, an image of his own manufacture, but it is also in some respects the creation of older publicists.

Indeed, in so far as unionism achieved its goals in 1912–14, success lay primarily in the area of salesmanship, of public relations. Carson was marketed with much the same vigour as was applied to Sunlight Soap, or to Dunville's whiskey; and it was of course Craig who acted as the marketing manager. Carson's electoral experience had been gained within a none too testing forum, Trinity College, Dublin, where unionism was routinely triumphant, and a unionist MP was guaranteed a comfortable tenure. Electoral management did not come easily to Carson, for it had never been necessary. Craig's political schooling, on the other hand, had been more rigorous, for he had come to prominence in the context of a divided and threatened unionism. Craig, his brother Charles Curtis Craig, William Moore and a handful of other, younger Conservative Unionists had, in the years before 1906, successfully warded off an electoral challenge from one of the most skilled politicians of the home rule era – Thomas Wallace Russell. Russell, an independent Protestant radical, had leached away unionist votes in key rural marginal constituencies – yet he had also, in effect, reinvigorated mainstream unionism in the north. He had compelled his unionist opponents to reconsider their electoral strategies in Ulster, after years of an enervated reliance on sectarian and party polarity. Craig was one of the younger generation of loyalist activists who successfully and creatively replied to Russell's onslaught. He became a vigorous platform speaker, and he carefully exploited other media of communication – from Orange and masonic contacts to the gewgaws of Edwardian electioneering (badges, rosettes, crude woodcut portraits and cartoons, and cyclostyled campaign messages; see Jackson, 1987).

Craig's training in electoral management and his flair for publicity were of central importance to the marketing of unionism between 1912 and 1914. He and his colleagues on the standing committee of the Ulster Unionist Council formulated images of cohesion and determination within unionism through carefully marshalled displays: they cultivated an image of leadership, and of the venerability of its purpose, choreographing Carson's movements, stage-managing his public appearances.[10] The skill with which Ulster unionism was marketed should not obscure the extent of the distortion which was involved. The appeals to antiquity were of doubtful persuasiveness, even judged in 1912. Public displays of unity only temporarily bolstered a unionism which had been characterised by schism since its institutional foundation in the 1880s. Yet – crucially – these were the images which lasted. It was the skill of the image-builders, rather than the complexity or elusiveness of their subject, which shaped subsequent attitudes towards the events of 1912–14. The apparently sustained success of unionist negativism in 1912–14, chronicled admiringly by McNeill and his historiographical successors, supplied a para-digm for subsequent unionist behaviour. In so far as the ways in which Ulster said 'no' in 1912–14 were echoed in the ways in which Ulster said 'no' in the 1980s, then contemporary unionist activists have shown themselves both to be historicist and to have been directed by their reading of their own past.[11]

This should surprise less if one examines fully the achievement of the image-makers of 1912–14. Craig, for his part, helped to transform the uncom-fortably histrionic and highly sensitive Carson into an object of popular loyalist devotion. Craig managed his visits to Ireland, the demonstrations at which he spoke, the photo-calls. It was evidently Craig who suggested that the signing of the Covenant by Carson and the other luminaries of the movement should be filmed for the benefit of country audiences and the education of the British. It was Craig who fabricated a political genealogy for Carson and for Ulster unionism by evoking comparisons with William III and with seventeenth-century Calvinist Dissent. He was largely responsible for obtaining a banner which had been carried before William in 1690 and which was reused as Carson's standard in 1912.[12] The Covenant of 1912, again partly Craig's inspiration, and on which the first signature was Carson's, carried echoes of the Scots' Covenants of 1638 and 1643. Indeed the invocation of God in the Covenant, and its pious language, suggested even more ancient, Judaic, precedents for loyalist strategy in 1912 (Ervine, 1949: 221).

Yet what is most impressive about the marketing of unionism in 1912 is, perhaps, the comprehensive application of Edwardian technology to this task. Film was exploited to publicise unionist festivals and demonstrations. Even Copeland Trimble, commander of the Enniskillen Horse, demanded a full turnout of his men in May 1913 'because of the presence of cinematographic operators'.[13] Motor vehicles and motorcycles were deployed within the UVF, drivers advertising their unionism through brass fender-badges.[14] The resources of the printing industry were exploited to the full. That central medium of communication in Edwardian Ireland, the halfpenny postcard, was used to carry loyalist propaganda, from coy depictions of unionism in the form of pugnacious little boys or vulnerable young women through to images of Carson (Killen, 1985: 55, 72). Carson's grimly ironic features appeared everywhere: in dozens of poses on tens of thousands of cards; on mass-produced lapel badges; on charity stamps. German porcelain manufacturers supplied parian busts of Carson and Bonar Law to the china cabinets of suburban Belfast. If, as Ronan Fanning has pointed out, the homes of the Irish Republic were adorned with the triptych of Pope John XXIII, Robert and John F. Kennedy in the early 1960s, then the unionist household gods were the king-emperor, William III, and – above all – Carson.[15] The commercial classes of Belfast may occasionally and discreetly have questioned the latter's leadership, but their business sense outran their political equivocation.[16] Carson's image was marketable, and these classes responded creatively to the challenge of retailing their leader.

Through signing the Covenant, through wearing their badges or joining the UVF, unionist men and women were bound to their leadership in an unprecedented way. In a limited sense, to return to an earlier analogy, Carson and Craig reformulated O'Connell's political achievement, politicising their constituency as thoroughly as the Liberator had done with his people 90 years earlier. In mechanical terms their task was easier in that they had the resources of the Edwardian advertising industry and the machinery of modern party organisation at their disposal; but, like earlier populist nationalists, they conveyed a simplified political creed with considerable effect. On the other hand, the success of their salesmanship has tended to obscure the substance of their policies; and, in so far as this is true, subsequent unionists, in looking back to 1912, are devoted to an ideal, rather than pondering an actuality.

The UVF and the 1914 gunrunning coup

The comparatively small amount of research conducted on unionist politics in the period has only now begun to illustrate the vulnerability of the unionist leadership and, by implication, its success both in preserving a unified public front and in persuading contemporaries that its resources were rather more considerable than in fact was the case. W. S. Rodner and others have identified the degree of backbench English Conservative disquiet over loyalist militancy and the capacity for schism within Conservatism over Ulster.[17] Tensions within the Ulster unionist leadership over the crucial issue of compromise, conflict between Belfast businessmen and their political commanders over finance, the comparative success of government surveillance of loyalist activity – these and much else have been revealed by recent research.[18] A. T. Q. Stewart chronicled the failure of successive gunrunning expeditions in his pioneering *The Ulster crisis* (Stewart, 1967: 91–102). There is considerable evidence among the manuscript material in the Public Record Office of Northern Ireland to suggest that the figures for UVF membership (nominally 100,000) conceal a much more patchy local reality. It seems clear, for example, that truancy was a marked problem in certain UVF regiments, and that officers found it much easier to mobilise their men for a weekend at camp, or for a day out in Belfast, than for sustained training programmes.[19] The recreational dimension to the UVF should not be underplayed: at the risk of mixing the institutional analogies, the young men of the UVF – and probably two thirds were under 35 – preferred to play at being boy scouts than at being soldiers.[20]

Ritual displays of unity and cathartic mass demonstrations were merely the skin of a much more complicated organism. Historically, whether in 1912 or in 1985, the unionist command has shown itself capable of occasionally mobilising its resources; but it has also proved to be much less adept at coping with its own transient success – at supplying coherent direction or a long-term, flexible plan of campaign. The fragility of unionist unity and the variety of unionist origins have been much more striking influences on the development of the movement than atypical and unsustainable displays of cohesion, whether at Belfast City Hall in 1985, or at the same venue in 1912.

One well-documented episode in the unionist campaign of 1912–14 may be used to illustrate the strategic dilemma faced by the leaders of the movement and the success with which setbacks and complexities were concealed. On the night of 24–25 April 1914, militant unionists, led by the quixotic Major Fred Crawford, landed some 25,000 rifles and three million rounds of ammunition, principally at Larne, in County Antrim. These weapons were swiftly distributed and effectively concealed: some caches were in fact so well hidden that they have only come to light in the routine searches for weapons conducted by the British army since 1969. The gunrunners had apparently achieved an unequivocal military as well as political victory. They had achieved, as Townshend has commented, both 'a crude amplification of the UVF's firepower' and a grim corroboration for their rhetorical challenge (Townshend, 1983: 253). The event was thoroughly publicised, with celebratory demonstrations, the compilation of a souvenir booklet, and extensive coverage in the British and European press. The gunrunning was chronicled by McNeill in his illuminating, if partial, *Ulster's stand for union* (1922); and Crawford and other, less significant, conspirators subsequently committed their individual testimonies to print (Crawford, 1947; Adgey, n.d).

The centrality of this episode for the historical perceptions of contemporary unionism may be gauged by the attitudes of a leader like Paisley as well as by the number of popular accounts at present available. In April 1964 Paisley and O'Neill, promoting their rival definitions of unionism, held separate commemorations of the gunrunning. O'Neill, speaking at Larne on 25 April, attempted to mitigate his political revisionism by appealing to loyalist fundamentals – but his celebration of the morbidly anti-Catholic Crawford came only a day after a pioneering visit to a Catholic school (Our Lady of Lourdes in Ballymoney, County Antrim). In successive editions of the Belfast *News Letter* O'Neill featured first as an ecumenical, photographed smiling beneath a Catholic crucifix, and – immediately afterwards – as the bowler-hatted successor to the Edwardian militants. Paisley's appeal was less open to misinterpretation; moreover his commemorative meeting in the Ulster Hall, Belfast, on 25 April, attracted 1,800 pious unionists compared with the 500 accompanying O'Neill at Larne. The contrast between the ambiguities of O'Neill's policies and the apparently uncomplicated loyalism of the gunrunners was the theme of Paisley's address, with the unspoken implication that the true inheritor of Crawford's vision was Paisley himself: 'whether willingly or unwillingly, aware or unaware, Captain O'Neill has, by countenancing the Roman idol [i.e., Catholic imagery], given food to the Roman propagandists . . . Ulster needs far more men with the spirit of the gunrunners today'.[21]

The Ulster Society, founded in 1985 'to make people aware of their distinctive Ulster-British heritage and culture', has published several works devoted to unionist history in the period 1912–14, and to April 1914 in particular.[22] Their *Covenant and challenge* (1989), a volume of essays written by the Rev. Brett Ingram, includes a lecture celebrating loyalist activity in these years, and reprints a newspaper article on 'The Chauffer [*sic*] who Carried Guns to Donegal' (in 1913). Gordon Lucy's *The Ulster Covenant* (1989) includes some important photographic material relating to the gunrunning of April 1914. David Hume's well researched and frankly celebratory *'For Ulster and her freedom'* (1989) is the most comprehensive expression of contemporary loyalty to the memory of unionist militancy in 1912–14. Other recent unionist publications refer piously to the opponents of the third Home Rule Bill. *Lillibulero!* (Ulster Society, 1988) – a volume of loyalist songs – includes a number of Orange ballads which evoke the achievements of Carson and the gunrunners. The ballad 'The Union Cruiser' (sung to the air of 'The Yellow Rose of Texas') indirectly but unmistakably celebrates the April 1914 gunrunning:

I can see the stormy ocean in our happy northern home,
Where our countrymen are arming to resist the wiles of Rome,
I can see the Union Cruiser in the harbour of Belfast
And the Orange flag of liberty is floating from her mast (Ulster Society, 1988).

The invocation of Crawford and the gunrunners perhaps reached a peak in 1986–7, in the months following the Anglo-Irish Agreement. Larne, and the events of 1912–14 in general, have for long had a symbolic significance within loyalism, but their relevance was apparently underlined in the aftermath of the Hillsborough accord. Unionist militancy at the time of the third Home Rule Bill, reaching a crescendo at Larne, was a measure of the distance between loyalism and the mainstream of British politics, and it reflected mutual distrust and incomprehension even between loyalism and British conservatism. Equally the Anglo-Irish Agreement confirmed the distance between the British parties and contemporary loyalism, with the unionist political and social command being treated to near-comprehensive English Conservative disdain. The suspicion that an English governing class regarded loyalism as a colonial subculture evolved into a certainty in November 1985.[23]

Thus the isolation of 1914 became the isolation of 1985, and the political expedients of 1914 became the suggested strategies of 1985. Just as in the era of O'Neill, so in the aftermath of Hillsborough the unionist establishment as well as populist loyalism turned to Carson and Crawford for validation.[24] Paisley and O'Neill had vied for the legacy of Carson in the 1960s, while since 1985 radical loyalists in the Ulster Defence Association (UDA) and elsewhere have sustained a populist challenge – though against a unionist establishment whose chief ornament is now Paisley himself. In the months following Hillsborough the ideologues of the UDA recalled Crawford and the unionist commanders of 1914 in highlighting the perceived inadequacy of the party leaders in the 1980s ('students of history will contrast and compare the snivelling wrecks of manhood who masquerade as political leaders in the 1980s with the giants of Ulster').[25]

Unionists of different hues have sought to jog memories of April 1914, even though the re-enactment (in 1989) of the events at Larne – the Larne pageant – may yet join the Closing of the Gates at Derry and the Sham Fight in the mystery cycle of loyalism's evolution.[26] The iconography of 1914 has been revived in other ways: a postcard of an armed and defiant young woman ('Ulster 1914: Deserted! Well I can stand alone') has been deployed with a particular and grim enthusiasm.[27] The first wall painting depicting an image from 1912–14 appeared in 1987 – part of a revival of loyalist mural art originating in 1984–5 (Lyttle, 1988; Rolston, 1988: 10–11; Rolston, 1987: 23; Loftus, 1990; Rolston, 1991: 39, 44–5).

Yet setting aside the imagery and hyperbole current in Orange pubs and clubs, it is arguable that, as with the contemporaneous gunrunning at Howth, the usefulness of Larne lay as much in the publicity which was generated as in any more tangible achievement. The gunrunning reflected and generated a much more complicated debate inside unionism than the publicists were willing to recognise, or their audience – which includes contemporary unionism – has sought to elucidate.

'Revisionist' zeal has apparently spent itself within Irish historiography, and counter-revisionist texts have reminded the profession of the value of empathy as an interpretative tool. It would be misleading in any case to undervalue the commitment of loyalist militants in 1914, and pointless to bewail the role that their actions play, and have played, in the historical perceptions of loyalism (Bradshaw, 1989: 350–1). Judged as a response to British government policy – judged in terms of the personal devotion involved, or in terms of logistics – the gunrunning *was* a spectacular tactical success; and its celebration in loyalist popular culture (songs, ballads, community history) is not difficult to understand.

Yet it is possible to offer other, in certain respects more complicated, perspectives on Larne. Judging the distance between the popular celebrations of loyalist achievement and the surviving evidence of their activity is one measure of the success of unionist publicity. It is also, arguably, a measure of loyalist self-delusion. Given the role of 1912–14 in loyalist folklore, both before, but especially after 1985 (the actions of leading politicians, the form of demonstrations, and the celebratory publications), it is possible that unionists are being swayed by a particular rendering of their own past. A Whiggish reading of 1912–14, and of its consequences, shapes both historical perceptions and also the unionist response to contemporary demands. As with aspects of contemporary nationalism, a simplified version of the past helps to validate simplified responses to contemporary demands.

Some 30 years ago, Patrick Buckland rightly distinguished the bellicosity of the UVF from the convictions and priorities of the unionist political leadership: 'most of the political leaders of Unionism hoped and thought that the UVF would not have to fight' (Buckland, 1973: 64–5). Archival evidence made available since this comment was published (in 1973) has confirmed the hesitancy of the unionist leadership, the distance between their qualms and their rhetoric.[28] The UVF was useful as a demonstration of unionist conviction as well as a means of channelling loyalist emotion away from the kind of street confrontation which had been so damaging, both politically and financially, in 1886 (Townshend, 1983: 247, 249). But the usefulness of the UVF depended on the strength of its morale, and this in turn depended on its being gainfully employed. In these contingencies lay a very profound political dilemma for unionism in 1913–14. Thus Asquith's 'masterly inactivity', based as it was – if only indirectly – on intelligence reports of the condition of unionism, had perhaps a more solid rationale than some commentators have allowed. Simply by doing nothing Asquith could permit the unionist leadership to become prisoners of their own logic, penned in by their own indecision over violence, and by their own supporters' desire for a more assertive command. Aggression, on any realistic assessment, threatened sympathy in England; inertia threatened morale in Ireland, as was increasingly clear by late

1913. In so far as unionist leaders showed themselves willing to negotiate, even in the potentially most compromising of venues, and in so far as they radically scaled down their demands in 1911–12 and 1914, then Asquith's 'strategy' was rather more than a euphemism for ignorance or idleness.[29]

Viewed in this light the Larne episode emerges as one further stage in the process by which unionists backed themselves into an impasse. Some of the most influential of the unionist leaders grasped that the interests of the movement lay in threat rather than in action, and were accordingly unhappy about the importation of arms, and certainly unhappy about their distribution. Police reports of unionist gatherings in 1913 and early 1914 suggest that the hardliners were decidedly in the minority.[30] Before 1914 extremists like Crawford had been fed relatively small amounts of money, and thereby temporarily diverted from any apocalyptic project into small-scale operations. The unionists had brought guns into Ireland from as early as 1910, but such projects were designed partly to mollify the hawks (a fact occasionally perceived even by Crawford), and partly to alarm the government.[31] The Ulster Unionist Council was not yet investing enough money for these projects to be serious efforts towards equipping an army; but they certainly occupied the conspiratorially minded, and gave both the Royal Irish Constabulary and Sir James Dougherty, the under-secretary for Ireland, some cause for reflection. Such activities may be perceived as a further means by which the political leadership sought to condition constitutional negotiation.

By early 1914, however, these allusions to violence were having as little impact as the wholly rhetorical challenge laid down by organised unionism in 1886 and 1893. Asquith had not responded with substantial concessions, and the unionist political leadership was therefore left in the talons of the hawks within the UVF. The preliminary decision to fund a major gunrunning expedition was taken only in January 1914, in the context – significantly – of the abortive private negotiations conducted between Carson, Bonar Law and Asquith. It represented a climb down by the political leadership of unionism, and a recognition of the futility of the strategy which had been pursued up to that point. In this sense the Larne gunrunning, dazzling as a tactical coup, also reflected a profound strategic failure for Carson and for his political intimates.[32]

Carson's increasingly apocalyptic rhetoric in the spring of 1914 – reminiscent of Pearse at his most lugubrious – indicated the quandary which he felt unionism to be in. Violence for Carson was certainly an option – the last option – but he perceived violence in icily realistic terms: that is to say, as honourable, but also as suicidal. After Larne, when the penalties of incitement were inescapable, Carson softened his tone.[33] It was as if Larne was an end in itself – as if it alone had been sufficient to satisfy the military honour of the Ulster unionist movement and the personal honour of its leaders.

The effective value of the gunrunning, beyond the undoubtedly central issues of morale and publicity, is questionable.[34] It consolidated the firepower of the UVF; but then, given the Curragh Mutiny, such an exercise was largely redundant – for the British were no longer in a position to impose a settlement. Moreover the UVF did not need Larne in order to overwhelm the poorly organised and poorly equipped Irish Volunteer movement. Did Larne strengthen the debating position of the unionist leadership? The presumption must be that it did, though there were certainly few tangible benefits before August 1914. At the same time the likelihood of a disastrous breach of discipline, of some form of violent incident, was considerably greater after April. The discipline of the UVF, surprisingly good, given the history of popular sectarian confrontation in Ulster, was by no means absolute: any local and armed aggression by the loyalists would have had disastrous implications for support in England, and within English Conservatism (Buckland, 1973: 63–4). If Larne made the unionist leadership a more formidable adversary in the eyes of the Liberal government, then it also made a negotiated settlement all the more desirable – and for *everyone* concerned, pre-eminently the unionists.

Nor did the gunrunning give unionists the means to fight a war. Strongly swayed by British army personnel and precedent, the UVF favoured a 'stand-up fight' rather than guerrilla tactics. Indeed guerrilla warfare had been damned in the eyes of the loyalist tacticians through its associations with the Boer campaign of 1899–1902: the involvement of northern Irish regiments of the British army in this war had been considerable, with loyalist leaders such as Craig, Crawford and Robert Wallace having enlisted and served.[35] Accepting conventional and confrontational warfare meant acquiring a formidably stocked arsenal as well as a thoroughly trained army. The UVF was capable of impressing susceptible English journalists, but there are good reasons for supposing that its morale was flagging before April 1914, and that its general efficiency was questionable.[36] Moreover the fruits of the Larne gunrunning, even taken in combination with earlier weapons importation, did not constitute an adequate arsenal. The Larne episode increased UVF firepower, just enough for this firepower to be a political liability and yet not sufficiently for it to be an unequivocal military asset. The threat of violence was certainly increased, but not the threat of formalised violence. Informal sectarian or political confrontation was now a greater risk, but the ritualised and 'honourable' warfare envisioned by the UVF tacticians was still out of the question. Thus the UVF had only the capability to fight a 'dirty' war, which would certainly have sacrificed political opinion in England to the point where Asquith could have imposed a settlement with impunity.

As has been observed, 25,000 rifles and three million rounds of ammunition were shipped into Larne in April 1914. Several thousand weapons had been smuggled into Ireland in 1910–11 and in the spring of 1914; in addition there was a relatively large number of arms in Ulster, even before 1910 – partly owing to the troubled recent history of the province, and partly because weapons were used extensively by the farming population. On the other hand, many of the weapons in circulation were extremely old, souvenirs from the 1798 rebellion, or antiques from the age of the flintlock; and the British police had been relatively successful in locating and impounding weapons bound for loyalist militants. From the perspective both of propaganda and military credibility, the Larne gunrunning was of disproportionate significance for the UVF. Until Larne it was a toy army, while the effort to shift away from playground battles had been half-hearted, and in any case had been publicly thwarted by the British authorities. Larne was effectively publicised, its significance exaggerated, precisely because it stood in the context of sustained failure. But building on the success of Larne inside Ireland was rather more challenging than persuading the British public of its significance. And it seems clear that neither the political nor the military leadership of loyalism had any firm idea about future action.

But 25,000 rifles were not sufficient to arm a body which claimed a membership of 100,000. Three million rounds of ammunition spread over 25,000 offered little scope for weapons training or for anything other than a momentary confrontation. The rifles were, as Townshend has pointed out, of three different makes, and no scheme of rationalisation was ever drawn up: it is hard to disagree with his conclusion that 'in a full-scale military clash the UVF weaponry would have created a logistical nightmare' (Townshend, 1983: 255). Larne, therefore, turned an unarmed force into a badly armed force. In both its military and political implications the gunrunning highlighted the Ulster unionists' difficulties without providing solutions. Carson recognised that violence was the politics of suicide – but his ideological successors have been rather more sanguine in interpreting 1914.

Conclusion

Yet the cult of 1912–14 and April 1914 is central to the historical consciousness of modern unionism. Why this should be so demands some further and final illumination, for the events and personalities of 1912–14 constitute on the face of it only one of numerous historical resources open to exploitation. The Boyne and the Somme, 1690 and 1916, continue to resonate through loyalist popular culture, yet other bloody or rhetorical struggles are forgotten. The campaigns of 1886 and, to a lesser extent, of 1893, against the first and second Home Rule Bills, were of vital importance in the formulation of modern unionism; yet they, and the first leader of organised unionism, Edward James

Saunderson, play only marginal parts in contemporary loyalist apologetic.

The importance of 1912–14 lies partly in that it was the first mobilisation of unionism to take place in the context of commercial and industrial dominance within the movement – the first mobilisation to occur in the context of a relatively marginalised landlordism, and a politically passive farmer class. I have argued this case more fully elsewhere (Jackson, 1989a: 230–5, 320–6), but an outline of the thesis is worth presenting because of its particular relevance to the concerns of this chapter. The campaign of 1912–14 was, quite simply, the first 'modern' mobilisation of Ulster unionism. It was also the first truly popular mobilisation of unionism (Hobsbawm, 1983a, 1983b). The socio-economic leadership of unionism was different in 1912–14 from that of 1886, and it more clearly prefigured the distribution of power in what would become Northern Ireland. The loyalists of 1912, and the imagery which they generated, were more accessible and more relevant to the unionist rulers of Northern Ireland; and the loyalists of 1912–14 could, in any case, be more credibly depicted as the political originators of the state.

The pervasiveness of the imagery of 1912–14 is impressive, and has a bearing on this argument. It may be an oversimplification to suggest a relationship between commercial domination within unionism and the commercialisation of unionist imagery. In the light of the work of Eric Hobsbawm it may be more reasonable to suggest a link between the popularisation of unionist politics and such commercialisation (Hobsbawm, 1983a, 1983b). Yet it is unquestionable that the movement was marketed with much greater vigour and imagination in 1912–14 than in any earlier period. This is certainly a secondary explanation for the unique success of unionist mobilisation in these years. Moreover, given the survival of tens of thousands of Ulster Covenants, of UVF rifles, of UVF lapel badges, and given the survival of multifarious images of Carson, it is also clear that the successful marketing of unionism in 1912 has indirectly influenced subsequent generations. By implication it may be contended that, with this tangible legacy, the contemporary memory of 1912–14 has been tailored by dead partisans to a degree unusual even in twentieth-century Ireland.

Omnipresent images of 1912–14 have been obvious targets for political exploitation. Carson and Craig have been revered by unionist governments and by unionist critics of unionist government: within loyalism they have been a touchstone of political orthodoxy. A political creed characterised by reductionist responses to political debate has found sanction in a reductionist version of its own past. A political movement of recent origins has sought validation and venerability through its own recent past – through the politicians of 1912, who in turn were evoking a much more ancient political pedigree by their Covenant and their ritual. Reality has become entangled somewhere in the skeins of historical reference.

The constrained historical vision of loyalism – what Terence Brown has caustically labelled the 'poverty' of unionist historical awareness – is illustrated, therefore, by the interpretations of 1912–14 (Brown, 1988: 223). Arguably, and at the risk of oversimplification, this vision is related, in turn, to the limitations of unionist ideology – a monochrome present created from a monochrome past. Certainly the 'history' which the unionist state chose for itself was not only irrelevant to its nationalist population, but was also more generally inadequate as a means of legitimisation. Celebrating its fiftieth anniversary in 1971, unionist ministers could only express their anxieties and loyalty through the model of the Solemn League and Covenant. In a confused historical analogy these men defended devolved government by reference to an integrationist text, and commemorated 1921 by evoking 1912: this was indeed 'pissing in the gale of history', to borrow the vigorous language of Ron Hutchinson's *Rat in the skull* (quoted in Cairns and Richards, 1988: 150).

Unionist Ulster failed in 1972 partly because Northern Ireland had never been a coherent aspiration, and partly because the ideology and ceremonial of the state, the history exploited by the unionist movement, illustrated this fact with a brutal clarity. As one perceptive observer put it, 'the failure of the twentieth-century democracies is in part attributable to their failure to invest the state with ceremonial' (Cannadine, 1987). Unionist Ulster failed partly because it was failed by its own past.

Chapter 8

Contemporary republicanism and the strategy of armed struggle

Joseph Ruane

Introduction

The Good Friday Agreement of 1998 proved more difficult to implement than had been originally anticipated. By mid-2003, the institutions were suspended and there was no prospect of an early restoration. There was still no agreement on the final disposal of arms or on the new policing service. Support for the anti-Agreement Democratic Unionist Party (DUP) was growing; armed groups on both sides remained committed to violence; sectarian strife continued at the points of communal interface. On a pessimistic view, it might be asked whether much had changed at all. At another level, the situation was profoundly different. The scale of violence had reduced dramatically and the parties who originally supported the agreement declared their continued commitment to it. Uncertainty continued to surround IRA intentions on the disposal of its weapons, but most of these appeared already to have been placed 'beyond use'. The demand of the Ulster Unionist Party (UUP) for complete disarmament by the Provisional IRA (IRA),[1] and the complete cessation of its intelligence and other activities, sprang more from political principle, and concern that Sinn Féin might profit politically from low level IRA activity, than from fear that the war might be resumed. The Continuity IRA (CIRA) and the Real IRA (RIRA) still presented a security problem, but they had little standing within the wider republican community and lacked political wings capable of securing a significant portion of the nationalist vote. Republican violence had not ended, but it was not an integral part of the political process as it had been from the 1970s to the 1990s.

Assuming that armed conflict has now drawn to a close,[2] we can, with a certain distance and detachment, attempt to map its parameters, examine its causes and consequences, and seek to learn from it. Why did such intense conflict initially break out and why did it last so long? Has the Good Friday Agreement finally legitimated Northern Ireland as a political entity? Is political violence likely to continue in some form, and could it conceivably return on the scale of recent decades?[3]

The structural basis of the conflict

There was much that was conjunctural and contingent in the political destabilisation of Northern Ireland between 1968 and 1970, but this has to be seen in the context of structural forces operating over a much longer time period (Ruane and Todd, 1996). Two features of the *longue durée* are particularly important. The first is the changing balance of power between Protestants and Catholics in Ireland. Irish Catholics were comprehensively defeated in the religious wars of the sixteenth and seventeenth centuries; power was subsequently concentrated in the hands of Protestants of British stock and was underwritten by the British state (Canny, 2001). From about the middle of the eighteenth century, a Catholic recovery was under way (Bartlett, 1992: 45–65). At first slow and halting, it became increasingly rapid in the latter part of the nineteenth century; by its end Catholics were the predominant political force on the island. Their power was, however, geographically uneven, and power in the north-east was in Protestant hands. The partition of the island in 1920 respected that power balance. Catholics secured the independence of the territory that they already overwhelmingly controlled; Protestants gained control over the devolved government of Northern Ireland. Despite unionist control over the state in Northern Ireland, the long-term tendency for power to shift in favour of Catholics or nationalists continued at the level of the island as a whole (Ruane and Todd, 1996). This continuing shift in the balance of power was the structural condition for the destabilisation of the northern state in 1969.

The second feature of the *longue durée* is the interaction between two different forms of power – structural and institutional – and the crises associated with this. Structural power arises from control over demographic, military, cultural, economic and organisational resources; institutional power arises from access to positions within the state apparatus and political system. The two forms of power intersect and each can be used to defend or advance the other. They tend, therefore, to converge. But gaps open up, particularly when structural power increases and an adjustment has yet to take place at the level of institutional power. The opening and closing of such gaps go far to explain the cycles of low- and high-intensity conflict that have been a consistent feature of the conflict since the mid-eighteenth century. The periods of high-intensity conflict have occurred when Catholic structural power has increased and they have used it to press for greater institutional power. Protestants typically resist, and Catholics intensify the pressure until at least some of their demands are met. When institutional and structural power are again in line, conflict subsides. But the settlements which bring such conflicts to a close are invariably temporary: the increased institutional power is used to effect a further shift in the structural power-balance, opening the way for a new challenge and a further period of intensified conflict (See Ruane and Todd, 2001).

Violence has played a central role in this conflict from the outset. The initial imbalance of Protestant and Catholic power was established by the military victory of British Protestant settlers and the British state over Old English and Gaelic Irish Catholics. It was subsequently maintained by the concentration of coercive power in British and Protestant hands. As a conventional military force, Catholics never recovered from their seventeenth-century defeat; the closest a military uprising came to success was the United Irish rebellion of 1798. Much later Catholics acquired the capacity for guerrilla-type violence. Guerrilla violence may act as a prelude to conventional war, when, for example, it is used to demonstrate that an enemy is weaker than it appears and that a popular uprising can be victorious. Much guerrilla violence is, however, of a more limited kind (for examples, see Beckett, 2001). Its goal is not to defeat the enemy militarily, which it has no possibility of doing, but to undermine its legitimacy, to impede its ability to maintain order and to exact a higher cost to maintaining the status quo than it considers acceptable. The success of guerrilla tactics depends on a complex set of conditions: the tactical abilities of the governmental and guerrilla forces (military and propagandistic), the nature of the political regime (for example, authoritarian or liberal democratic), the nature of its interests in the territory (economic, strategic, national), the nature of its claims on this territory (part of its recognised national territory, a colony), and the balance of international interests and sympathies. When – and only when – the balance of these conditions is favourable, guerrilla warfare can be highly cost-effective, achieving its goals at relatively low cost to the guerrillas and their community.

The capacity for coercion recovered by Catholics in the nineteenth century was uniquely of the second – guerrilla – kind. It was limited in scope and effective only when, and to the extent that, Catholics already possessed major structural power. The clearest example of this is the War of Independence (1919–21) which, despite the limited scale of the violence, secured a higher level of independence than would otherwise have been offered. On the other hand, independence could only be achieved for those counties where the balance of structural power was already overwhelmingly in the Catholic favour. Once the limits of this structural power had been reached, there was little to be gained by further violence (Ruane and Todd, 1996: 46–7).

This would remain the case in the decades that followed, as nationalists were well aware and as the IRA repeatedly discovered. The failure of nationalists to support a republican military campaign had little to do with a principled rejection of violence. Nationalists may have exaggerated the extent of Catholic inequality and anti-Catholic discrimination during the Stormont period, but both were in evidence and most Catholics saw little hope of a solution within the context of Northern Ireland. For those who were nationalist – and most were – partition was a further source of grievance, and violence was widely considered to be a legitimate means to bring it to an end. The objection to it centred not on its legitimacy, but on its impracticality and low chance of success. After the collapse of the IRA's campaign of 1956–62, its futility was obvious even to the IRA, and the thrust of Catholic, nationalist and republican strategic thinking lay elsewhere. The emphasis shifted to remedying Catholic grievances within Northern Ireland, using new forms of political struggle: community self-help, media campaigns, and radical – but legal – street politics (Feeney, 2002: 218–27).

In the second half of the 1960s a process of Catholic mobilisation began under the banner of 'civil rights'. In a very short space of time, the tactics went from a low-key media and lobbying campaign to provocative street protests, and the goals went from limited reforms to a direct challenge to the state itself at least in the case of People's Democracy (Farrell, 1976: 249). But even People's Democracy-style street politics was of the dramatic, non-lethal, publicity-seeking kind. No one envisaged or anticipated the lethal form of violence that would soon emerge, embed itself and become a seemingly permanent feature of life in Northern Ireland. How did this happen?

The crisis of the state

The primary condition of the violence that became endemic in Northern Ireland from the 1970s was the crisis of the state. There were two distinct but interlocking dimensions to the crisis: on the one hand, the destabilising of the Stormont regime; on the other hand, the virtually total delegitimising of British rule in the eyes of a large section of the nationalist population. The structural basis of the Stormont regime was undermined by the continuing shift in the balance of power in favour of Catholics. Over time Northern Catholics developed into a more cohesive and politically resourceful community. By the 1960s their principal external ally – the Republic – had overcome the difficulties of a young and impoverished state and (later) the price of its wartime neutrality. The Northern Ireland economy was becoming increasingly dependent on a British subvention and on external investment, and unionists were becoming more vulnerable to pressure from the British government. Britain itself was in transition from a first-rank imperial state to a second-rank European state, more sensitive to international and particularly American opinion. There was a new concern internationally with minority rights and new opportunities for political mobilisation around such issues, in particular using the mass media. By the 1960s these changes had left unionists exposed and vulnerable, although the extent to which this had happened was not yet clear (Ruane and Todd, 1996: 125–6). The granting of a monopoly of political power to Protestants in Northern Ireland in 1920 was predicated on the assumption that they could control the Catholic community. By the 1960s they had lost that capacity. A challenge of some kind was inevitable. What remained to be determined was its form, its timing and the manner of its unfolding.

The delegitimising of British rule was a more conjunctural and contingent development, though it also had structural roots. To understand it, it is necessary to distinguish between *foundational* and *practical* legitimacy. Foundational legitimacy relates to whether a state should exist in the first instance; practical legitimacy relates to its particular form and how it behaves. The British state lacked foundational legitimacy for nationalists in Northern Ireland by virtue of its Britishness; they rejected its claim to sovereignty over any part of Ireland and they actively disliked its symbols. But their anger and resentment during the Stormont period were almost entirely focused on the Unionist government, Unionist-dominated local authorities and the local security forces. Indeed, they had long sought greater British involvement in the affairs of Northern Ireland as a way of setting limits to unionist excesses. The British state was the actually existing state. It was the ultimate source of the key social services on which Catholics depended (health, education, social welfare), and its policies in the post-war period were markedly more progressive than those of the Republic. As a result it enjoyed considerable practical legitimacy, with the potential for much more. In the event, the manner of its intervention in Northern Ireland from 1969 onwards cost it its practical legitimacy, while confirming its lack of foundational legitimacy.

The crisis was precipitated by the confrontations between the civil rights marchers and the loyalists and security forces, but the violence that exploded in Derry and Belfast in August 1969 was fundamentally communal in nature. The arrival of British troops restored order in the short term, but in the longer term created the conditions for a deepening crisis. The British government decided to manage the crisis through the existing structures of government. The intention was to provide the Stormont government with security backup, and in return to insist on reforms. Unionists welcomed the security backup, but resisted the reforms. For nationalists, the only thing that mattered was reform; they wanted far more than unionists were willing to concede, and rioting was a means to achieve it. The stage was set for a wider confrontation. Security policies against rioters became increasingly harsh and were noticeably more severe against Catholics than against Protestants. The IRA emerged in the first instance as community defenders, but from the summer of 1970, with the support – or at least tolerance – of the embattled Catholic communities, it went on the offensive, with attacks on the security forces and on public buildings. The battle lines hardened, and whatever potential there had been for a neutral British security presence had now dissipated. The security forces responded with the internment of IRA suspects and the shooting dead of unarmed marchers and rioters. A vicious cycle was in place, fed by fear, insecurity and grievance on both sides, and sustained by the violence of the IRA, the security forces and the loyalist paramilitaries. Violence had now acquired its own momentum.

The success of the IRA in exploiting the post-1969 crisis to extend and consolidate its base was due in the first instance to the oppositions inherent in the situation. But it was also a mark of its strategic and tactical skills: military (to secure and stockpile arms, mount attacks and defend itself against counterattack), organisational (to ensure a chain that could at once be effective and resistant to infiltration), and ideological (to persuade the community to give it support – or at least acquiescence – and to secure allies farther afield). It had to do all of this in the face of the harsh security measures – internment, non-jury courts, brutalising interrogation techniques as well as daily harassment – and the bombs and random assassinations of loyalist paramilitaries. The measures adopted by the security forces were often so severe and so indiscriminate that they helped rather than hindered the IRA's campaign – by alienating the local Catholic communities and making it easier for the IRA to secure support. But that support could never be taken for granted. The local communities were paying a heavy price for the campaign: a massive and oppressive security presence in their areas, deaths and injuries, including those of small children, very high unemployment, run-down neighbourhoods, and an all-pervasive culture of war and violence.[4]

How, in those circumstances, was the IRA able to secure popular support and retain it right up to the end? There were two separate phases. During the first, the Catholic community felt under attack from both loyalists and the forces of the state, and the most exposed local communities demanded that the IRA (whether Official or Provisional) act as communal defenders. A new situation developed, however, when the proactive nature of the IRA's campaign became clear, and it was evident that its actions were aggravating the situation. Some now turned against it; others became enthusiastic supporters; still others moved between opposition, tolerance and guarded support. Those whose opposition became too vocal ran the risk of ostracism, a beating or being forced out of their areas. If they went further and became informers, they faced death (Moloney, 2002: 118–25). But these were always a minority; the majority was willing at the very least to tolerate the IRA's campaign. Their willingness to do so sprang in each case from a complex set of motives, but common to all was the conviction that there was no other way of having their long-standing grievances addressed and of ending the loyalist and state violence that was now being inflicted on them. They had never expected anything from unionists, but they had nurtured the hope that the British government would be more even-handed. Now, it seemed, the British government was no better. That this was the conclusion reached owed more than a little to the behaviour of the British security forces, but it was also due to the success of republicans in disseminating their version of Irish history and analysis of British rule.

This was no small task. Republicans were thin on the ground in 1969, and had lost considerable face because of their failure to defend exposed communities from loyalist attack in August 1969. Very many – perhaps most – Catholics had learned or absorbed a nationalist understanding of Irish history which formed a cultural substratum on which a republican analysis could be built. But this was primarily a historical narrative which many in the 1960s had difficulty applying to the present. A view of the British army as an imperial force met with little response when British forces first arrived in Derry in 1969, as Bernadette Devlin discovered (Bardon, 1992: 669). In fact, at that time, very many in the working-class Catholic communities of Belfast and Derry saw the British army (unlike the Northern security forces) in neutral terms, the army they would automatically think of joining if the job appealed to them, one whose regimental insignias they would without hesitation place on the walls of their parlours. This army was now to be ideologically reconstructed as an 'army of occupation', just as the British government – the source of the Butler education act and the welfare state and the long sought counterbalance to unionist excesses – was to become what Gerry Adams would later call a 'monster of imperial power' (Adams, 1986: 69).

The British contribution to that process of ideological reconstruction was internment, the torture of prisoners, the daily harassment of ordinary Catholics, the shooting of unarmed rioters, the imperious tones of politicians such as Roy Mason and Margaret Thatcher, and a reform process that appeared always to be subject to a unionist veto. But even in the face of British imperiousness and partisanship, and the confused and polarised conditions of the time, the distinctive agenda of republicans was clear, as was the offensive and brutal nature of their campaign.[5] Traditional republicans gave the campaign uncritical support, but they were not numerous enough to sustain the kind of struggle that had now been embarked on. A wider penumbra of support had to be created and maintained, and this was more difficult. At the level of ideology, it was achieved through the articulation of a clear message, endlessly repeated. This 'republican analysis of the situation' consisted of the following propositions which for republicans had the status of axioms: the British government was an imperial presence in Ireland; partition was a denial of the Irish right to self-determination; as long as the British remained there would be people who would resist by force of arms; Northern Catholics could never get equality while partition remained; the British government and establishment could not be negotiated with or trusted; only violence would persuade it to withdraw; the campaign of the IRA was a war, and as in all wars innocent people would die; this time the war had to continue until the British left; the war would succeed.

Not all nationalists, still less all Catholics, could be persuaded to accept each and every one of these propositions. But enough were persuaded to constitute a core republican community, and enough accepted sufficient of them to sustain the ambivalence on which the armed struggle depended. Even allowing for the intensity of the polarisation on both sides – and the emotional indifference to the pain of the other side – it required constant ideological work by republicans to explain again and again, for example, why actions that risked or resulted in the deaths of children were militarily necessary, why ordinary Protestant workmen could be 'legitimate targets', why kin, neighbours and friends suspected (sometimes wrongly) of giving information to the security forces deserved to die, why the goal being sought justified the terrible means being used to achieve it. The IRA justified such casualties on the grounds that this was a 'war' and that in all wars 'innocent people die'. Such statements were described by hostile observers as 'mealy-mouthed'; in their view, this was nothing more than the violence of psychopaths and fanatics. That this underestimated the political seriousness of the IRA[6] and the strength of their conviction was dramatically revealed in the hunger strikes of 1981, when ten men starved themselves to death to vindicate their claim that what they were engaged in was not terrorism, but war.

The persistence of the campaign

The effect of the conflict was to intensify the fear, hostility, bitterness and grievance which had produced it in the first place. How then was it to end? There was no possibility of it ending while each of the protagonists doggedly pursued victory. But even when there was an openness to a negotiated settlement, someone had to make the first move. In the end it was republicans, and perhaps it could only have been republicans. Why did they do so, and why did it take so long? One answer to the last question is implicit in Séamus Mallon's much quoted comment that the Belfast Agreement of 1998 was 'Sunningdale for slow learners'. In Mallon's understanding, the more perceptive recognised very early the only way this conflict could end; it took lesser minds rather longer to work it out. Mallon's observation can be read as simply a claim to the superior wisdom and foresight of the SDLP, but it is strikingly consistent with the observations of John Stoessinger (1993) on the causes and endings of wars:

There is a remarkable consistence in the self-images of most national leaders on the brink of war. Each confidently expects victory after a brief and triumphant campaign. . . . A leader's misperception of his adversary's power is perhaps the quintessential cause of war. It is vital to remember, however, that it is not the actual distribution of power that precipitates a war; it is the way in which a leader thinks that power is distributed . . . Thus, on the eve of each war, at least one nation misperceives another's power. In that sense the beginning of each war is a misperception or an accident. The war itself then slowly, and in agony, teaches the lesson of reality (Stoessinger, 1993: 217–18).

On this understanding, the Northern conflict continued until each side had learned the 'lesson of reality'. Why did the lesson take so long to learn? It is too simple to attribute this to the supposed learning difficulties of those involved, all of whom, indeed, showed considerable strategic ability.[7] It arose in part because of the enormous gap between their initial positions. The minimal demands of nationalists were for power sharing (with or without an 'Irish dimension'); the maximal demand was Irish unity as soon as possible. From the beginning there were unionists willing to accept power sharing, but few of these were willing to consider an 'Irish dimension', and many more wanted a return to (unionist) majority rule. The British government insisted on power sharing and (to a lesser extent) an 'Irish dimension', but it was unwilling to impose this on unionists (and, in any case, fearful of even trying to do so); in the meantime it hoped to defeat the IRA. It would inevitably take time before each side – and in particular the more radical tendencies – would consider scaling back their aspirations to a point at which a settlement became possible. But there was also the dynamic of war itself. If a war does not end quickly, it takes on a life and logic of its own. Each side soon invests so much that victory becomes an imperative. There are always new weapons to acquire, new tactics to try, and new alliances to forge, some of which may conceivably tip the balance. In this conflict each new weapon or tactic made a difference, but not enough, or not the one intended. It took time for this to become clear, and in the meantime each side was tempted to underestimate the resources and staying power of the other.

A stalemate is all the more likely in a situation where long-established power structures have collapsed and the new power balance is difficult to read. Was there some point at which the British government would throw in the towel and walk away? It is clear now that there was not, but it was less clear then. More than once the British government was tempted to cut its losses and leave the Irish to their fate (Dixon, 2001b: 158–62). There was also the possibility that a major escalation in the republican weaponry of war might force the issue. But was there also some point at which the IRA's organisation and morale would collapse? Was there a chance that, in a scenario once outlined by Danny Morrison, the women of the Falls would dig up the weapons and throw them into the street? We know now that there was not, although some believed that it would eventually happen. Was there some point at which the British government would give up its policy of 'conciliating nationalism', return the province to unionist control and let them get on with the job of restoring order? There was not, but many unionists thought it worth holding out for, not least when they received assurances from the British government that it would never negotiate with terrorists.

The republican 'peace process' began in 1988. Why at that time? There are two basic types of explanations: those which stress the weakness of the movement, and those which emphasise its command of new resources. One version of the weakness argument holds that the ability of the IRA to maintain the armed struggle was in fact running down. The number of failed operations was growing, suggesting either improvements in security or informers quite high in the ranks, and loyalists were successfully targetting IRA and Sinn Féin members based on information from the security forces. A different version of the argument (one which appeals to republican dissidents) stresses the ageing of the leadership, its reduced energy, and desire for a reward for the effort it had put in. Once the opening presented itself, the glow of international approval, the appeal of celebrity status and the lure of power proved irresistible. Moloney (2002) offers a particular twist on the weakness argument. He argues that the political leadership was open to a political strategy from the early 1980s. The militarists were not, however; and in the mid-1980s they planned to escalate the conflict with an offensive modelled on the 1968 'Tet Offensive' of the Vietcong, which convinced the US government that the Vietnam war was unwinnable. The plans were already at an advanced stage when the final shipment of the necessary weaponry was captured on the *Eksund*. When hope of a military breakthrough was gone, the way was open for a political strategy (Moloney, 2002: 3–33). Meanwhile the capacity of the IRA to function militarily was declining, and by the end of the second ceasefire (1997), the campaign had fallen to pieces (Moloney, 2002: 458).

The alternative explanation accepts that there was a military stalemate, but places the main emphasis on changes in the wider political situation and on the emergence of alternatives to violence. Many nationalists saw in the Anglo-Irish Agreement of 1985 the first real evidence that the British government was taking the question of equality and the 'Irish dimension' seriously, and was willing (unlike in 1974) to stand firm in the face of determined unionist opposition. This perception was reinforced by the passing of stronger fair employment legislation in 1989. The situation was changing in other respects as well. Catholic numbers continued to grow as a proportion of the total population; the nationalist vote was rising steadily; and the economic position of middle-class Catholics was strengthening, as was their cultural self-confidence. The Irish government had shown in the Anglo-Irish Agreement its commitment and ability to negotiate an agreement favourable to nationalists. Irish-Americans were becoming more attentive to what was happening and more assertive on issues such as fair employment and human rights; the White House was showing an increasing interest in Northern Ireland. The hunger strikes had improved the international image of the IRA. Republicans had shown their ability to get elected. The perception was gaining ground that they were 'working with the grain of history' (Ruane and Todd, 1996: 139–46). The IRA could sustain the armed struggle indefinitely, but there might be an easier and more effective way of getting the same result.

It will take some time before a full explanation of the origins of the peace process is possible. What must be said is that, whatever gains the Catholic community may or may not have made between the abortive Sunningdale Agreement and the Good Friday Agreement,[8] republicans certainly made gains. The Sunningdale Agreement of 1973 (which loyalists and unionists rejected) would have assured moderate nationalists a place in the new political order. It offered nothing to republicans. They did not want that kind of settlement at that time, but it had little to offer them had they wanted it. Sinn Féin was unsure of how much popular support it enjoyed and had very limited experience of electoral politics. The British and Irish governments viewed them as mindless militants to be defeated or marginalised. By the end of the 1980s the situation was very different. Sinn Féin had proved its staying power, and the policy was now to bring the republicans into the political system. The result was an agreement which guaranteed Sinn Féin a position in government and the possibility of becoming the major nationalist political party in Northern Ireland.

The negotiation of a settlement

By the 1980s the conditions for a settlement had emerged, but the conflict had still to be ended. This would not be an easy task. If it is true, as de Toqueville observed, that a state is never more vulnerable than when it begins to reform, it is also true that parties to a conflict are never more vulnerable than when they begin to negotiate a settlement. The Sinn Féin leadership faced by far the biggest task. It had built a movement, waged a costly war, and sought electoral support – all on an analysis of the situation from which it now proposed radically to depart. For two decades it had ruled out negotiations with the British government on anything other than a British withdrawal. Now negotiations would begin, based on the Downing Street Declaration of 1993, on the assumption that British sovereignty and Northern Ireland would remain for as long as this was the wish of the people of Northern Ireland. The territory that Sinn Féin had insisted was a wholly artificial entity, the product of a gerrymander conducted on the basis of a sectarian headcount, was now to be accorded a right (however qualified) to self-determination.

It would take time before the full implications of the peace process became clear to Sinn Féin's supporters, and it seems certain that many of the concessions they ultimately agreed to would not have been contemplated at the outset. The people who had to be convinced first were IRA volunteers, particularly those in prison. Most of these had devoted years to the struggle, and many had borne the loss of family members and friends. After that it was necessary to convince the wider republican community, whose support (or tolerance) had been a condition of the military phase of the struggle and whose political support would now be crucial. There was an ever-present risk of a split in the ranks of the IRA, the possibility that key figures would desert to dissident groups and provoke an internal civil war; the leadership ran the risk of assassination; there was a danger that the entire political strategy would be undermined if the republican vote collapsed in anger or apathy. There was the further complication that the change had to be managed under the glare of opponents: constitutional nationalists, the two governments, the unionist parties, and political commentators deeply hostile to republicans.

The success of the leadership in keeping the movement together through the period of transition is a tribute to its political skills. There has been speculation about measures taken to sideline, or even to eliminate, potential opponents before the ceasefire, and reference to later intimidation and violence to silence critics and dissenters. But the overwhelming evidence is that the acceptance of the new strategy was secured through persuasion. It was not achieved overnight; on the contrary, the process was a deliberately gradualist one, with carefully worded ambiguities, the tailoring of different messages to different audiences, strategic delays, statements made and then retracted or qualified, and firm undertakings that were later abandoned. But despite the cloud of ambiguity that hung over the process, it soon became clear that the 'republican analysis of the situation' was not simply being abandoned, but stood on its head. Talk of imperialism and colonialism receded and references to the goal of Irish unity became fewer. The emphasis now was on justice, rights, fairness, equality and human dignity, and it was affirmed that with appropriate legislation and institutions, all of this could be secured within Northern Ireland. In a complete reversal of the analysis of the past, it was being argued that not alone was all this possible without Irish unity, it would pave the way for unity.[9]

The initial response of Sinn Féin's supporters was shock, or even dismay, followed by a gradual – in some cases, unenthusiastic – acceptance of the logic of what was now proposed. The key factor among those who accepted it was their willingness to trust the leadership. Not all were willing to do that; a minority denounced what was happening as a betrayal and became disenchanted, disillusioned or cynical.[10] The republican leadership showed formidable political skills in charting the new direction, but the question remains as to why the bulk of republican supporters was willing to go along with them. Two very different approaches to explanation have been adopted. One is to argue that the specifically *republican* roots of Catholic or nationalist politics during these years were much shallower than they seemed at the time. Eamonn McCann has advanced the most radical version of this argument with the claim that the movement which fought the war was not republican at all, but a civil rights movement which simply adopted the ideological and organisational framework of a pre-existing republican tradition.[11] On this account, once it became clear that the civil rights concerns of the Catholic community could be comprehensively addressed, the central republican concern with Irish unity and the illegitimacy of the British presence faded from view. An alternative version of the argument is that the crisis of 1969–70 allowed republicans to get control of the most disadvantaged members of the Catholic population, and to manipulate or coerce them into supporting a political cause which, deep down, was not very important to them.[12]

The other approach to explanation takes seriously the claim of the leadership that there was no essential contradiction between the peace process and republicanism. The leadership emphasised the continued strength of republicanism, including the undefeated status of the IRA, and presented the change as simply the adoption of a new, more effective, strategy to achieve traditional republican goals. The armed struggle had reached the limits of what it could achieve, at least for the present, and while it could be continued indefinitely, it was a barrier to further progress. Other resources were becoming available – popular political support, the support of the Irish government or of influential Irish-Americans – which could not be accessed while the armed struggle continued. The best strategy now was to set the armed struggle aside, and to secure an agreement which would deliver equality within Northern Ireland, underpin the continued Catholic demographic advance, strengthen the links between North and South, and steer Northern Ireland towards reunification with the rest of the island. This line of argument did not convince the entire republican movement, but it ironed out (or obscured) enough of the contradictions to overcome the charges of betrayal and sell-out by dissenters, and to carry the majority with it.[13]

The British and Irish governments had a similar – though less demanding and less risky – task of ideological revision to perform. The British government was going to defy its declaration that it would never negotiate with 'terrorists', and instead ensure them a place in government even while they held on to their weapons, and refused to declare that the war was over. On the other hand, once a ceasefire was in place, the wider British public was little troubled by the prospect of its government 'negotiating with terrorists'. It was well aware of the precedents for this: every colonial conflict had ended the same way.[14] Above all it was relieved that the conflict was now coming to an end. For the British government itself, there was almost no loss of face: there was no question of withdrawal and republicans had accepted the 'principle of (majority) consent'. The Irish government faced a public that was potentially more hostile: for two decades political commentary in the South had been extremely critical of republicans, and there was a pervasive fear of being tainted by association with them. But the southern government could also cite precedents: previous generations of republicans had used violence and had then abandoned it to enter the political process; the two largest parties in the South had themselves travelled the same route. The use of violence had been wrong, but the priority was to facilitate the transition to constitutional politics, not to dwell on the past. Those long opposed to republicanism viewed the process with suspicion and hostility, but the wider public was willing to put its reservations aside to secure peace.

One of the striking aspects of the way in which the process was handled by the governments was the acceptance that what had been taking place was a 'war' rather than 'terrorism'. The IRA had always claimed to have been fighting a war, and Sinn Féin entered the peace process on the assumption that it was about bringing an end to a war. It praised the courage of the IRA in calling a ceasefire and demanded that Sinn Féin be allowed to enter political negotiations without the IRA disarming, on the grounds that 'an undefeated army' does not unilaterally disarm before a peace settlement. But up to then the terminology of war was not used outside the ranks of Sinn Féin; any hint of it invited the suspicion that the person using it was a 'republican fellow-traveller'. Now it entered mainstream discourse. It was a gradual process and one with which the governments, particularly the British government, were not entirely comfortable. But it proved strategically useful in the search for a settlement and, without it, it is not clear that a settlement would have been possible.

This is because war, unlike terrorism, has a certain respectability in human affairs. Terrorism is evil; wars are tragedies from which people have to move on. Killing by terrorists is murder and should meet with the full rigours of the law; in war it is legitimate, it can gain medals and lead to promotion. The killing of innocent bystanders by terrorists is a heinous crime; the killing of civilians in wartime is regrettable but inevitable. Prisoners of war can expect to be released as soon as peace is established; those jailed for terrorist offences are expected to serve out their sentences. The goal in defeating terrorism is to disarm and punish the terrorists; in wars undefeated enemies do not surrender their weapons before peace negotiations begin, and do not do so afterwards.

Indeed, armies defeated in war may soon be rearmed by their conquerors in the interests of defence and internal order. Without the notion that what had been taking place in Northern Ireland was – in some sense – a war there could have been no inter-party talks, no early release of prisoners, no settlement while arms remained to be decommissioned, no assured positions for republicans in the government of Northern Ireland, and no suggestion that they might be future members of police boards.

Not everyone accepted this redefinition of what the conflict had been, and certainly not on the terms demanded by Sinn Féin. Some commentators (notably Conor Cruise O'Brien) argued that the entire process was betraying the fundamental principles of democracy that the governments were pledged to defend. There was, however, political method in this apparent constitutional madness. War implies the absence of an overarching governmental framework. It normally refers to conflicts between sovereign nations, but it is also applied to situations of ethnic or civil conflict when a governmental framework is absent, weak or contested. That the governmental framework in Northern Ireland was contested was not in question. The purpose of the negotiations was to bring this contestation to an end by establishing a framework that would have legitimacy and where the normal rule of law would henceforth apply. The governments went along with – rather than endorsing – Sinn Féin's definition of the IRA's campaign as a war in order to secure an agreement which would prevent violence ever being legitimated in such terms in the future.

Achievements of the peace process

The best hope of those who launched the peace process and negotiated the Good Friday Agreement was to bring a complete and permanent end to all forms of political violence in Ireland; the priority goal was to end the campaign of the IRA. Are these goals being realised? It is unlikely that the best hope of the negotiators will be fulfilled in the near future. Since the wars of the seventeenth century there have been three basic kinds of extra-legal political violence in Ireland: armed loyalism, armed republicanism, and inter-communal attritional violence. Each of these is now over two centuries old. Armed republicanism shows no sign of disappearing. The IRA has not yet completely abandoned the field, and it has yet to become clear whether, or in what form, it plans to do so. The CIRA and RIRA are still active. Inter-communal attritional violence continues, particularly at the communal interfaces, but it is not limited to that. It was an important component in the violence of the past 30 years, running alongside, but also animating, the more politically orientated paramilitary violence. There is no reason to expect it to disappear.

Indeed, on past experience, it is likely to get worse as the two communities come closer to demographic and economic parity.

In normal circumstances the scale of republican and attritional violence is low. The major problem lies in the outbreak of prolonged periods of intense violence. There were two of these in the twentieth century. Is it possible that this was a phase in Irish political history which is now over? The first question is whether the most recent one is itself over, or in what sense it is over. The signs are more contradictory than it might first seem. It is clear that Provisional republicanism, in both its political and military forms, wants to move to a completely political strategy. The IRA has deliberately run down its capacity to conduct an armed campaign. It appears to have put most of its weaponry 'beyond use'. It has allowed a degree of laxity to creep into its organisation, and may now be more easily penetrated by the security forces. Sinn Féin has nurtured a climate of opinion and public sentiment which would make a return to violence very difficult. It has abandoned the arguments that it used to defend its past campaign, and has adopted a much more conciliatory tone. It has made important concessions of principle, particularly in respect of legitimacy.[15] None of this was entered into lightly. It was high-risk activity and required a complex choreography involving governments and political parties, each with its own agenda and concerns. It would take an extraordinary development for Sinn Féin now to walk away from this. On the other hand, it remains unclear what IRA intentions for the future actually are. It is resisting suggestions that it disband and Sinn Féin clearly wishes to retain the centre ground of radical republicanism. In this context, it is significant that it is retaining the title of 'Sinn Féin'; when the Southern parties embraced constitutional politics, they abandoned it (only if the Provisional movement splits irrevocably is there a prospect of a name-change). One must also assume that, despite the running down of its operational effectiveness, the IRA retains the capacity to re-emerge as a significant paramilitary force. Until it actually disbands, there remains a degree of ambiguity as to whether, or in what sense, the current phase is truly over.

There is the further question of whether, at some future date, a new crisis could occur which would lead the IRA to relaunch its campaign, or allow another republican group to launch a campaign and get command over the republican centre ground. Two factors make this unlikely (though not impossible). First, crises of the order of 1969 do not easily happen. As we saw, it took a multiplicity of factors at different levels to produce that crisis and the destabilisation that followed. Its most general condition was the change in the underlying balance of power between Protestant and Catholic, unionist and nationalist. But conjunctural factors were also important (for example, the changing nature of the Northern Irish economy and the post-war British state, and the development of new forms of minority political struggle). The process also depended on a host of contingent developments (for example, the founding of People's Democracy and its decision to march from Belfast to Derry in January 1969, the split in the IRA which led to the formation of the Provisional IRA, the British general election of June 1970, which returned the Conservatives to power and brought a much tougher security regime). The crisis required a complex alignment of forces, all pushing in the same direction, and then a further deterioration in conditions before the process of political destabilisation became truly irreversible. More than 30 years on, if peace can be established and the institutions of the agreement can be got to function, a similar destabilisation will be difficult to achieve.

Second, the launching and sustaining of a campaign similar to that just waged by the IRA is far from an easy task. Apart from the crisis needed to set it in motion, it depends on two key factors: motivation and capacity. Motivation has three separate components: normative (belief in its legitimacy), cognitive (belief that it will enable it to achieve its goals) and affective (willingness on the part of those supporting it to bear its emotional and psychological costs). Capacity likewise has three components: organisational effectiveness (the recruitment of members, the maintenance of discipline and morale, and preventing infiltration), logistics (the procurement of weapons, and the ability to mount attacks) and political support (of the community on behalf of whom the struggle is to be waged, as well as more wide-ranging networks). These are demanding conditions. The IRA succeeded in meeting them, but conditions in the early 1970s were truly extraordinary, and maintaining them subsequent to that required constant work.[16] There is little to suggest that the current alternative IRAs, with their small numbers, poor organisation, infiltration by the security forces and low standing in the republican community, could meet those conditions. Could the IRA repeat its performance of the early 1970s? Despite its currently depleted organisational state, and the ideological hostages to fortune which its political leadership has given, the chances are that it could. It still occupies the political centre ground of republicanism and, though it would be difficult, it could renew itself militarily. On the other hand, neither Sinn Féin nor the IRA shows any interest in doing this, and their occupancy of the centre ground of republicanism actually prevents more militant groups from getting a foothold.

There are, however, two considerations which give cause for concern for the future. One centres on the effects of the past 30 years of cultural learning. It might safely be assumed that the experience has taught the different parties much about how to avoid such crises and conflicts in the future. But cultural learning under conditions of conflict is Janus-faced: if the ability to contain conflict and to make peace is learned, so too is the ability to make war. The communities have a long history of conflict, but in 1969 they still had a lot to learn about how to wage war against each other on the scale of the 1970s and

1980s, and – in the case of republicans – to do so against the modern British state. They now have that knowledge; it is part of their cultural repertoire, and circumstances may one day conspire to reactivate it. This is not to present a wholly imaginary situation. Past crises have been produced by a change in the balance of power between Catholics and Protestants. That change continues. It may stop at a point of rough parity between the communities. It is more likely to continue beyond that, possibly to a point where nationalists form an overall majority in Northern Ireland and are in a position to push for Irish unity. The agreement sets down the conditions and procedures to be followed in such an eventuality. It is unlikely to happen smoothly or consensually. At this point, we may expect the third strand of political violence in Ireland – armed loyalism – to come forcibly into play, with the clear possibility of a wider destabilisation.

Chapter 9

Contemporary unionism and the tactics of resistance

Paul Dixon

Introduction

Unionists have used both constitutional and extra-constitutional, violent and non-violent, *tactics* in order to resist incorporation into a united Ireland and to achieve their *strategic goal* of securing the union between Northern Ireland and Great Britain. David Trimble, for example, supported the militant Ulster Vanguard group in the early 1970s when the union appeared to be threatened, yet he has been the champion of the peace process since he became Ulster Unionist Party leader in 1995. In the propaganda war waged over Northern Ireland, unionists are often portrayed as suffering from a 'siege mentality' or as paranoid and irrational in their resistance to various British–Irish const-itutional initiatives.[1] By contrast, this chapter argues that there is evidence to substantiate unionist concerns about British policy and their place within the union, concerns which date back at least to the start of the recent conflict. This argument is illustrated with evidence from two periods of high unionist insecurity. The first covers the years 1970–6, which saw the failure of the first peace process, the power-sharing experiment (1972–4). The second is the aftermath of the Anglo-Irish Agreement (1985–94), which was the prelude to the second peace process, dating from the IRA ceasefire of 1994.

There are four principal elements to the argument:

- First, British interests in Northern Ireland – while they are not static – are not as strong as unionists would like them to be. For much of the period since partition, Britain has had no *overriding* selfish, strategic or economic interest in Northern Ireland, beyond stability.

- Second, as a result of this lack of interest – as well as a lack of identification with Ulster unionism – the British do not provide the support for unionism that the southern Irish provide for nationalism, and there is no other external force to take up this role. The isolation of unionism compounds its insecurity over the constitutional future of Northern Ireland.

- Third, as a result of British 'untrustworthiness' and unionist isolation during periods of heightened constitutional insecurity, unionists (whether 'constitutional' or 'unconstitutional', 'respectable' or 'unrespectable') tend to shift towards more militant and violent tactics to defend the union. Such tactical forms of unionist resistance to Irish unity during the recent conflict are not necessarily irrational, paranoid or counter-productive in achieving their strategic aim.

- Fourth, the political leaders of unionism operate within a political context that both constrains and enables them to lead their parties and followers towards accommodation with nationalists. In periods of heightened constitutional insecurity, their ability to control their followers, prevent violence and promote accommodation with nationalists is more limited.

The argument presented here is less about morality – and the intention here is not in any way to legitimise unionist violence – than about trying to understand unionist tactics for preserving the union and the constraints operating on unionist politicians. A 'realistic' appraisal of these constraints is important in understanding just how far unionists can move towards a more inclusive civic unionism (Dixon, 2004) and towards an accommodation with nationalism. The chapter is divided into four parts: first, an assessment of the degree to which Britain remains committed to the union; second, a discussion of unionist insecurity and its militant tactics of resistance, 1970–6; third, an analysis of the dilemmas of unionist leadership after the Anglo-Irish Agreement; and finally, a discussion of the relationship between power, democracy and violence.

Great Britain and the union

Republicans have traditionally argued that British imperialism is determined to hold on to its 'first and last colony'. Particularly since the end of the 1980s, however, some within the republican movement have begun to reassess this analysis and to some extent accept that Britain has 'no selfish strategic or economic interest' in Northern Ireland. Alongside this has developed a more sophisticated understanding of how the British state operates and of the tensions within it – for example, between the 'securocrats' and the political elite. The nationalist Social Democratic and Labour Party (SDLP) has argued that Britain has 'no selfish strategic or economic interest' in Northern Ireland since the early 1970s (Dixon, 2001b). It is worth considering three aspects of the unionist response to this changed political context: first, unionist perceptions of the level of British commitment to the union; second, the consequences of the asymmetrical relationship between the unionist and nationalist communities, on the one hand, and their external allies, the British and Irish governments, on the other; and, third, the political response within unionism in periods of heightened constitutional insecurity.

British attitudes

Unionism has been divided in its attitude to the British state and its policy towards Northern Ireland. In the 1960s the moderate unionist prime minister Terence O'Neill favoured a compliant attitude towards British intervention, while unionist hardliners were more resistant. As British governments were perceived to adopt a more 'interfering' and pro-nationalist stance, so unionists took a more sceptical view of British policy, and the more trusting approach of moderates was undermined. The problem for moderate unionists is that their willingness to reach an accommodation with nationalists is often interpreted by outsiders as a sign of weakness on the union. Unionists are more likely to vote for hardline candidates to communicate the strength of their opposition to Irish unity if the election of moderates is seen by the British government as indicating a softening on the union.

The integrationist wing of unionism, which saw its heyday in the late 1980s, was remarkable for the trust which it placed in the British state. It argued that Northern Ireland should be treated like any other part of the United Kingdom, and was therefore opposed to devolution there. The leader of the Ulster Unionist Party (UUP) during the period 1979–95, James Molyneaux, was unusual for being a hardline unionist who felt that he could trust successive Conservative governments to defend the union. The Anglo-Irish Agreement (1985) and the Framework documents (1995) undermined Molyneaux's approach of trusting Conservative prime ministers Margaret Thatcher and John Major. Bob McCartney, a leading integrationist figure in the UUP, later formed the United Kingdom Unionist Party (UKUP) and, echoing the Democratic Unionist Party (DUP), expounded a highly negative view of British policy. Since partition, he argued, the British government's strategic aim had been to gradually ease Northern Ireland out of the union.

Unionist perceptions of the treachery of British policy and the threat to their constitutional position have often been dismissed (particularly by republicans who hold a strongly contrasting view) as unfounded or even paranoid. There is, however, plenty of evidence to support the sceptical position adopted by unionists towards British policy during the recent conflict (Bew, Gibbon and Patterson, 1979; Patterson, 1986; Dixon, 2001b). British 'untrustworthiness' dates back at least to partition, when the British imposed a devolved parliament on the unionists and introduced safeguards for the nationalist minority. The British government's apparent offer of unity to the Irish government if it would enter the Second World War on the side of the allies was, for unionists, an important example of British weakness on the union. The Ireland Act, 1949, gave unionists the guarantee that Ireland would not be united without the consent of the Northern Ireland Parliament. The prospect of a Labour government at Westminster apparently committed to civil rights and an interventionist approach to the economy revived unionist anxieties that their position in the union could become undermined. Harold Wilson's 'surrogate nationalism' and sympathies for Irish unity, although shallow, further alarmed unionists (Bew, Gibbon and Patterson, 1979; Dixon, 2001b: 60–4). The principal objection of the Labour governments (1964–70) to Irish unity appeared to lie in the opposition of unionist opinion rather than any over-riding selfish, strategic or economic interest. This was based on the view that premature unification would result in a unionist backlash, implying that nationalists would have to conciliate Protestants if they wanted a united Ireland (Dixon, 2001b: 109).

Unionist fears of British treachery may have been exaggerated, or they may have been misperceptions of the intentions of the Labour government; but there was nonetheless evidence to suggest that there was substance to these beliefs. The case studies presented below of British policy in 1970–6 and 1985–94 illustrate the substance of continuing unionist concerns over their place in the union. On 9 November 1990 the Secretary of State for Northern Ireland, Peter Brooke, announced that 'The British Government has no selfish strategic or economic interest in Northern Ireland, our role is to help, enable and encourage'. While his words have been presented as a sea change in British policy, this stance was apparent in the early 1970s. Britain did not have any overriding interest in retaining the union; it is retained because it offers the best prospect for a stable solution to the conflict. Northern Ireland had long ceased to be a net contributor to the British exchequer and was a 'drain' on the rest of the United Kingdom. Any economic interests could have been secured in a united Ireland. Ireland's geographical proximity makes it of strategic interest to Britain, but these interests could be ensured in a united Ireland and it does not appear to be of overriding importance to British policy makers. The Irish government may well have given the British security guarantees in exchange for Irish unity.

The end of the Cold War made even more obvious Britain's lack of strategic interest in Northern Ireland (Dixon 2002a). Opinion polls and British political discourse suggest that Northern Ireland is not seen as a part of the union and the 'British nation' in the way that England, Scotland and Wales are. Since the mid-1970s opinion polls have shown consistent support for British withdrawal from Northern Ireland. The need for stability in the island of Ireland best explains Britain's continuing presence in Northern Ireland. British withdrawal and Irish unity or an independent Ulster threatened to plunge the island into civil war, with overspill effects in Britain, particularly in cities with a large Irish-descended population. The Irish government could be destabilised and the island made vulnerable to a republican takeover, a development that would not be in Britain's economic interest, as the Republic is a leading trading partner. It might also draw severe international criticism, particularly from Europe and the USA. The integration of Northern Ireland into the United Kingdom would not accommodate nationalist aspirations and was likely to undermine nationalist 'moderates' and reduce the co-operation of the Republic of Ireland. The consequences could well be an upsurge of republican violence and reduced prospects of a stable settlement.

The British political elite considered withdrawal, independence and integration in their search for a stable settlement to the conflict in Northern Ireland, but these options were rejected on the grounds that they were likely to worsen the conflict. The constraints on British policy were such that the only stable solution appeared to lie in a package somewhere between power sharing on its own and power sharing with an Irish dimension (Dixon, 2001a; Dixon, 2001b: ch. 7). Any British politician making progress towards a settlement in Ireland could also calculate on receiving a reward from the British electorate for removing such an intractable problem from the political agenda.

Asymmetry and unionist isolation

As suggested above, the British government has not been the sponsor of Ulster unionism in the way that the Irish government has supported Irish nationalism. This is not only the result of a lack of British interest in the union with Northern Ireland but arises also from the government's perceived need to act in an 'even-handed' manner towards unionists and nationalists. While the British government must act as 'champion of the union' to reassure unionists that their place in the union is guaranteed by the British, the British government is also under pressure from nationalists to act as a 'neutral arbiter' between all parties to the conflict in order to reassure them that they will be dealt with fairly in a peace process. In addition, the British government pledges that it will end the union with Northern Ireland if that is the desire of a majority of people living there.

The asymmetrical relationship between the unionists and nationalists, in terms of the backing they receive from the British and Irish governments respectively, leaves unionism vulnerable. Significantly, according to opinion polls, the citizens of the Republic are more likely to regard Northern Ireland as part of their nation while the British on the whole do not. The plight of nationalists in the North has a resonance among political and public opinion in the Republic in a way that the plight of unionists does not in Britain; the unionists cannot draw on the same sympathy and support in Britain that the nationalists can in the Republic and further afield. British public opinion has consistently favoured withdrawal from Northern Ireland since the mid-1970s and there is only limited, qualified support for the retention of the union with Northern Ireland (Dixon, 1995b). Indeed, an opinion poll as far back as June 1967 showed 45 per cent of a British sample approving of the proposition that the British government encourage Northern Ireland to join up with the Republic (19 per cent disapproved and 36 per cent didn't know). Unionism's alienation from British public opinion is not the recent, dramatic shift that some pundits would like to suggest (*The Guardian*, 21 Aug 2001).

The lack of *overriding* British strategic, economic or political interests in Northern Ireland has further fed unionist insecurity about Britain's commitment to the union. Among the political elite there is limited sympathy with the unionist cause in either the Labour or Conservative parties, as even pro-union Conservatives have admitted (see below, pp. 140–2). During the history of the recent 'troubles' it has been only in exceptional periods (when the support of Ulster Unionist MPs in the House of Commons has been sought after) that British governments have paid close attention to unionist interests. The British Labour Party's support for Irish unity, and sympathy for this option among some Conservatives, underline the asymmetrical relationship and isolation of unionism. In addition to this, northern nationalists have worked effectively to cultivate support and influence in the USA and Europe. It is this array of national and international forces ranged behind the nationalists (the so-called 'pan-nationalist front') which goes some way to explaining the oft-cited siege mentality of unionists.

Given the 'unreliable' record of successive British governments on Northern Ireland, it is hardly surprising that unionists have regarded both the first (1972–4) and second (1994–) 'peace processes' with considerable suspicion and treated the notion of joint authority with even greater hostility (Dixon, 1995b). If constitutional methods seem unlikely to guarantee unionists their place within the union then they are likely to turn towards more militant tactics, including violence, to prevent their incorporation in a united Ireland, an outcome that makes the prospects of accommodation with nationalists less likely.

While ambiguity over Northern Ireland's constitutional position may contribute to paramilitary violence, it is possible that the opposite is also true – that declarations of total constitutional security may also be counterproductive (if not seen as devoid of credibility). In an interview in 1989 Peter Brooke referred to the example of Cyprus: in 1954 a British minister declared it would 'never' leave the Empire but by 1960 the island had won its independence. If the British government, as some urge, was to declare that Northern Ireland will be forever part of the United Kingdom then this might inflame nationalists and republicans (along with the Republic of Ireland and international opinion), destabilise the situation further and contribute to an upsurge of violence. Leaving open at least the possibility of Irish unity by consent and peaceful means would seem to be not only democratic but the minimum required incentive if the (Provisional) Irish Republican Army (IRA), or other republican paramilitaries, are to be induced to become involved in the democratic process. The consent formula is democratic, has widespread agreement, as demonstrated by its presence in the Good Friday Agreement, allows nationalists to retain their aspirations and gives unionists some guarantee about their future in the United Kingdom.

Unionist constitutional insecurity

During periods of high insecurity about their constitutional position, unionists have generally been readier to advocate more violent *tactics*, against both the state and republicans, to achieve their *strategic* aim: defence of their position within the union. These perceptions of British policy may be exaggerated, but there is a rational basis to them (Dixon, 1996: 132–3). When non-violent tactics and constitutional methods appear to be failing to secure Northern Ireland's place in the union, then unionism shifts towards less constitutional methods of influencing British policy.

The sharp dichotomy between 'constitutional' and 'unconstitutional' unionism disguises the grey area in which unionist politics has often operated. The UUP and the DUP are often portrayed as 'constitutional', although the UUP appears 'more respectable' than the DUP. The loyalist paramilitary organisations are seen as 'unconstitutional' and their associated parties, the Progressive Unionist Party (PUP) and, until recently, the Ulster Democratic Party (UDP), at best 'semi-constitutional'. The advent of the peace process has to some extent complicated this picture. The UDP and PUP came out in support of the process while the DUP continues to oppose it, having been joined by the 'Liberal Unionists' (Porter, 1996: ch. 4) of the UKUP and the Northern Ireland Unionist Party (NIUP), the paramilitary Loyalist Volunteer Force (LVF) and an influential faction within the UUP itself.

The principal unionist parties (UUP, DUP) have operated in the grey area between the poles of violent and non-violent tactics, veering towards one pole or the other depending on the wider political context. In particular, it will be suggested that unionists have tended to shift towards more direct and violent methods of political action when they fear – often with good reason – that their position within the union is becoming undermined. When these fears are heightened, the room for unionist political elites to contemplate accommodation with nationalists (in British-sponsored initiatives) is constrained. Political leaders can act either to incite or control violence, depending on the constraints and opportunities operating on them. Assessing these constraints and opportunities is difficult and controversial. For example, a speech by a unionist leader using aggressive rhetoric could represent an attempt to increase tension and incite violence against nationalists. On the other hand, the unionist leader may be attempting to head off a militant challenge and act as a safety valve to express unionist concerns. In this way, steam can be let off and passions can be channelled away from more violent expression. An understanding of the constraints and opportunities operating on unionist leaders enables a more nuanced – and less stereotypical – understanding of unionist politics (see Dixon, 2002b, on the various political skills deployed in Northern Ireland).

A unionist shift towards more violent tactics and failure to engage with British initiatives for resolving the conflict can undermine unionist strategic aims. Intransigence and violence – if they are taken too far – could further endanger British support for the union with Northern Ireland and provoke an anti-unionist response.

Unionist insecurity, phase 1: 1970–6

The election of a Conservative government in June 1970, with its traditional links with unionism and more repressive approach to security policy, may have initially contributed towards settling unionist anxieties. The 'firm hand' that many unionists welcomed on the security front resulted in the introduction of internment without trial in August 1971, and most tragically in the 'Bloody Sunday' deaths of January 1972. Nevertheless, the Conservative government confronted unionism and made concessions to nationalism. It was, after all, a Conservative government that prorogued Stormont in March 1972, that introduced the notion of power sharing in a white paper in March 1973 and that did a deal with the Irish government in December 1973 proposing a significant 'Irish dimension'.

Indeed, it was clear that following internment leading politicians in both the Conservative government and the Labour opposition were becoming more sympathetic to the goal of Irish unity. The British prime minister, Edward Heath, in his Guildhall Speech to the City of London on 15 November 1971, declared that nationalists' aspiration for Irish unity by democratic and constitutional means was legitimate and that if a majority in Northern Ireland wanted Irish unity 'I do not believe any British government would stand in the way'. There were reports in newspapers that Conservative ministers were sympathetic to Irish unity. Such expressions were necessarily off the record in order to minimise their impact on unionist opinion. In January 1972 *The Economist* reported that 'ministers have made little secret of their belief that the most satisfactory solution in the end would be if a political solution were created over the years in which the Protestant majority in the north could come to recognise a future for itself in a united Ireland' (Patterson, 1986). Peter Jenkins wrote in *The Guardian*:

Ministers would like nothing better than to be shot of the problems of Northern Ireland. Some privately conceded that probably the only permanent long-term solution to the problem of Ireland is its reunification. They would be happy in the meanwhile to see the Stormont [*sic*; parliament] cut down to size as the Belfast Urban District Council. These views are even more prevalent and more strongly held within the civil service (*The Guardian*, 8 Nov. 1971).

According to these reports, reunification was not seen 'as a dramatic act of policy' but 'as the eventual result of a growing together process'. This modernising view (Dixon, 2001b: ch. 3) suggested that the longer-term interests of the people of Northern Ireland required convergence: 'The development of common interests between the two islands, facilitated by common membership of the European Community, must become the basis of co-operation, between the two communities in Northern Ireland' (*The Guardian*, 22 Nov 1971; see Bew, Gibbon and Patterson, 1995: 169 for further evidence of Conservative sympathies for Irish unity).

The Bloody Sunday inquiry has uncovered cabinet documents revealing the extent of the Conservative cabinet's ambivalence over the union with Northern Ireland in 1972. Reviewing the minutes of a cabinet meeting shortly after Bloody Sunday, Eamonn McCann points out that 'The minutes suggest that the British government was far from dogmatic about the constitutional future of the North. None of the ministers is recorded expressing a straight-forward defence-of-the-realm position' (*Sunday Tribune*, 26 Sept. 1999). The Defence Secretary, Lord Carrington, even argued that expecting nationalists to wait 20 years for a united Ireland was asking too much, which may suggest that there was no overriding defence objection to Irish unity (Bew, Gibbon and Patterson, 1995: 169). Unionists were enraged by the 'softly, softly' security policy of the Conservative government, by the introduction of direct rule (a key IRA demand) and by secret talks between the Conservative government and the IRA in July 1972, shortly after the Conservatives had said they would not negotiate with terrorists.

The conflict, particularly on the left, was seen increasingly by the British political elite as a colonial one rather than as a problem that was internal to the United Kingdom. The corollary of this position was British withdrawal and Irish unity. In November 1971, Harold Wilson put forward a 15-point plan for Irish unity by consent. Conservative reactions to Wilson's proposals were notable by their restraint. In December 1971 Wilson declared that 'No democratic politician can negotiate with people who are murdering people' (*The Times*, 7 Dec. 1971). In March 1972 the Labour leader secretly met the IRA. Senior Labour politicians began to discuss British withdrawal under the code name 'Algeria' so that they could publicly deny any such discussions (Haines, 1977). Although the Labour Party was in opposition, it was a credible alternative party of government, so unionists had good reason to fear these developments in party thinking.

Significant sections of the British political elite publicly and privately favoured Irish unity as a means to extricate Britain from a problem in which it had little interest other than stability. The untrustworthiness of the British political elite undermined those unionists who wanted to trust British guarantees on the union and share power with nationalists. Hardline unionists could credibly argue that power sharing was a British-inspired policy to ease Northern Ireland out of the union. The shift in British political elite attitudes towards Northern Ireland, along with a poll in September 1971 showing 59 per cent public support for withdrawal, was noticed by unionist opinion (Patterson, 1986). A unionist backlash developed, encouraged by what unionists saw as the appeasement of the IRA by the British political elite. The British-driven, power-sharing experiment was opposed by loyalists as a step down the road to Irish unity.

The British government might well have gradually eased Northern Ireland out of the union had some hardline unionists not demonstrated their ability to bring Northern Ireland to the brink of civil war. The loyalist mobilisation was apparent in demonstrations, strikes and in the sectarian murder of Catholic civilians. Hardline unionists were dissatisfied at the failure of their own government and the British government to take a more vigorous approach in the face of growing IRA violence. The introduction of internment in the same month precipitated a rapid escalation of violence and in its wake loyalism mobilised. The mass-based Ulster Defence Association (UDA) was formed in September 1971 as an umbrella body for loyalist vigilante groups. At its peak in 1972, it was estimated to have 40,000 members (Elliott and Flackes, 1999: 474). The same month Ian Paisley and his Protestant Unionist Party joined forces with the working-class unionism of Desmond Boal in establishing the hardline DUP.

The Ulster Vanguard group embodied the overlap between the 'respectable' unionism of the UUP and paramilitarism. It was formed in early 1972 as an umbrella organisation to overcome party divisions. Significantly, it recruited members from the 'respectable' UUP even though it had direct links to the Vanguard Service Corps, a paramilitary organisation. The rhetoric of the Vanguard leader, William Craig, was aggressive. He told a rally in March 1972 that 'if the politicians fail, it will be our duty to liquidate the enemy'. In Autumn 1972 Craig declared his willingness 'to come out and shoot and kill'. David Trimble – signatory of the Good Friday Agreement, Nobel Peace Prize winner and leader of the UUP – was an active member of Vanguard as were David Burnside, later MP, and Sir Reg Empey, later a pro-agreement member of the UUP. Ulster Vanguard was highly sceptical of British policy (Trimble argued that it had perhaps mortally wounded the union), opposed direct rule and reluctantly flirted with Ulster nationalism and independence. While Ulster independence has not been a popular option among the unionist electorate, it might be hinted at by unionists as an attempt to threaten the British government that in the event of a 'sell-out' unionists would have an alternative option to Irish unity.

During 1972–3 loyalist mobilisation proceeded, raising the prospect of the British army facing a war against both loyalist and republican paramilitaries. Loyalists, fearing that the truce with the IRA was the prelude to a betrayal by the British government, began to establish their own barricades in loyalist areas. On 3 July 1972 a standoff between 8,000 members of the UDA and the outnumbered army threatened to lead to heavy bloodshed if soldiers were forced to fire on advancing loyalists. An historian of the army in Northern Ireland argued that such a clash 'would have put the army in an unenviable and probably impossible position' (Hamill, 1985: 110). While to some extent the army was prepared to take on loyalists, there were limits to how far they could go without provoking an unsustainable war on two fronts, against both the IRA and loyalist paramilitaries. There were also concerns as to how far the locally recruited security forces would police their own community (Dixon, 2001b: 98–128).

The loyalist backlash culminated in the Ulster Workers' Council (UWC) strike of May 1974 which succeeded in bringing down the power-sharing experiment, and with it the collapse of British policy as it had evolved since 1972. The loyalist mobilisation of 1971–4 demonstrated the power of unionism, and British government policy shifted away from power-sharing, and perhaps the hope of Irish unity, towards accommodating the new reality of unionist power. British (and Irish) calculations altered radically; independence rather than Irish unity appeared to be the best route to British withdrawal. For all the Irish government's nationalist posturing, British withdrawal represented a considerable threat to the southern state most likely resulting in a civil war in which the Irish government would have found itself embroiled. By the mid-1970s, the British calculated that normalisation (implying 'Ulsterisation' and 'criminalisation') and containment offered the best prospect for insulating itself from the conflict and minimising instability. Whether or not the British government had been serious about easing Northern Ireland into a united Ireland through power sharing and an Irish dimension, the ability of unionists to mobilise and threaten civil war may well have scuppered those hopes.

Unionist insecurity, phase 2: 1985–94

Between 1974 and 1976 there was a widespread expectation that the British were about to withdraw from Northern Ireland. After 1976, as British policy makers took steps to reassure unionists, these fears subsided and loyalist violence decreased. The assertion of unionist power in 1971–4 had changed calculations as to what was politically possible in Northern Ireland, in the unionists' favour. The finely balanced House of Commons also gave leverage to unionist MPs, forcing the British government and Conservative opposition to attend more closely to their interests. There followed a period in 1976–9 that was without a major constitutional initiative to raise unionist concerns. The loyalist strike of 1977, unlike the UWC strike, failed. The parameters of British policy had been tested; neither independence, integration nor withdrawal appeared likely to produce the stability that the British desired. While Ian Paisley went on the 'Carson Trail' in 1980 over Anglo-Irish initiatives that developed into the Anglo-Irish Agreement of 1985, loyalist paramilitaries remained relatively quiet. The Anglo-Irish Agreement was signed by the British and Irish governments on 15 November 1985 by Margaret Thatcher, the British Prime Minister (1979–90) and Garret FitzGerald, the Irish Taoiseach (1982–7). The agreement gave the Republic of Ireland a consultative role in British policy towards Northern Ireland. FitzGerald claimed that the Agreement was 'as near to Joint Authority as one can get'. Unionist resistance to the agreement was impressive and, once again, shifted towards more militant tactics to secure the union.

The unionist revolt: violence and the union
In retrospect, there was probably more reason for unionists to fear that British policy in the early 1970s was about manipulating Northern Ireland out of the union than was the case later with the Anglo-Irish Agreement. The legacy of previous British policy may have influenced unionist perceptions about the agreement. Margaret Thatcher's intention was probably not to push Northern Ireland out of the union but to increase security co-operation with the Republic of Ireland. Others with influence on British policy probably saw the agreement as a step towards an historic accommodation between unionism and nationalism. The unionist sense of betrayal and insecurity was heightened by the fact that it was a Conservative (rather than a Labour) government, led by an avowed unionist, which had betrayed them. English unionists differed from their Ulster counterparts; they tended to prioritise the security of British soldiers (over locally recruited forces) and were prepared to 'compromise' the constitutional position of Northern Ireland (Dixon 2001b: 201–2).

British and Irish politicians underestimated the strength of unionist opposition to the Anglo-Irish Agreement. Unionists saw the agreement as a step towards a united Ireland, and their reaction was overwhelmingly hostile. Even the moderate Alliance Party was threatened with a split. On 23 November 1985 there was a huge demonstration, with 250,000 demonstrators (out of a total unionist population of about a million), 'the biggest rally of the Protestant people since . . . 1912' (Needham, 1998: 76–7). On the first anniversary of the signing of the agreement a further protest attended by about 200,000 people took place, and there was rioting in loyalist areas. A petition against the agreement in January–February 1987 raised 400,000 signatures. A *Sunday Times*/MORI opinion poll published on 24 November 1985 found 83 per cent of Protestants did not think the agreement would improve the prospects for peace while just seven per cent thought it would. The poll asked those opposed to the agreement to indicate their support for different ways of protesting: 53 per cent favoured signing a petition; 44 per cent a mini-general election; 39 per cent mass demonstrations; 27 per cent strikes; 15 per cent rent and rate strikes; 14 per cent refusal to pay water/electricity charges; 14 per cent a declaration of independence; and 10 per cent armed revolt (*Sunday Times*, 24 Nov. 1985). The unionist MPs at Westminster resigned their seats so that a poll could be taken in Northern Ireland on the Anglo-Irish agreement. In the following by-elections 418,230 votes were cast for anti-agreement candidates, representing 43 per cent of the electorate as a whole, although one unionist lost his seat to Seamus Mallon of the SDLP. The vote for the centrist Alliance Party slumped. Unionist councils refused to set rates and were fined.

Constitutional politics could not guarantee the union; the unionist MPs could easily be outvoted in the House of Commons and, as the Anglo-Irish Agreement appeared to demonstrate, the unionism of their Conservative allies was suspect. To prevent Northern Ireland being rolled out of the union, unionist politicians took politics into the streets and used the threat of violence to demonstrate to the British and Irish governments (and perhaps the nationalists) the limits to which unionists could be pushed – underlining the parameters of British policy. Had unionists failed to mobilise and demonstrate the strength of their opposition to the agreement, then the two governments might have taken that as a signal that the British–Irish process could be accelerated towards joint authority (Seldon, 1997: 432). Sammy Wilson of the DUP argued that unionists could not afford to be positive in the first two years after the agreement because 'you could have clouded the issue' (Cochrane 1997: 236). Unionism had to communicate the depth of its hostility to the agreement and to any further initiatives to undermine the union. The unionist dilemma was that 'constitutional' unionists by threatening violence could encourage and legitimise the position of those who actually used violence. The leaders of the 'constitutional' unionist parties,

Molyneaux and Paisley, were entering a grey area in which it was difficult to discern whether their intention was to incite or contain violence. Unionist politicians were not only expressing the outrage of unionist opinion but were also attempting to mobilise unionist power and were using the threat of violence to set limits on British policy. At the same time, unionists ran the risk of inciting and escalating a level of violence that would split unionism, worsen relations with nationalists and further damage the union. A new organisation, the Ulster Clubs, was formed shortly before the Anglo-Irish Agreement was signed. It occupied the political ground between constitutional and unconstitutional politics, symbolised by the fact that John McMichael of the UDA had a place on its steering committee (Bruce, 1994: 104). The chairperson of the Ulster Clubs, Alan Wright, argued 'Ultimately, because my faith, my province and my children matter, if violence is the only way that I can uphold these things then I will, while not being a violent man, resort to force' (quoted in Kenny, 1986: 120). David Trimble, future leader of the UUP, was a member of Ulster Clubs and he described the 'unionist dilemma':

> If you have a situation where there is a serious attack on your constitutional position and liberties – and I regard the Anglo-Irish agreement as being just that – and where the Government tells you constitutional action is ineffective, you are left in a very awkward situation . . . do you sit back and do nothing, or move outside constitutional forms of protest? I don't think you can deal with the situation without the risk of an extra-parliamentary campaign. . . . I would personally draw the line at terrorism and serious violence. But if we are talking about a campaign that involves demonstrations and so on, then a certain element of violence may be inescapable (Cochrane, 1997: 157–8).

While unionists like Trimble encouraged more militant tactics for defending the union, the problem was that this could play into the hands of the paramilitaries at the expense of the political parties, and damage the union. Chris McGimpsey argued that the dilemma facing the unionist community was 'how to maintain opposition to the agreement which does not, as a by-product, also weaken the union' (Aughey, 1989: 72).

Unionist politicians: leading or following?

At the end of February 1986, Molyneaux and Paisley appeared willing to try to reach agreement with Thatcher. At a meeting in Downing Street, the leaders of the DUP and UUP were assured that the Anglo-Irish Agreement would be operated sensitively and were offered concessions on new arrangements for enabling unionists to make their views known to the government, on consultations about the handling of Northern Ireland business at Westminster and on the need for discussions on devolved government (*The Irish Times*,

26–7 Feb. 1986). Molyneaux and Paisley agreed to reflect on the British government's proposals and the UUP leader expressed the hope that a forthcoming loyalist strike might not go ahead. The unionist leaders had shifted from saying initially that they would accept no part of the Anglo-Irish Agreement to agreeing to discuss devolution if the agreement was suspended. The British government wanted to be seen to be meeting unionist demands and calming their misgivings about the agreement (*The Irish Times*, 27 Feb. 1986). Secretary of State Tom King claimed that after devolution only cross-border security and economic co-operation would be dealt with by the Intergovernmental Conference that had been established under the agreement. When the unionist leaders returned to Belfast they were forced to retreat by their supporters and subsequently announced that they would hold no further talks with the prime minister unless the agreement was scrapped (*The Irish Times*, 27 Feb. 1986). Thatcher continued to oppose suspending the agreement, and it was a 'gap' in the meeting of the Intergovernmental Conference that allowed the all-party 'Brooke Talks' to get under way in 1991.

The significance of this episode is that it illustrates the constraints operating on the unionist political elites and the problems that they were to have in managing unionist opposition to the Anglo-Irish Agreement. Molyneaux and Paisley had worked hard to find a compromise with the government and 'this was almost their undoing' (Aughey, 1989: 89; Bruce, 1994: 113). According to the *Sunday Times*, it was obvious that Molyneaux and Paisley had been 'running to keep up with the pace of events in Ulster', and it would require some effort for the constitutional politicians to reassert their leadership (Owen, 1994: 61, 75–76). The British prime minister recognised the dilemma of unionist leaders. As Thatcher recalled, 'Ian Paisley was in the forefront of the campaign against the agreement. But far more worrying was the fact that behind him stood harder and more sinister figures who might all too easily cross the line from civil disobedience to violence' (Thatcher, 1993: 403).

The unionist party leaders struggled to contain and control unionist protest against the Anglo-Irish Agreement. On 3 March 1986 a loyalist strike against the agreement was accompanied by intimidation and rioting in which police were shot at 20 times and 47 RUC officers were injured. Attacks on police homes followed. The UUP leader, James Molyneaux, roundly condemned the violence and declared that future strikes would not be supported by his party. He was criticised by the DUP for giving up at least the threat of another day of action and the leverage this gave unionists against the British government. The DUP argued that the level of violence had been exaggerated and that unconstitutional action had to be 'bold and unapologetic' if it was to be effective against the British. In April a young Protestant, Keith White, was killed by a plastic bullet during rioting in Portadown. In the wake of this incident, Paisley hardened his rhetorical stance against rioting, risking the opposition of radicals within his own party (Cochrane, 1997: 149–50, 153). Unionist leaders were concerned that protest might escalate beyond their ability to control it. Molyneaux commented, 'the reality is that Mr Paisley and I . . . have been overtaken by the people of Northern Ireland' (Owen, 1994). On 23 April 1986 a programme of protest and civil disobedience was launched to assert the control of politicians rather than paramilitaries over the anti-agreement campaign.

On 10 November 1986 a paramilitary-style militant loyalist group, Ulster Resistance, was formed. Ian Paisley participated in this group, although it has been argued that he played a moderating role within the organisation, attempting to keep control of protest and ensure that it did not turn into revolt (Aughey, 1989: 76–7, see also Cochrane, 1997: 162, 159–60). Cochrane argues that

> the DUP hoped that by supporting Ulster Resistance they could manipulate and harness what was essentially an inexperienced political leadership and thus align it more closely with the priorities of the DUP. Additionally, Paisley hoped that his donning of the red beret would re-establish his Carsonite credentials with the radical elements within his own party, who were becoming restless with the pace of the anti-agreement campaign and disillusioned with the unionist pact (Cochrane, 1997: 159–60).

Whether unionist leaders exerted a moderating influence over their parties or not depends on the observer's assessment of whether the people they led within their party and their electorate tended to be more 'extreme' or 'moderate' than their party leaders. In other words, to what extent do the structures in which politicians operate constrain their ability to lead their parties? The 'orthodox nationalist view' would condemn the unionist party leaders for stirring up loyalist opposition to the agreement and encouraging it onto the streets with the resulting violence and intimidation. This view would suggest that the unionist people are more 'moderate' than their unrepresentative politicians and that, generally, it is the politicians who cynically stoke up and exploit sectarian sentiment to further their own political ambitions. The constitutional pretences of unionist politicians are contrasted with the violence which follows from their political rhetoric.

An alternative (some would say unionist) perspective would recognise the role that Paisley and Molyneaux played in attempting to avert confrontation in February 1986. Finding unionist party opinion, and perhaps also public opinion more generally, opposed to negotiation, the two party leaders attempted to restrain and control unionist protest by leading that protest and channelling it, to some extent, into non-violent tactics. This view would emphasise the importance of unionist leaders being seen to represent and articulate unionist grievance, in order to maintain their leadership positions, but at the same time attempting to control and restrain the political expression of that grievance. In this view, the unionist electorate tend to be more 'extreme' than their political leaders. Molyneaux took 'the long view' that the existence of a united unionist front on the Anglo-Irish Agreement was an end in itself, maintaining unionist morale and allowing the letting off of steam 'which had it not been released, may have been used for more destructive purposes' (Cochrane, 1997: 193). Protest would continue until the British realised that the agreement was not working. An indication that there was more extreme loyalist opinion than that being expressed by DUP leaders is apparent in the emergence and relative electoral success of the 'extremist' Protestant Unionist George Seawright. Seawright was expelled from the DUP for anti-Catholic remarks but subsequently succeeded in winning significant support as a 'Protestant Unionist' and was elected to Belfast City Council (Bruce, 1994: 143–5).

Power, democracy and violence

Behind the façade of constitutional democracy lies the unequal distribution of power and the threat of violence and force that has played a continuing role in the conflict over Northern Ireland. Both 'constitutional' nationalist and unionist politicians have benefited (and suffered) from the threat and use of violence, whether or not they have encouraged it. The border was formed after threats of violence by unionists. Since partition, unionists have employed state violence to maintain their dominance, while republicans have employed violence to challenge the state. Nationalists during the civil rights campaign demonstrated the effectiveness of taking politics into the streets, with the threat to violence that this implied. The civil rights movement swiftly won its demands, but by then republicans were exploiting the mobilisation of the Catholic community to reopen the border question by escalating conflict with the British army. The rising tide of violence was successful in shifting the political agenda away from civil rights and towards the border question, eventually resulting in the suspension of Stormont and the power-sharing experiment. British ambiguity over Northern Ireland's constitutional position, its record of withdrawal from Empire and evidence of withdrawal sentiment in Britain encouraged republicans to believe that they were on the verge of victory over the British. The continuing violence of the IRA's campaign during 'the troubles' has contributed significantly to the polarisation of public opinion and enormous suffering. But it has also proved a powerful tool for drawing the attention of the British government to republican grievances. The mobilisation of republicans during the 1980–1 hunger strikes and Sinn Féin's successful entry into electoral politics were catalysts of the Anglo-Irish Agreement in 1985. For some unionists, it is the continuing IRA threat of a return to violence that has driven the British government's 'appeasement' of the republican movement during the peace process.

In the wake of the Anglo-Irish Agreement unionists mobilised once again to set limits on British policy. Unionist politicians, as they had in the early 1970s, entered the grey area between democratic politics and advocacy of violence. Without strong unionist resistance they feared – with some reason – the extension of the Anglo-Irish Agreement and their coercion into a united Ireland. Unionists, by taking politics into the streets, used the threat of violence and the reality of limited violence against the British government. Employing the rhetoric and threat of violence could incite some to actual violence, legitimise paramilitary activities and enhance the power of paramilitaries over party politicians. This ran the risk that violence could escalate out of control and damage the union. On the other hand, however, a more passive response to the agreement might have failed to communicate the depth of unionist attachment to the union and determination to preserve it, encouraging British politicians to move towards joint authority and Irish unity.

The political realities of Northern Ireland have led to 'constitutional' unionist and nationalist politicians benefiting (and suffering) from the activities of violent paramilitaries and having contacts with them. This is not to say that they necessarily condone those activities, and 'constitutional' politicians from all of the major parties (UUP, DUP, Alliance Party, SDLP) have been strong in their condemnation of paramilitary violence. The paramilitaries have also been contemptuous of the 'constitutional' parties. But the benefits that these politicians have received through the use and threat of violence – and a perception that they have from time to time actually inspired or promoted that violence – has coloured the other community's view of their intentions. The SDLP benefited from the republican campaign by using the leverage that this violence gave them to win the Anglo-Irish Agreement and concessions during both 'peace processes'. Similarly, unionist constitutional politicians benefited from loyalist violence in the early 1970s and mid-1980s, since this helped to establish the parameters to British policy in a way that purely peaceful protest might not have done. By taking politics into the streets, unionist and nationalist politicians were employing the threat of civil disturbance to influence policy.

During the recent peace process, 'constitutional' unionist politicians have continued to operate in the grey area between 'constitutional' and 'unconstitutional' politics. While David Trimble refused to talk with Sinn Féin, he did engage in talks with Billy Wright, leader of the paramilitary LVF, to discuss the impasse at Drumcree. In September 1997, the UUP entered all-party talks with nationalists, flanked by the political representatives of the loyalist paramilitary parties, the PUP and the UDP.

The DUP have had a closer relationship with loyalist paramilitaries than the UUP. Leading members of the party have shared platforms with loyalist paramilitaries, while others have acted in ways that could be interpreted as lending legitimacy to the LVF. There are advantages to the DUP in its ambiguity on the use of violence and association with loyalist paramilitaries. This ambiguity allows the DUP to present a different face to the different constituencies which it is trying to court. On the one hand, it can reach out to those hardliners in the unionist community who support a militant and perhaps violent defence of the union, helping to keep the DUP in control of this extremist constituency and preventing the emergence of an even more extreme loyalist party. On the other hand, the ambiguity over violence and paramilitarism allows the DUP to present a more 'respectable' image to appeal to mainstream unionists and those who have voted for the more respectable UUP. The political parties of the loyalist paramilitaries have been notoriously unable to win significant electoral support, and the Vanguard Unionist Party suffered electorally from its association with paramilitaries (Bruce, 1986).

The attempts of various parties and governments to incorporate republican and loyalist paramilitaries into the democratic process have been brought about by accommodating – to some extent – the power of the gun. 'Absolutists' decry any dealings with paramilitaries on the grounds that they undermine elected representatives and thereby compromise democratic principles – yet this group includes politicians who themselves have had links with paramilitaries. Most politicians would probably accept to some extent the 'realist' position that compromise is legitimate, on the grounds that 'the ends justify the means'. Realists would argue that politics is a dirty business and deception and manipulation are justified on the grounds that they hold out the promise of peace and a lasting settlement (Dixon, 2002b). The problem lies in trying to distinguish shades of grey. At what point does compromise with paramilitary organisations invalidate the objective of creating a democratic society? Are politicians seeking to exacerbate or contain paramilitary violence? Is there a moral equivalence between Sinn Féin, which has a private army, and has engaged in violent rhetoric, and the DUP which has consorted with paramilitaries and engaged in violent rhetoric?

Conclusion

The strategic objective of unionists is to preserve the union between Great Britain and Northern Ireland. Until 1972 unionists wielded power within the Northern Ireland state to secure this objective. Since the 1960s some unionists have also used unconstitutional tactics to defend their place in the union. The shift from constitutional to unconstitutional methods has in part reflected a perception among unionists that the British government and its guarantees could not be trusted, and that constitutional methods were failing to secure the union. This was most starkly apparent during the period 1970–6 when there was evidence of sympathy among the British political elite for Irish unity, suggesting no overriding British interest, beyond stability, in preserving the union. If the British had been intent on edging Northern Ireland out of the union during this period, then the loyalist/Protestant backlash of 1971–6 – while morally repugnant – might well have succeeded in preventing the British from withdrawing. The British believed that withdrawal was likely to lead to civil war, destabilising the island of Ireland and perhaps also Britain. By demonstrating the power of unionism, the backlash set parameters to British policy.

In retrospect, the union was not as threatened by the Anglo-Irish Agreement as it was by British policy during the early 1970s. However, the strength of the unionist reaction to the agreement was a reminder of continuing opposition to Irish unity and a warning to British policy makers not to push unionists too far – for example, by extending the Anglo-Irish Agreement into joint authority – because of the risk of civil war. While unionist politicians shifted to more militant 'unconstitutional' tactics to defend the union, there were limits to how far they could contain their supporters. The danger was that if violence got out of control, which it threatened to do, this could further damage the unionist cause in Britain. Widespread violence might also see further polarisation in Northern Ireland, with the result that power would shift from the hands of the elected politicians and towards the paramilitaries. Unionist politicians had to walk a fine line in the grey area between constitutional and unconstitutional tactics. A shift by unionists towards more militant tactics did not come without risk to the overall strategic objective, defence of the union. But if unionists could no longer accept the union on British terms then some contemplated independence.

The political career of David Trimble illustrates the dilemmas facing unionists. Trimble was driven to despair by British policy and joined Ulster Vanguard, an organisation that was prepared to flirt with paramilitarism. Following the Anglo-Irish Agreement he expressed again the tactical dilemma that unionists faced in setting limits on British government policy. If constitutional methods failed, then more militant tactics were necessary to defend the union. In 1998, Trimble signed the Good Friday Agreement on behalf of the UUP. The agreement was endorsed by unionists in a referendum on the assumption that Sinn Féin would not enter government without some decommissioning of IRA weapons. Trimble gambled that British policy, of which he had long been sceptical, would be sufficiently supportive to protect him and his more proactive and positive tactics for defending the union from hardline unionist critics. This trust appears to have been misplaced, as his support within the Ulster Unionist Party has gradually leaked away and the rival Democratic Unionist Party has made impressive gains at the ballot box. Trimble's tactical skill may have secured the agreement and, strategically, it may have promised to secure the future of the union, but this could be at the cost of his own future and that of his party.

Chapter 10

The Northern Ireland peace process and the impact of decommissioning

John de Chastelain

Introduction

For the purpose of this chapter I characterise the current peace process as having started in 1994, although there were several attempts to reach a lasting political settlement in Northern Ireland after the Troubles began at the end of the 1960s. The Sunningdale Agreement of the early 1970s, the Anglo-Irish Agreement of 1985, the strand one and two talks of 1991 and 1992, and the Downing Street Declaration of 1993, all represented significant moves in an attempt to broker an enduring peace. But I start my examination in 1994 because that was when the back-channel contacts between paramilitary representatives and government officials, combined with the work of political leaders, led to the paramilitary ceasefires which initiated the current process, soon after which the decommissioning of paramilitary arms became a significant issue.[1]

Decommissioning has been a principal issue running through each phase of the current peace process, and in the minds of many its satisfactory resolution has been essential to the success of that process. It is only one of a complex series of issues awaiting resolution, and while the practical aspect of ridding the island of Ireland of large amounts of illegal weaponry is significant, in the minds of many the symbolism of arms decommissioning as a practical demonstration of the end of paramilitarism is equally or even more important.[2]

Here I will discuss decommissioning in the context of several distinct phases, grouped for the sake of convenience into two broad periods, with the Good Friday (or Belfast) Agreement of 10 April 1998 (hereafter referred to as 'the agreement') as the dividing point between the two. The first period was one in which decommissioning, while important, was not an insurmountable obstacle to political progress. While the issue of decommissioning almost prevented the political negotiations from even starting – and once started, from getting down to substantive negotiations – the agreement finally reached in April 1998 was achieved without any actual decommissioning having taken place (IBDA, 1996: paras 33 to 35).[3] In the second period, the significance of decommissioning continued but in a different form. Now the issue was one of implementation, not of agreement in principle; painful issues would have to be addressed in practice, and representatives of opposing perspectives would no longer be able to rely on abstractions. That this was so became clear in the first phase of this new period, which started in the summer of 1998 with the implementation of the agreement, and ended in July of 1999 in the failure to form an executive. The second phase of this period covers the Mitchell Review from September to November of 1999. The third begins with the initial implementation of the Review in November 1999 and ends in February 2000 when the Executive was suspended. The fourth begins with the efforts leading to the re-establishment of the Assembly in May 2000 and ends with its suspension again in October 2002. The final phase of the period covers the efforts to get the institutions re-established before the Assembly elections, which were due to take place at the beginning of May 2003 but which were subsequently postponed.

The decommissioning issue before the agreement

The paramilitary ceasefires and the International Body

In August 1994 the Irish Republican Army (IRA) declared a ceasefire and in October the two main loyalist paramilitary groups, the Ulster Volunteer Force (UVF) and the Ulster Defence Association/Ulster Freedom Fighters (UDA/UFF) did likewise. They did so on the basis of giving politics a chance to achieve what the use of arms by either side had failed to bring about: on the republican side a united Ireland, and on the loyalist side the guarantee that Northern Ireland would remain a part of the United Kingdom. The scene was set for political talks to agree on the implementation of an inclusive government with devolved powers in the North, on the relationships to be put in place between North and South, and on the relationships to be established between Dublin and London – strands one, two and three. But in March 1995, in a speech in Washington, the Northern Ireland Secretary of State, Sir Patrick Mayhew, suggested that paramilitary groups would have to give a demonstration of their peaceful intentions by decommissioning some of their arms before their associated political parties could take part in the political discussions. The IRA regarded this suggestion as a precondition that had nothing to do with their voluntary ceasefire and by the autumn of 1995 the ceasefires seemed likely to fail. Thus even before the political talks started, decommissioning seemed likely to present a serious obstacle.

On 28 November 1995 the Prime Minister and the Taoiseach – John Major and John Bruton – launched a twin track process to get political discussions under way. The first track called for a three-person International Body to report on the decommissioning issue. The second track was to be a series of talks involving the two governments and the Northern Ireland political parties to deal with the first two strands, with the British government and the Northern Ireland political parties involved in strand one, and the two governments and the Northern Ireland political parties involved in strand two. The two governments alone would address strand three. The International Body was to start its work right away and to report its findings to the two governments by 15 January 1996. The governments made it clear that neither they 'nor any other party cooperating with the work of the body, is bound in advance to accept its recommendations which will be advisory. The two governments will consider carefully any recommendations it makes and give them due weight on their merits' (British and Irish Governments, 1995).[4] In terms of the second track, the governments announced they would convene preparatory talks 'with a remit to reach widespread agreement on the basis, participation, structure, format and agenda to bring all parties together for substantive negotiations aimed at a political settlement based on consent' (British and Irish Governments, 1995).

The International Body
The International Body comprised former Senator George Mitchell of the United States who was named chairman, the former Prime Minister of Finland, Harri Holkeri, and me (at the time I was completing a term as Canada's Chief of the Defence Staff). The Body was given a two-month mandate to report on two issues: the willingness of the paramilitary groups to decommission their arms, and mechanisms by which that might be achieved. The fact that the United States was asked to provide the Body's chair was recognition of President Clinton's active interest in the search for a solution, and an acknowledgement of Senator Mitchell's year-long experience as the President's adviser on economic affairs on the island of Ireland. The other choices were dictated by the need to maintain balance. The Irish government wished to choose a distinguished individual from a Scandinavian country, and the British government wanted someone with military experience from a Commonwealth country.

After two months of study and interviews the Body concluded that paramilitary groups on ceasefire would consider decommissioning, but not before the talks started. We so reported on 22 January 1996 and at the same time suggested how decommissioning might be accomplished. But it was also clear that a lack of trust existed between the political parties, as well as within the paramilitary groups and the general population, and we believed that this mistrust should be addressed. We moved outside our remit and addressed the lack of trust between political parties by suggesting six principles of democracy and non-violence that we believed the parties could be invited to adopt if they were to take part in the talks. The parties were thus invited to commit themselves:

- To democratic and exclusively peaceful means of resolving political issues;
- To the total disarmament of all paramilitary organisations;
- To agree that such disarmament must be verifiable to the satisfaction of an independent commission;
- To renounce for themselves, and to oppose any effort by others, to use force, or threaten to use force, to influence the course or the outcome of all-party negotiations;
- To agree to abide by the terms of any agreement reached in all-party negotiations and to resort to democratic and exclusively peaceful methods in trying to alter any aspect of the outcome with which they may disagree; and
- To urge that 'punishment' killings and beatings stop and to take effective steps to prevent such actions (IBDA, 1996: paras 33 to 35).

We also suggested that a number of confidence-building measures might be addressed to answer the concerns within the population as a whole. These included issues like human rights, policing, prisoners, 'the disappeared', the use of baton-rounds by the security forces, and the suggestion that 'an elective process could contribute to the building of trust' (IBDA, 1996: paras 51 to 57). To address the lack of trust within the paramilitary groups, we listed six criteria that we believed should apply if decommissioning were to be successful. These included: avoiding the perception of surrender or defeat, prohibiting the forensic testing of decommissioned arms for the purpose of prosecution, and insisting that the process of decommissioning should be complete, safe, mutual, and verifiable to the satisfaction of an independent commission.

We proposed four methods of decommissioning, while not suggesting that these were exclusive. They were:

- The transfer of armaments to the Commission or to the designated representatives of either Government, for subsequent destruction;
- The provision of information to the Commission or to designated representatives of either Government, leading to the discovery of armaments for subsequent destruction;
- The depositing of armaments for collection and subsequent destruction by the Commission or by representatives of either Government; and
- Destruction of arms by the paramilitary groups themselves (IBDA, 1996: para 44).

As noted in the six principles for the conduct of decommissioning, we recommended that whatever method was used, verification should be provided by the independent commission if the process were to be convincing. We presented our report to the two governments on 22 January 1996 and two days later made it public at a press conference in Belfast. Then the International Body disbanded. Some republicans believed that the British government gave the report inappropriate attention, focusing on its recommendation concerning elections to a Forum from which the delegates to the political talks could be chosen. On 9 February 1996, a little more than two weeks after the report was made public, the IRA broke its ceasefire with a bomb attack at South Quay, Canary Wharf, in London.

The beginning of political talks, June 1996

In spite of the IRA's return to violence, the political talks went ahead on 10 June 1996 with the two governments and nine political parties participating. Sinn Féin was excluded given the lack of an IRA ceasefire. Two other political parties associated with paramilitary groups – the Progressive Unionist Party (PUP) linked with the UVF, and the Ulster Democratic Party (UDP) linked with the UDA/UFF – were admitted to the talks as their respective paramilitary groups were on ceasefire. The three members of the International Body were invited back to chair meetings of the Plenary Committee, the Business Committee, the strand two talks and any sub-committees where both governments were represented. The parties that wished to participate in the talks were required to state their acceptance of the six principles of democracy and non-violence suggested by the International Body – by now known as the Mitchell Principles. But there was initial resistance by the parties to the ground rules, the agenda, and the rules of procedure developed by the two governments, and the talks started on an unofficial basis until rules of procedure and the agenda had been agreed by all the participants.

Agreeing on rules of procedure was to take almost two months (Northern Ireland Office, 1996), and progress was then impeded by failure to agree on the agenda. Again, decommissioning was the reason. Unionists wanted decommissioning to be the first subject addressed. They argued there could be no place at the table in democratic talks for parties which had connections with illegal armed groups. They had reluctantly agreed to take part in the talks without prior decommissioning, but they wanted to ensure that this issue was addressed before the political ones. The nationalist Social Democratic and Labour Party (SDLP) agreed that decommissioning was important and that it had to be addressed, but its members noted that the talks were about political issues, and they argued that these should not be held up by a failure to agree on decommissioning.

The impasse lasted for more than a year. It was not until September 1997, after general elections in both the Republic of Ireland and the UK, and after the declaration of a second IRA ceasefire and the inclusion of Sinn Féin in the talks, that an agenda was finally agreed. Then it was only after the new Taoiseach and the new Prime Minister (Bertie Ahern and Tony Blair) agreed that the talks must end within a year – and after they had put in place the Independent International Commission on Decommissioning that had been authorised in legislation passed separately in the Dáil and in Parliament the previous February[5] – that the talks were able to get down to substantive discussion of the three strands.

The Independent International Commission and the talks process

When the talks resumed in September 1997 it was without the Democratic Unionist Party (DUP) and the United Kingdom Unionist Party (UKUP), which left when Sinn Féin took their seats around the table. Thus the talks started with eight political parties, the two governments and the Independent Chairmen; together their representatives constituted the Plenary Committee.[6] The first priority for the Plenary Committee was to agree on the agenda, which was done swiftly, with a programme of discussion for the first two strands scheduled by a Business Committee enabled for that purpose. Meanwhile the decommissioning body began its work independently of the political discussions.

The Independent International Commission on Decommissioning (IICD) was brought into being on 26 August 1997 by an agreement between the two governments (British and Irish Governments, 1997). It included commissioners from the same three nations as those involved in the International Body and in providing the Independent Chairmen for the talks in 1996, that is Finland, the USA and Canada. Brigadier Tauno Nieminen from Finland and Ambassador Donald Johnson from the United States were named as two of the commissioners; I was named as the third and as chairman of the body.[7] The task given us was fourfold: to consult widely, to recommend methods of decommissioning to the governments and the parties, to facilitate the execution of decommissioning, and to report. Initially we were to report to the Plenary Committee through a Liaison Sub-committee on Decommissioning chaired by Harri Holkeri. Once the Plenary Committee ceased to exist, we were to report to the governments alone. The legislative basis for the Commission's work was provided by the British and Irish arms decommissioning acts of February 1997, each of which called for the destruction of paramilitary arms, with destruction being defined as rendering them 'permanently inaccessible or permanently unusable'. It was with this direction that the Commission began its consultation.

Working from offices in Dublin and Belfast we informed the parties that we believed the only way in which we could carry out our task was through the appointment by each paramilitary group of a representative with whom we could work out the details. Almost immediately the UVF named a member of the PUP, Mr Billy Hutchinson, as its representative. The IRA and the UDA/UFF declined to do so. After consultation with those whom we believed could represent the views of the IRA and the UDA/UFF, and having received the views of the UVF, we proposed two methods of decommissioning that gave promise of being accepted by the paramilitary groups and we recommended that these should be incorporated in a procedural document by the governments. These were two of the four recommended by the International Body: information leading to the discovery of arms for subsequent destruction, and destruction by the paramilitary groups themselves, both with verification by the Commission. The Liaison Sub-Committee on Decommissioning, which included representatives of each of the parties in the talks as well as the two governments, approved the recommendations, and these were then submitted to the governments to be formalised in a procedural document (referred to hereafter, to reflect its different description in the two jurisdictions, as 'scheme / regulations').[8]

The decommissioning issue after the agreement

The context within which decommissioning had been discussed heretofore changed immediately following the adoption of the agreement on 10 April 1998. Up to this time, the focus had been on matters of general principle concerning each of the subjects discussed in the negotiations, but now it shifted to the minutiae of implementation. Hard practical issues had to be confronted. As some observers noted at the time, while the agreement was a signal achievement in itself, where its implementation was concerned the devil was in the detail.

The agreement addressed decommissioning by saying:

1. . . . the resolution of the decommissioning issue is an indispensable part of the process of negotiation. . . .

3. All participants accordingly reaffirm their commitment to the total disarmament of all paramilitary organisations. They also confirm their intention to continue to work constructively and in good faith with the Independent Commission and to use any influence they may have, to achieve the decommissioning of all paramilitary arms within two years following endorsement in referendums North and South of the Agreement and in the context of the implementation of the overall settlement (Northern Ireland Office, 1998a: part 7).

Some aspects of the agreement were left imprecise to assure cross party approval. Significantly, the date by which decommissioning was to be completed was specified, but the date by which it had to start was not.

Efforts at implementation, 1998–9

Shortly after the agreement was approved, the two governments put in place the scheme/regulations formalising the two decommissioning methods proposed by the IICD. But there was little progress on setting up the political bodies approved by the agreement – the Executive and the North/South bodies. Once again decommissioning played a major role. The Ulster Unionist Party (UUP) refused to sit in the Executive with Sinn Féin in the absence of a start on decommissioning. They noted that while prisoners were being given early release, the Patten Commission on policing had begun its work, and the British Army had begun the process of normalisation (or demilitarisation), there was no movement on decommissioning by either republicans or loyalists. Unionists reiterated once more their reluctance to sit in government with parties that had private armies.

Republicans and nationalists pointed out that the agreement's statement on decommissioning talked in terms of it taking place in the 'context of the implementation of the overall settlement', and noted that two years had been contemplated for the decommissioning process. It was thus expected to be completed by 22 May 2000. They insisted that it was only by setting up the approved political structures, and by having an inclusive government with devolved powers being seen to be working, that the conditions in which decommissioning would happen would likely be achieved. Once again, the Commission appealed unsuccessfully to the IRA and the UDA/UFF to name points of contact, although Sinn Féin named Mr Martin McGuinness as that party's representative to the Commission. Over the period of the next year there was little progress on setting up the political institutions or on decommissioning, except for an event on 18 December 1998 in which arms belonging to the Loyalist Volunteer Force (LVF) were publicly decommissioned. This event was conducted in front of television cameras at the LVF's insistence, and while the amount of weapons, ammunition, explosives and detonators was small, it was sufficient to give the Commission an opportunity to practise methods of destruction.

During the first half of 1999 the Taoiseach and Prime Minister made several attempts to break the deadlock: at Hillsborough in April, at Downing Street in May and at Stormont in June. None had the desired result of securing the establishment of the political bodies and a start to decommissioning. But at Stormont at the end of June, the IICD was asked to produce a progress report in which, among other points, it was invited to define when it believed the process of decommissioning was deemed to have started. Citing, in part, statements in the governments' decommissioning scheme/regulations, the IICD said it believed that the process started when a paramilitary group:

(a) gives an unambiguous commitment that decommissioning will be completed by 22 May 2000, and

(b) commences detailed discussions of actual modalities (amounts, types, location, timing) with the Commission through an authorized representative (IICD, 1999–2003: 2 July 1999, para 17).

The IICD believed that it should only be a matter of days between the nomination of a representative and a first meeting, and only a matter of weeks between that meeting and the start of decommissioning.

In July one change occurred in the Commission when the American Commissioner, Ambassador Donald Johnson, returned to the State Department in Washington. His replacement as Commissioner was Andrew Sens, a former member of the US State Department who had been with the Commission since its beginning. Continuity was thus maintained. Also in July 1999, in another attempt to break the deadlock, the Secretary of State, Mo Mowlam, convened the Assembly. Doing so required the Presiding Officer to call on the four major parties to nominate their candidates for the Executive. But the UUP boycotted the Assembly meeting, and the Secretary of State's initiative collapsed. The two prime ministers invoked the review clause of the agreement and invited Senator Mitchell back to Belfast to conduct it.

The Mitchell review
Senator Mitchell conducted his review over a three-month period, starting in September 1999, and he based it on three issues: the need to establish an inclusive government with devolved powers, the need for decommissioning by 22 May 2000, and the need for this decommissioning to be carried out in a manner determined by the IICD. Pressure to find a solution to the decommissioning issue thus remained at the forefront. The review consisted largely of bilateral meetings between Senator Mitchell, the UUP, Sinn Féin and the SDLP. At its conclusion in November 1999, an agreed solution prescribed a number of choreographed events:

- agreement by the UUP to set up the Executive and the North/South bodies

- the naming by all the paramilitary groups of a representative to the IICD

- a meeting between the IICD and these representatives, and

- a report on those meetings from the IICD to the governments in December 1999 (Mitchell, 1999b).

The IICD's principal role in the review was to meet with Mitchell and provide him with an assessment of the decommissioning situation. Once the review was complete, the three Commissioners believed that while there might have been no firm agreement on decommissioning, there was an understanding that substantive discussions on it would start in December and lead to actual decommissioning in a matter of weeks. Given the Christmas break, this realistically meant decommissioning starting in January 2000, and our December report was expected to include a commitment to report again at the end of January.

Implementing the review and setting up the institutions
The Assembly met and the Executive was appointed on 29 November 1999. Powers dealing with six main areas were devolved to the Assembly, from Westminster, as of midnight on 1 December. After nearly thirty years Northern Ireland had its own government again, but now it included Sinn Féin. On 2 December the IRA named a representative to the Commission and the UDA/UFF did likewise on 8 December. Shortly afterwards we held separate meetings with each and gave the governments a written report on them. This report reflected the fact that both the UVF and UDA/UFF had confirmed their willingness to consider decommissioning their arms, but the UVF specified it would not do so until the IRA declared 'the war is over', and the UDA/UFF said it would not start before the IRA did so. The IRA's representative gave us a reaffirmation of their intent to maintain their ceasefire, and their commitment to a peaceful and democratic path to achieve their goals, but did not address the technical aspects of decommissioning (IICD, 1999–2003: 10 Dec. 1999).

That the IRA was not more forthcoming at this first meeting may have been its reaction to the announcement by the UUP that the Ulster Unionist Council would meet at the end of January to review the situation, which gave the impression that if there had been no move on decommissioning by then, the UUP would reconsider its involvement in the Executive. Republicans and nationalists reacted negatively to this announcement, pointing out that such unilateral reviews were not part of the agreement. Through the month of January 2000 the IICD met separately on several occasions with the IRA, UVF and UDA/UFF representatives. The latter two agreed with us on methods of decommissioning and on general supporting issues, but they maintained their position of not moving before the IRA's intentions were clear. The IRA representative reiterated the IRA's commitment to the ceasefire and the peaceful resolution of the issues, and the IRA issued a statement in which it declared it was not a threat to peace. But the representative would not discuss actual decommissioning pending further progress on the overall implementation of the agreement. At the end of January we reported to the governments that we had made no progress on actual decommissioning, adding that if at any time we believed decommissioning would not happen, we would recommend that we be disbanded.

While acknowledging that a start date for decommissioning was best worked out in co-operation with the representatives, we repeated a point made in our December report in which we said: '. . . the Commission is prepared, if necessary, to state that actual decommissioning is to start within a specific period' (IICD, 1999-2003: 10 Dec. 1999, para 6). Having been given estimates of the paramilitary groups' arms inventories by the security forces North and South, and the opinion that these were likely held in widely dispersed locations, we also said we were prepared to announce the kind of timetable we felt would be necessary to ensure completion by 22 May 2000 (IICD, 1999–2003: 31 Jan. 2000, para 6).

The UUP deferred its Council meeting to 12 February and in the intervening time the governments, the parties and the Commission worked to seek a more positive response on decommissioning from the IRA and loyalist groups alike. On 11 February, in a meeting with the IRA representative, we were given a statement which offered some promise of movement. This was to the effect that the IRA would 'consider a process to put arms beyond use' in the context of the overall implementation of the agreement and the resolution of the causes of conflict. While the statement did not say that the IRA would decommission, and while it seemed to put political conditions on their doing so that were outside our mandate to consider, it nonetheless contained words which the representative had not used before. In our report that day we welcomed 'the IRA's recognition that the issue of arms needs to be dealt with in an acceptable way and that this is a necessary objective of a genuine peace process', as well as their apparent willingness 'to initiate a comprehensive process to put arms beyond use, in a manner as to ensure maximum public confidence' (IICD, 1999-2003: 11 Feb. 2000, paras 6–7).

Given the lack of an unconditional agreement to start decommissioning by any of the paramilitary groups, Secretary of State Peter Mandelson suspended the Executive and re-imposed direct rule on 11 February 2000. Shortly afterwards, the IRA representative contacted us to say he would soon announce he was breaking off contact with us and withdrawing the proposals given us to date. Days later he did so. Once more decommissioning was the issue holding back political progress.

Re-instatement of the institutions and further challenges

During the two months immediately after the suspension of the institutions, strenuous efforts to bring the process back on track were led by the Taoiseach and the Prime Minister. In a statement on 5 May 2000, the two governments asked the Commission to investigate whether decommissioning methods other than the approved two might more readily achieve our mandate for arms destruction. Furthermore, the governments joined in saying that they believed that all aspects of the agreement could be brought to completion by June 2001 and committed themselves to that goal. The next day the IRA announced they would re-open contact with the Commission. They also said that as a confidence-building measure, they would open some of their arms dumps to international inspectors, who would report on their findings to the Commission. Significantly they stated that:

> the IRA leadership will initiate a process that will completely and verifiably put IRA arms beyond use. We will do it in such a way as to avoid risk to the public and misappropriation by others and ensure maximum public confidence.[9]

An important component of this announcement, compared to the 11 February one, was the addition of the adverbs 'completely' and 'verifiably' – words that echoed recommendations made in the International Body's 1996 report on the requirements for decommissioning. Significant also was the statement that the IRA would 'initiate a process' rather than 'consider' one.

The IRA chose Cyril Ramaphosa of the African National Congress and former President Martti Ahtisaari of Finland to carry out the inspections of selected arms dumps. These two distinguished and respected international figures would work independently of the Commission and would report their findings to it only after they had completed an inspection. Many welcomed this move by the IRA, although the secrecy with which the two would conduct their activities undermined, within some parties, the confidence that the IRA hoped to engender.

On 29 May 2000 the British government restored the Executive with its devolved powers and the Assembly recommenced sitting on 5 June. Later that month the IRA representative phoned the Commission, reopening contact, and on 25 June the two inspectors reported to us that they had inspected IRA arms dumps and put in place measures to ensure that they would know, when they next saw them, if the arms there had been used. The inspectors also told us that prior to conducting their inspection, they had consulted with weapons experts to ensure that they knew what to look for. We so reported to the governments (IICD, 1999–2003: 25 June 2000).

Throughout July and August there was no movement on decommissioning, perhaps not surprisingly given the activities of the marching season and the summer hiatus. But in early September the Commission made efforts to re-engage with each of the paramilitary representatives. One aim was to find out exactly what the IRA meant by 'putting arms beyond use', and to ascertain if it met our mandate to facilitate the complete destruction of paramilitary arms. We also wanted to find out if there had been any change in the position of the two loyalist paramilitary groups, particularly given the feud that had erupted between them during the summer.

By October 2000 we had not been able to persuade the representatives to meet with us. Political parties explained why they believed this was so. In the IRA's case it was suggested that insufficient implementation of the Patten report on policing, and the slow pace of demilitarisation by the British Army, as well as concern over the future of former IRA members – who were 'on the run' and still sought by the authorities – were preventing them from re-engaging with us. In the loyalist case it was believed that the ongoing feud was the reason.

We made it known to the paramilitary groups that we would submit a report to the governments towards the end of October and that we hoped for engagement with the representatives before then. Such an engagement would allow us to make the report as complete and informed as possible. But only the UDA/UFF representatives met with us. These assured us of their continuing commitment to the peace process and to decommissioning, but they reiterated their insistence on making no move before the IRA, and they made it clear that the ongoing nature of the feud made early decommissioning extremely unlikely, if not impossible.

In late October the two inspectors reported to the IICD that they had carried out a second inspection and verified that the arms they had inspected in June remained undisturbed. The IRA subsequently confirmed publicly that the inspection had taken place and that the reason for its failure to re-engage with the Commission was its concern over the British Government's slow implementation of the agreement's other requirements. Furthermore, the IRA stated 'We have also decided to resume discussions with the IICD when we are satisfied that the peace process will be advanced by these discussions.'[10] We reported the inspection to the two governments on 26 October but noted that we had made no progress on actual decommissioning (IICD, 1999–2003: 26 Oct. 2000).

The Ulster Unionist Council met again on 28 October and voted to bar Sinn Féin members from participating in meetings of the North/South Ministerial Council. It also called on the Commission to be more proactive in meeting its mandate, specifically by insisting on meetings with the paramilitary representatives, by setting deadlines and schedules, and by producing more frequent written reports to the governments. Towards the end of the year senior officials from the two governments held intensive meetings with the political parties in a bid to resolve the issues of policing, demilitarisation and decommissioning. They did this against the background of an imminent visit by President Clinton to the Republic and Northern Ireland, and continuing efforts by dissident republicans to carry out attacks on government targets and the security forces. In December 2000 the UVF and UDA/UFF announced an end to the loyalist feud, and on 12 and 13 December President Clinton visited Dublin and then Belfast. The visit was generally well received, but it led to no breakthrough on the problem issues.

On 22 December the Commission produced an end of year report to the governments in which it noted that it had still not resumed meetings with the IRA representative, although a meeting with the UVF representative and discussions with UDA/UFF representatives confirmed the loyalist paramilitary groups' earlier conditional commitments on decommissioning. We reiterated a point made in our report of a year earlier, to the effect that sufficient time still remained for decommissioning to be carried out by June 2001. But we also pointed out once again that we would specify the date by which we felt we would have to start decommissioning, if we were to carry it out by June, and the schedule that would be needed to do so (IICD, 1999–2003: 22 Dec. 2000, para 7).

The year 2001 began with continued efforts by government officials to resolve the demilitarisation, policing and decommissioning issues. But concern was expressed that if these were not soon addressed successfully, the lead-up to Northern Ireland council elections and an anticipated British general election in the spring might result in a diversion of the political parties' attention and possibly to a suspension of the institutions. Moreover, a hiatus until June, with the prospect of the imminent marching season and the summer break, meant that the June target for decommissioning would not be met and substantive re-engagement on the issues might not be possible until September.

In mid-January, and still with input from officials of the outgoing Clinton administration, the two prime ministers became personally engaged in the negotiations, with Prime Minister Blair visiting Belfast on 17 January and making public his ongoing contact with the Taoiseach. February saw a continuation of intense discussions between officials from the two governments and the parties principally concerned. These were carried out against the background of a change in government in the USA and the question of whether the new Republican administration of George W. Bush would place the same emphasis on seeking a resolution of the Northern Ireland situation as the Democratic administration of Bill Clinton had done. They also occurred against the background of an increase in dissident republican attacks on targets in both Northern Ireland and England, including a mortar attack against Ebrington Barracks in Londonderry in February and a bomb attack outside the BBC building in London in early March. The period also witnessed a continuation of loyalist bomb attacks in and around Belfast, although UVF and UDA/UFF leaders maintained that the loyalist feud had not re-opened.

On 8 March 2001 the Taoiseach and the Prime Minister met with the pro-Agreement parties at Hillsborough. The same day the IRA announced it would reopen contact with the Commission and later the same day it reported that it had done so in a telephone call. After the Hillsborough meetings the two governments reported:

In a statement on 6 May 2000, the IRA undertook to initiate a process that would completely and verifiably put IRA arms beyond use. Today, they have announced that they will enter into further discussions with the IICD, on the basis of their earlier commitment. This is a welcome development. Discussions should now start promptly and lead to agreement on the ways in which IRA arms will be put completely and verifiably beyond use. We look forward to early and positive reports from the IICD about progress made. It remains vital that all paramilitary groups engage fully and actively with the IICD, so that the issue of paramilitary arms is definitively resolved.

The two Governments believe that once the IICD reports that, as a first step, the IRA will agree with the IICD a scheme for putting IRA arms beyond use to enable the Commission to discharge the mandate given to it by the two Governments in May (i.e., to consider 'whether there are any further proposals for decommissioning schemes which offer the Commission greater scope to proceed in more effective and satisfactory ways with the discharging of its basic mandate'); and that it expects agreement to be reached before long, this will have helped create the context in which the objectives set out in the two Governments' statement of 5 May 2000 can be secured.

On 14 March the IRA issued a statement:

On Thursday 8 March the IRA leadership announced that we would enter into further discussions with the IICD on the basis of our commitment to resolving the issue of arms as contained in our statement of 6 May 2000. The IRA representative has since met with the IICD and set out the basis for discussions. The IRA has honoured its commitments and will continue to do so.[11]

Weston Park meeting and decommissioning

The Commission's resumption of meetings with the IRA representative notwithstanding, there was no progress on actual decommissioning. The remainder of the spring saw increased dissident republican bomb attacks in London, the harassment of Catholic children walking to school in the Ardoyne area, and the murders of both Protestants and Catholics throughout the province, claimed predominantly by loyalist groups. On 8 May, expressing increased impatience over the continued lack of progress on decommissioning, the UUP leader David Trimble announced he would resign as First Minister on 1 July unless the IRA began to decommission its arms. This announcement remained in effect after the IICD reported on 30 May that the inspectors had carried out their third inspection (IICD, 1999–2003: 30 May 2001). Once again, the issue of decommissioning appeared likely to impede the implementation of the political process.

Significantly, and perhaps reflecting concern on all sides over the slow progress towards complete implementation of the agreement, the 7 June 2001

UK general election saw both Sinn Féin and the Democratic Unionist Party increase their numbers of seats in Parliament and their percentage of the popular vote. For the first time, Sinn Féin became the larger of the two nationalist parties.

Concern over the lack of progress was not improved at the end of June when the Commission reported to the governments that there had been no action on decommissioning and the June target called for by the governments the previous year had been missed. The Commission concluded its report by noting that:

> Some people have said they believe our inability to engineer a start to decommissioning has called into question our usefulness to the process and suggest we now withdraw from it. Others have urged us to remain engaged and to continue to press paramilitary groups to begin decommissioning. We have given both views careful consideration.
>
> Given the conditions the IRA, the UVF and the UFF say they require before they will put their arms beyond use, we believe we cannot influence that activity by making demands or by setting deadlines. But we will continue to do what we can to implement our mandate through continuing contact and discussion with each of the paramilitary groups IICD, 1999–2003: 30 June 2001. paras 10–11).

The next day David Trimble resigned as First Minister and a week later the two prime ministers announced they would hold talks with the pro-agreement parties at Weston Park in Shropshire to address the outstanding issues arising from the agreement. The talks were held between 9 and 14 July, and on 1 August the Secretary of State, Dr John Reid, and the Irish Foreign Minister, Brian Cowen, published the results of their discussions in a draft implementation plan proposing ways of addressing the four main outstanding issues: policing, normalisation, the stability of the institutions, and decommissioning. They invited the parties to provide comments on the proposals within a week. The proposal on decommissioning noted that:

> In respect of the issue of putting arms beyond use, the two Governments repeat their view that this is an indispensable part of implementing the Good Friday Agreement. All parties to the Agreement recognize that; and that under the Agreement, this issue must be resolved in a manner acceptable to and verified by the Independent International Commission on Decommissioning in accordance with its basic mandate in law (British and Irish Governments, 2001).

The weeks following the governments' paper witnessed a number of significant issues that directly or indirectly had a bearing on the decommissioning process. On 6 August, in a report to the governments, the Commission said that:

In a recent meeting with the Commission, the IRA representative proposed a method for putting IRA arms completely and verifiably beyond use. We are satisfied that this proposal meets the Commission's remit in accordance with the Governments' scheme and regulations (IICD, 1999–2003: 1 Aug. 2001, paras 1–2).

The UUP announced its disagreement with the governments' newly proposed implementation plan and said that agreement alone on a decommissioning method provided insufficient progress – following which the IRA withdrew its offer of that method on 14 August. The Secretary of State issued a 24-hour suspension of the Assembly to prolong the period before which elections of the First and Deputy First Ministers were required, and the British and Irish governments approved a new scheme/regulations to supplement the ones already in existence. At this point two events on the other side of the Atlantic changed the climate within which the decommissioning issue was unfolding. On 13 August three people linked to the Irish republican movement were arrested in Colombia for alleged terrorist offences. Almost a month later, on 11 September, the World Trade Centre towers in New York were demolished in a terrorist attack and the United States Government announced a war on terrorism.

IRA decommissioning

Some felt that the terrorist attack on the United States might have a spillover effect on decommissioning and believed the IRA might decide to carry out an event shortly afterwards. This belief was heightened by the fact that President Bush's representative on Northern Ireland, Ambassador Richard Haass, was in Dublin and Belfast on 11 September. No such event took place, and on 18 October David Trimble announced the resignation of his three ministers from the Executive, saying: 'We take this decision with no pleasure – it has been a long time in coming. Ever since the IRA failed to keep its promise to put its weapons beyond use this problem became inevitable.'[12]

The first IRA decommissioning event
That action left the Secretary of State facing the need to collapse the Executive or call Assembly elections unless the parties returned within a period of seven days. However, on 23 October the IICD reported to the governments that the Commissioners had witnessed an event in which the IRA had put a quantity of arms beyond use, and the same day the IRA issued a statement in which they said:

The political process is now on the point of collapse. Such a collapse would certainly and eventually put the overall peace process in jeopardy. There is a responsibility upon everyone seriously committed to a just peace to do our best to avoid this. Therefore in order to save the peace process we have implemented the scheme agreed with the IICD in August.[13]

The announcement met with a mixed response. Many saw it as an historic event, but the secrecy surrounding it left others sceptical and wondering exactly what had happened. In our report we said we regarded the event as 'significant', but we were silent on the quantity of armaments put beyond use, other than to note that they included arms, ammunition and explosives (IICD, 1999–2003: 23 Oct. 2001, para 2). In carrying out the event the IRA opted for confidentiality as allowed by the scheme/regulations, although we cautioned that a lack of transparency could erode confidence in the Commission's reports. In response to subsequent queries we noted that three essential aspects of our mandate were respected during the conduct of the event, that is: the three Commissioners – Nieminen, Sens and I – had personally witnessed it; we had satisfied ourselves that it met the terms of the decommissioning legislation; and we had made an inventory of the arms involved for future reporting to the two governments.

In spite of questions raised over the lack of decommissioning details, arrangements were put in place to elect the First and Deputy First Ministers and to set the Executive up again. Due to growing unionist opposition, some members of the Alliance Party and of the Northern Ireland Women's Coalition redesignated themselves as unionists to secure a pro-agreement majority within the unionist bloc in the Assembly, thus securing the return of David Trimble as First Minister and of Mark Durkan (now leader of the SDLP) as Deputy First Minister.[14] The three UUP ministers rejoined the Executive and the Assembly resumed its role in governing the province. By the end of the year the Policing Board began its work, with members of the UUP, the SDLP and the DUP taking their places on it. Sinn Féin declined to do so, citing that the Patten recommendations had not been implemented in full, and concerns over accountability and the authority of the Chief Constable.

Also at the end of 2001 the UDP, heretofore the political wing of the UDA/UFF, and which had been unsuccessful in winning any Assembly seat in the 1998 election, announced that it was disbanding. While it had become increasingly inactive as a political party after the 1998 election, it had played an influential role in the talks leading to the agreement and its demise signalled an apparent end to political influence within the UDA/UFF. An increase in feuding within that body and between it and other loyalist groups seemed to confirm this was so. That issue was not helpful to the prospects for timely decommissioning by the UDA/UFF, particularly as the previous July it had announced that it was withdrawing its support for the agreement. In meetings held separately with the UVF and UDA/UFF representatives after

23 October 2001, the Commission sought to discover what influence, if any, the IRA decommissioning event would have on possible similar events by the loyalists. Both questioned whether one event by itself was a serious demonstration of the IRA's intent to deal with all of its arms, and the UVF representative noted that the IRA had still not announced that 'the war was over'.

The year 2001 ended with two events affecting the Commission. On 24 October Martti Ahtisaari informed the two governments that he and Cyril Ramaphosa would stand down as inspectors, believing that their role was no longer necessary now that IRA arms decommissioning had begun. The governments accepted the decision and thanked them for their work. At the end of November Brigadier Tauno Nieminen left the Commission for personal reasons and returned to Finland. As the Decommissioning Acts required the Commission to be comprised of no fewer than two Commissioners, the governments accepted the IICD's recommendation that it be left without a third one, at least until time or further developments dictated otherwise.

The second IRA decommissioning event

After the first IRA decommissioning event the Commissioners had urged the representative to arrange a follow-up one as soon as possible. We considered that a series of regular and frequent decommissioning events was desirable, both to get similar events started by the loyalist paramilitary groups and to further the overall political process. We also warned that any delay might encourage the idea that the October event had been a 'one-off'. Furthermore, we noted that delaying a second event until close to the Irish general election – scheduled for May 2002 – would give rise to suspicions that these events were being used for tactical reasons and not, as we hoped, as part of an ongoing process.

By the end of February 2002 there had been no repeat IRA arms event and when on 17 March a break-in occurred at one of the Belfast Police District Command Units at Castlereagh and sensitive documents were stolen, it seemed that another event was not likely to occur soon.[15] Republicans believed that the break-in was an inside job and that only members of the Special Branch would know how to gain access and what to look for.[16] Unionists believed that the IRA was to blame and a criminal investigation was still continuing in mid-2003. In parallel, the Secretary of State announced an independent review to examine the implications of this incident for national security. Unionists pointed to it as further evidence that the IRA ceasefire was not intact. Taken in conjunction with the recent jailing of IRA gun smugglers in Florida and the arrest of the three suspected IRA members in Colombia, unionists claimed that a pattern existed of continued IRA rearming, targeting and collusion with external terrorist groups.

However, on 8 April the Commission reported to the governments that a second event had occurred in which IRA arms had been put beyond use. In its report the two Commissioners said: 'we have witnessed an event in which the IRA leadership has put a varied and substantial quantity of ammunition, arms and explosive materiel beyond use' (IICD, 1999–2003: 8 Apr. 2002, para 1). The IRA issued a statement on the same day in which it said:

> The leadership of Óglaigh na h-Éireann has taken another initiative to put arms beyond use . . . This initiative is unilateral at a time when there are those who are not fulfilling their obligations . . . We fully appreciate the difficulties this causes for republicans, however the IRA is a highly disciplined and committed organisation.[17]

This second event was welcomed by many although the continued secrecy surrounding it left some unconvinced that it demonstrated a serious approach by the IRA to do away with its arsenal. When Sinn Féin increased its membership in the Dáil from one seat to five in the general election a month later, some claimed that it proved the IRA's April event had been timed with that in mind.

Over the next few months neither of the loyalist paramilitary groups took steps to decommission their arms, nor did the IRA follow up on the April action. That this was so might be explained in part by a series of events. Feuding broke out again within the loyalist groups and particularly within the UDA/UFF on the Shankill Road, where violence between C Company and other units of the group led to shootings, intimidation and families being forced to move. The Ulster Unionist Council met on 21 September, demanding the disbandment of the IRA and setting 18 January 2003 as the date by which they would leave the Assembly if disbandment had not occurred by then.[18] On 4 October the Police Service of Northern Ireland (PSNI) carried out a raid on the Sinn Féin offices at the Stormont Parliament Buildings, arresting a member of Sinn Féin on charges of possessing information likely to be of use to terrorists.

In response to these events the Secretary of State, Dr John Reid, suspended the Assembly at midnight on 14 October and shortly after returned to take up a new cabinet role in London. He was replaced as Secretary of State by Paul Murphy, who had been a Northern Ireland minister during the talks leading to the 1998 agreement. At the end of the month the IRA broke off contact with the IICD once more, giving the Assembly suspension as the reason, and the year ended with direct rule reimposed and the pending issues of policing, demilitarisation, the stability of the institutions and decommissioning unresolved. While the issue of decommissioning itself was not the sole cause of this recent setback, its slow progress had played a significant contributing role.

The year 2003 began with meetings between the parties and the prime ministers to find a way forward. But in January the UVF broke off contact with the IICD citing a lack of seriousness by the IRA on the process, and at the same time its associated political party the PUP broke off contact with Sinn Féin for the same reason. The UDA/UFF had, to all intents and purposes, ceased contact with the IICD when they withdrew their support for the agreement earlier in 2002. In February 2003 they ended their internal feud after one of their leaders was murdered by members of the UDA's C Company. This unit was forced to disband and its leaders fled Northern Ireland. An Ulster Political Research Group (UPRG) was formed to undo the damage done by the feuding and to give a political underpinning to the UDA/UFF's activities, and this group undertook to reopen contact with the IICD, with decommissioning becoming possible once the IRA engaged in 'genuine acts of completion'.[19]

Prime Ministers Blair and Ahern visited Belfast on 12 February and again on 3 March to discuss ways of addressing the outstanding issues. Tony Blair had called for acts of completion by the IRA in a Belfast speech on 17 October 2002,[20] and David Trimble had also demanded serious and visible acts of decommissioning by the IRA as the price for the Ulster Unionists re-entering the Assembly with Sinn Féin. In the absence of agreed solutions in March, the prime ministers undertook to return in early April to put to the parties a set of proposals that they believed should finally allow the full implementation of the agreement, and to have the forthcoming Assembly election conducted with that understanding in place. A last-minute announcement that President Bush would visit Belfast, also in early April, for discussions on the Iraq war and the Northern Ireland peace process, gave further impetus to the belief that such a result was possible.

Calls for clarity and election postponement

President Bush visited Hillsborough on 7 and 8 April for meetings with the two prime ministers and subsequently with the pro-Agreement parties. He pledged his personal support for progress in the peace process and said: 'This is an historic moment and I would urge all the communities in Northern Ireland to seize the opportunity for peace'.[21] The choreography surrounding the visit envisaged the two prime ministers returning to Hillsborough on 10 April, the fifth anniversary of the agreement, to publish their joint declaration laying out a road map for its final implementation. But it was not to be.

It was hoped that the publishing of the declaration would be followed by a statement from the IRA signalling an end to the war and a cessation of their activities, but when the probable content of that statement was passed on verbally to the two prime ministers they found it unconvincing. The publication of the declaration was postponed and efforts were made by both governments to obtain further clarity on the IRA's intentions. On 13 April it was reported that the IRA had given a statement to the prime ministers through Sinn Féin in which they focused on four main issues: the current disposition of the IRA and the status of its cessation; its future intentions; its attitude to a re-engagement with the IICD; and engagement in a process of putting arms beyond use.

Both prime ministers felt that what the IRA was offering differed little from the statement it had made in May 2000 and they called for clarification of its intention to cease all paramilitary activity and to put all of its arms beyond use. Mr Blair also signalled that while he wished the election to go ahead as planned, a lack of clarity over the IRA's intentions could delay it. Similarly on 12 April the Taoiseach told Gerry Adams and Martin McGuinness that he would not agree to publish the joint declaration unless the IRA offered greater clarity.[22]

Despite an assertion by Mr Adams that the draft IRA statement was 'clear and unambiguous', the prime ministers continued to delay publication of the declaration. Following days of continued discussions between the two over the issue, Mr Blair held a news conference in Downing Street on 23 April in which he said there were three questions concerning the IRA statement that needed answering:

> When the IRA say that their strategies and disciplines will not be inconsistent with the Good Friday Agreement, does that mean an end to all those activities inconsistent with the Good Friday Agreement – including targeting, procurement of weapons, so-called punishment beatings and so forth? Secondly, when they say they are committed to putting arms beyond use through the decommissioning commission, does that mean all arms – so that the process is complete? Thirdly, when they say they support the Good Friday Agreement and want it to work – does that mean that if the two governments and the other parties fulfil their obligations under the Good Friday Agreement and joint declaration – that means the complete and final closure of the conflict?[23]

Blair and Ahern were not alone in calling for greater clarity on the matter of the IRA's intentions. President Bush's representative, Ambassador Richard Haass, returned to Belfast hurriedly from Washington, saying that the United States supported the call for further clarity and describing the issue as a 'win-win or lose-lose' situation. In a speech at Stormont on 27 April, Gerry Adams addressed the three questions posed by Mr Blair and said, of the IRA's draft statement:

- Its logic is that there should be no activities inconsistent with this;
- Obviously this is not about putting some arms beyond use. It is about all arms;

- And thirdly, if the two governments and all the parties fulfil their commitments, this will provide the basis for a complete and final closure of the conflict.[24]

This statement was welcomed by the prime ministers who agreed that it gave satisfactory answers to the second and third questions, but Mr Blair said that the answer did not provide sufficient confirmation of the IRA's intention to cease all paramilitary activity. Until that was firmly understood, he said, 'there is no basis for progress'.

The arguments over the IRA's intentions took place amid growing concerns among the political parties that the election might be further postponed. It also occurred against the backdrop of a number of associated events. The IRA let it be known that they had re-opened a line of communication with the IICD and that they had been close to carrying out a third event to put arms beyond use. The UPRG announced that the UDA/UFF had reopened its contact with the Commission and that a meeting had been held at the IICD's offices on 16 April, with representatives of the UPRG and the UDA/UFF present.

However, at a republican meeting on 19 April, Brian Keenan, a senior republican figure, was reported as saying that he did not yet support the concept of republicans joining the policing board, which signalled, in the minds of some, that it was unlikely that Sinn Féin would join the policing board before the expected election.[25] One week later on 27 April, the British government dissolved the Assembly, which had remained suspended since the previous October.

On 1 May 2002, Mr Blair gave a press conference at his Downing Street office in which he announced that he was postponing the Northern Ireland Assembly election until the autumn and that he and the Taoiseach would publish the joint declaration immediately. He cited as the reason for the postponement the continued lack of clarity in the IRA's response concerning the end of its activities. In spite of a statement made by Gerry Adams the previous day in which he had included the word 'will' in regard to the IRA's peaceful intentions,[26] the Prime Minister made reference to the Joint Declaration and noted that 'there was a point blank refusal to rule out expressly the activities stated in paragraph 13 of the joint declaration'.[27]

The decision to postpone the election was greeted with dismay by most political parties in Northern Ireland, pro and anti-agreement alike. The Taoiseach also expressed disagreement with the postponement, saying that he believed that 'yet another postponement causes more problems for the process than it solves', but he added that nonetheless 'the strength and critical importance of the partnership between the two governments will endure'.[28]

Conclusion

A conclusion is perhaps an inappropriate way to end this chapter, as the peace process is far from concluded. Anti-agreement parties believe that the agreement has now been shown to be unworkable and that a new approach to the situation in Northern Ireland is necessary. Others claim that the interim period gives the governments and the parties an opportunity to address anew those aspects of the agreement that remain unresolved and to correct them. Mr Blair has ruled out the idea that the agreement is negotiable and he is supported by the Taoiseach, the United States and the pro-Agreement parties. There is varying support for his intention to implement some aspects of the Joint Declaration, in spite of the delay in the election. Republicans feel that implementation should go ahead apace, while unionists feel that moving on normalisation, in the absence of a clear statement of the IRA's intention to cease all paramilitary activity, is premature. Unionists have raised objections to the dismantling of two towers in South Armagh near Newry, particularly in light of ongoing dissident republican activity.

The situation in Northern Ireland in the period since the election postponement has been further complicated by the publishing of the Stevens Report on alleged past collusion between loyalist paramilitary groups and the British security forces, and the naming of the alleged agent Stakeknife, supposedly working within the upper echelons of the IRA leadership on behalf of the British security forces. But these issues have not deterred the two governments from continuing their efforts to bring the peace process to a satisfactory conclusion. Prime Minister Blair has said that he will now set up an independent body to monitor the implementation of the agreement, and he and the Taoiseach will implement other aspects of the joint declaration including equality, human rights, the Irish language, criminal justice and policing. Further moves on normalisation, including the reduction of troops and military bases in Northern Ireland, over a two-year period, will depend on the security situation.

The bill to approve the postponement of the Assembly election was proposed in the House of Commons by the Secretary of State on 12 May, and it subsequently received royal assent. It left to the Secretary of State the determination of a future date for the election. In the explanatory notes to the bill the reason for the election postponement is addressed:

> The Government's judgement is that, in the absence of clarity on an end to paramilitary activity in Northern Ireland, there is not sufficient trust and confidence among the Northern Ireland parties to permit the restoration of functioning devolved institutions immediately following a 29th May election. The postponement is intended to allow the two Governments to continue efforts

to rebuild the trust and confidence necessary for the restoration of effective devolved institutions.

Thus a new stage in the peace process has been reached. The Assembly remains dissolved, not simply suspended, and direct rule remains in effect. The majority in Northern Ireland seem very much in favour of a return to self-rule, enhanced with the further devolved powers anticipated in the joint declaration, while blame over the current situation remains divided. But whatever the root causes of the current setback, it is clear that concern over continuing paramilitary activity, both loyalist and republican, remains at the forefront. It is true that decommissioning applies to only one of those activities. But however symbolic the issue may be in the minds of some, it continues to be the principal source of concern for many in both north and south – as indeed it has been since the process began nearly ten years ago.*

---

* Editors' note: this paper reflects the position in July 2003 and does not take account of such later developments as the third IRA act of decommissioning on 21 October 2003.

Chapter 11

The legacy of political violence in Ireland

John Coakley

Introduction

In November 1913, Pádraic Pearse, a politically active schoolteacher destined to become an icon of independent Ireland, denounced what he saw as the unreserved embrace of parliamentary methods by Irish nationalists, and criticised their contempt for more militant methods. Contrasting this perspective with the unionist mobilisation that was then taking place in Ulster, he expressed a view that later observers, depending on their political standpoints, regarded as logical or as perverse: 'I think the Orangeman with a rifle a much less ridiculous figure than the Nationalist without a rifle' (Pearse, 1922: 185). At Easter 1916, Pearse and his fellow rebels followed up the implication of this position, becoming martyrs in the nationalist cause and thereby retrospectively legitimising one of their central ideological planks: 'the right of a minority to determine, in defiance of the ballot box, the future of the Irish people' (Edwards, 1977: 326). In this, they were explicitly following the example of another group that had embarked on a similar path, Ulster unionists led by Edward Carson.

The legacy of these positions over the decades that followed has been explored in the chapters that form the core of this book, which begin with the home rule crisis of 1912–14 (a juncture whose most marked feature was the taking up of arms by Ulster unionists) and end with the peace process that began in 1994 (an episode dominated by a debate over the disarming of Irish republicans). There are signs that the wheel may have come full circle. In September 1912 almost half a million Ulster unionists signed a solemn covenant in which they pledged to use 'all means which may be found necessary to defeat the present conspiracy to set up a Home Rule Parliament in Ireland'. At Easter 1916, the solemn proclamation of the rebels, later endorsed by an elected assembly, stated that 'In the name of God, and of the dead generations through whom she receives her old tradition of nationhood, Ireland, through us, summons her children to her flag, and strikes for her freedom.' Yet, over eight decades later, a majority of Carson's ideological descendants joined with almost all of the ideological descendants of Pearse in another solemn declaration, representing a reversal of past values, in referendums that endorsed a central principle of the 1998 Good Friday Agreement: 'We reaffirm our total and absolute commitment to exclusively democratic and peaceful means of resolving differences on political issues, and our opposition to any use or threat of force for any political purpose.'[1]

Any perception that political violence in Ireland can be neatly bracketed within the period 1912–94, however, would be misleading. Willingness by nationalists and unionists to resort to arms long predated this period, and refusal by both sides to give them up is likely to remain a significant theme for years to come. The need to provide a long historical perspective on the interplay between militant and conventional politics in Ireland has, indeed, been a central objective of this book. The aim of this concluding chapter is to review this process, and to set the Irish experience in yet another context: that of comparative political violence in the contemporary period. These two dimensions are addressed in the sections that follow.

Political violence: the Irish experience

In summarising an important legacy of the first two decades of the twentieth century, David Fitzpatrick (1996: 379) comments that 'the common rhetoric of militarism transcended political divisions in Ireland . . . For unionists, nationalists and republicans alike, soldiery was an ideal to be extolled rather than a menace to be confronted . . . Militarism was one of the few Irish stereotypes which evoked almost universal approbation in a bellicose era.' As the contributions to this volume show, the legacy of militarism was important from a number of perspectives. But the form taken by militaristic attitudes reflected a number of different perspectives before the First World War, and these were associated with four major groups: the Liberals, who governed the country either alone or in coalition; their British Conservative critics; a distinctive branch of British Toryism, Ulster Unionism; and nationalist Ireland. The Liberal government, endowed by democratic norms with the right and duty to use force to uphold the constitutional order, was accused by nationalist Ireland of failure to do this. The Tory opposition displayed an apparently reckless and paradox-laden willingness to subvert the constitution in order to defend it. But although mainstream British politics was able to recover from the excesses of this period, the two antagonistic Irish groups developed an enduring ambiguity towards the legitimacy of political violence, and, after almost five decades during which the political implications of this ambiguity went untested, it was confronted by a radically new political reality following the events of 1968.

Militarism and the break-up of the United Kingdom

One of the more generally acknowledged tendencies in the evolution of the modern state is the path by which the central government gradually gained legitimacy: rulers were eventually able to dispense with raw force, or even the threat of force, and could rely instead on the voluntary acquiescence of their subjects. Political sociologists may differ on the sources of popular deference, with explanations ranging from rational choice models (which emphasise collective interest in adhering to a common system of rule-making and implementation) to social psychological theories (which stress political social-isation and the imperceptible inculcation of values that legitimise the existing order). They may also disagree on the extent to which such patterns of deference are disseminated within specific societies; but few would disagree that, within western societies at least, the broad trend is towards popular endorsement of stable political structures.

The extent to which coercion has been sidelined as an instrument of government is not always obvious. Police forces continue to fight against organised crime, opportunistic anti-social behaviour and recreational violence. Public support for the state is often expressed negatively (in apathy, or refusal to rebel) rather than positively (in active support for and participation in the political process). Whole political systems disintegrated under the pressure of discordant popular pressures at the beginning of the twentieth century (as in the case of the Habsburg and Ottoman empires) and at the end of that century (as in the case of the Soviet Union, Yugoslavia and Czechoslovakia). But the phenomenon of organised military resistance against the state is undoubtedly less common in the Europe of the early twenty-first century than in earlier centuries.

It is interesting to look at the evolution of the United Kingdom in terms of this general trend away from political violence. On the face of it, there is some evidence that in the most rebellious part of this territory swords and pikes were being converted into ploughshares and hoes in the decades after the union of 1800 and, as we have seen in chapter 2, the primacy of parliamentary politics had been steadily established. By the middle of the nineteenth century, memories of the bitter wars of the seventeenth century and of the ferocity of the 1798 rebellion might still have been strong, but there was little evidence of desire to risk a repeat of these experiences. The two celebrated instances of nineteenth century rebellion may have illustrated the continuing attraction of military-style protest, but they also showed how difficult it now was to organise a military revolt. The Young Ireland rebellion of 1848 might indeed have followed the model of those of Austria, France, Naples and Sardinia, as one commentator dryly but apparently seriously remarked – 'had the children of Widow MacCormack of Boulagh Commons, Ballingarry, not been locked into a house full of police on July 28th, 1848'

(MacDonagh, 1945: 57).[2] The potentially more formidable Fenian rebellion of 1867 amounted to the short-lived occupation of a coastguard station and more widespread activities a few weeks later that were easily crushed; the total number of fatalities was about a dozen.

On the surface, then, it appeared as if militarism was being contained, or diverted down a less menacing path. Analogies with the contemporary period would be dangerous, but it is tempting to see parallels between the late nineteenth and the late twentieth centuries. Just as the successors to the Fenians were prepared to suspend their militaristic approach in the 1880s as part of an understanding with constitutional nationalism (which in turn was prepared to contemplate the more radical tactic of agrarian agitation), so too in the 1960s was the IRA prepared to suspend its support for militarism and to work de facto within the framework of the constitution (while moderate nationalists were prepared to take to the streets in civil rights protests). The analogy with the 1880s could be extended further – the role of John Hume in brokering an entente between constitutional nationalism and republicanism in the 1990s was not unlike Parnell's role in rallying the 'physical force' and constitutional traditions behind his 'new departure' more than a century earlier. Whatever the appropriateness of analogies of this kind, as discussed in chapter 2, there were signs that as the decades passed the lesson that parliamentary methods could secure valuable political ends had indeed been learned, first in the area of land reform and then in respect of the constitutional transformation of the United Kingdom itself. There were, however, as discussed below, also counter-indications, but these would have been more obvious to the intelligence branch of the Royal Irish Constabulary than to readers of the *Freeman's Journal.* As one experienced observer put it, describing the position up to 1910:

> For some time previously [to 1910] Irish politics had been almost as respectable and constitutional as a cricket match. Many old grievances had been eliminated. By the operation of Wyndham's Act, nearly three hundred thousand tenant farmers had become owners of their land; and those who remained tenants were well protected and had access to official guidance and arbitration. There was a very big export trade in the produce of the land, and the country was more prosperous than it had ever been before (Shearman, 1942: 129).

If the legitimacy of the parliamentary approach seemed, then, to have assumed a dominant position by the beginning of the twentieth century, it is necessary to ask how conventional politics became so seriously disrupted, and how the rest of the century became so bedevilled by political violence. There is little disagreement on the facts, if this question is answered in its strict and narrow sense: the constitutional process was disrupted by the Conservative parliamentary opposition and especially by its Ulster Unionist allies in an effort to subvert the third Home Rule Bill after 1912. There is rather less discussion of the embarrassing, long-term implications of this: it was British and Irish unionists, not Irish republicans, who pushed the gun into a central position in modern Irish politics. Of course, the position was not so simple; the Unionist argument was that home rule represented a change in the British constitution so fundamental that it required explicit endorsement by the people in a general election (a condition that was lacking, since this had not been an issue in Britain during the December 1910 general election). This argument was rejected by the Liberals, who argued that the issue of reform of the House of Lords – central in the December 1910 election campaign – had incontrovertible implications for that of home rule. While the Unionist argument may have been opportunistic and constitutionally implausible then, it nevertheless offered many convinced party members a moral defence for unconstitutional action.

This point emerges with some force in chapter 3, in Ronan Fanning's analysis of the corrosive effects of the slow progress of the third Home Rule Bill through parliament in 1912–14. As Fanning points out, the Parliament Act of 1911, by removing the absolute veto of the Unionist-dominated House of Lords, had allowed the Liberal party's home rule measure to get on to the statute book with Irish support; but by converting this veto into a suspensive one the Parliament Act had also legitimised the Lords' right to delay legislation, undermining the authority of the popularly elected chamber. This delay also allowed time for the mobilisation of extra-parliamentary opposition in Ulster with British Tory support, and, as Fanning reminds us, the threat of an army mutiny further impeded the government's freedom of movement, with alarming implications for Irish people's perceptions of democracy.

As suggested above, Irish political culture had, at least on the surface, moved a long distance down the democratic path by the early twentieth century. Conventional evidence supports this interpretation: in what was by now a substantially literate society (a characteristic that is commonly seen as a prerequisite to democracy), the popular newspapers overwhelmingly supported parliamentary politics, and voters consistently returned local councillors and MPs who reflected this perspective. It is true that from 1899 onwards there was a whiff of radicalism in local elections; but the Nationalist Party was as capable of fighting off threats in the South as the Unionist Party was in the North. This became clear in the biggest contest between Sinn Féin and the Nationalist Party before 1916 – the Leitrim North by-election of 1907, in which the Nationalists comfortably saw off a Sinn Féin challenge.[3] As late as 1915, Nationalist Party leader John Redmond could refer to Sinn Féin, without presumably denting his own plausibility, as a 'temporary cohesion of isolated cranks' (Dangerfield, 1966: 117). As Michael Laffan points out in chapter 4, by the beginning of the second decade of the twentieth century popular support for parliamentary politics had become so deeply ingrained that even militants recognised the hopelessness of their position.

Yet militants had not simply disappeared. The Fenians had survived military defeat in the 1860s and entente with constitutional nationalists in the 1870s and 1880s, and their organisation, the Irish Republican Brotherhood (IRB), continued; Nationalist MPs with pro-Fenian leanings were sometimes elected. The IRB also enjoyed a significant infusion of new blood in the early twentieth century. Sinn Féin might have been no electoral match for the Nationalist Party, but it continued to act as an effective pressure group and had a visible presence in Dublin Corporation and elsewhere at local level. Nationalist radicalism could also be detected in other quarters: although both the Gaelic Athletic Association (GAA, founded in 1884) and the Gaelic League (founded in 1893) had overtly non-political objectives, their potential significance for cultural nationalism was clear.

It was against this setting that, as Michael Laffan argues, a 'series of accidents' conspired to give a new breath of life to militant republicanism. The resort to arms by Ulster unionists provided nationalist Ireland with an excuse to follow suit; the absence of even-handedness on the part of the government in dealing with the two main factions in Ireland aggravated the nationalist sense of grievance; and what was perceived as harsh treatment of the 1916 rebels elevated those involved in the Easter Rising from deviant to heroic status. Acknowledgement by many members of the public that the militants might have had a point was complemented by the failure of the Nationalist Party to deliver home rule, especially in the course of the 1916 home rule negotiations. The net effect, as Laffan argues, was a discrediting of politics and an association of violence not with failure but with success – an expensive lesson to the competing Irish political traditions.

The Nationalist Party, however, faced a difficult choice, torn between long-standing nationalist rhetoric and contemporary reality. Militant mobilisation in Ulster shook not just the British government; the Irish Nationalist Party, too, came to appreciate the challenge posed by the political and military resources of northern unionism, and, as Paul Bew argues in chapter 5, in the final years of the party's dominance most of its leadership came to accept, at least privately, that it would be at best unwise to seek to coerce Ulster into a home-rule Ireland. Such views were to be heard also within Sinn Féin, though more rarely; that movement was preoccupied with its agenda of ending British rule, and this implied the removal of the British from all of Ireland. It also entailed crushing proponents of a more moderate perspective and, as Bew shows, it did this with some ruthlessness in rooting out the influence of the Nationalist Party and its activists.

Militarism in partitioned Ireland

Paul Bew has also pointed to the pragmatism of the British that resulted in the settlement of 1921–2, and to the remarkable similarity between the events that led to this and the peace process of the 1990s. Had the earlier settlement worked, of course, there would have been no need for the later peace process; the reality is that the settlement of the 1920s turned out not to be stable. In the south, a section of the paramilitary movement took over as the army and government of the new state, but faced a continuing challenge from its erstwhile more radical components. In the north, unionist rebels against home rule had a new state thrust on them, inherited the remnants of the Irish security apparatus (the Royal Irish Constabulary) and were allowed in effect to convert their paramilitary wing into a reserve special constabulary; but the legitimacy of their rule was never accepted by the nationalist minority.

The instability of the new arrangement was initially most obvious in the south. Paul Bew and Michael Laffan both draw attention to the single-minded commitment of the republican side to attainment of their goals by military methods in the early 1920s. As Laffan points out in chapter 4, this commitment could extend to a contempt for public opinion, and could survive devastating electoral setbacks (of a kind that de Valera and his anti-Treaty supporters suffered in the general elections of 1922 and 1923). Eunan O'Halpin describes, in chapter 6, the circumstances in which republican militarism survived in the early decades of independent Ireland, sometimes (as in the 1930s and the 1960s) by reorientating itself in a more left-leaning direction. This orientation may well have been compatible with the IRA's pursuit of external allies, but, as O'Halpin argues, attempts to procure assistance from the communist bloc and from other left-wing regimes in the early years of the state and during the Cold War were motivated by pragmatism rather than by ideology, as were the similar overtures to Germany during the two world wars. It was what O'Halpin describes as the 'hoary maxim' that 'England's difficulty is Ireland's opportunity' that best explains Irish republicanism's choice of external partners.

But during its bleakest years republicanism did not have to rely on external allies to secure its survival. At one level, it was sustained by the official ideology of the southern state, especially after Fianna Fáil's accession to power in 1932. Whatever the divergence between de Valera and his former radical republican allies, the early Fianna Fáil party shared with the most fundamentalist of republicans a common formal goal (establishment of an all-Ireland, independent republic). Furthermore, both groups rejected what later became seen as a key hurdle in the path towards this goal: the so-called principle of consent, understood as the right of Ulster unionists (or, more precisely, of the people of Northern Ireland – a very different category) to opt out of any such constitutional settlement. But while neither of the two groups accepted the notion of a northern veto, they differed in one crucial respect in terms of their strategy for achieving unity. For Fianna Fáil, to the extent that a strategy for unity was articulated at all, this rested on the assumption that it was up to the Irish government to do a deal with the British in accordance with which sovereignty over Northern Ireland would be transferred from London to Dublin (though the enthusiasm of the party leadership for this strategy varied considerably over time).[4] For militant republicans, the strategy was more straightforward: Irish unity could be achieved only by the military defeat of the British presence in the island of Ireland.

In addition to this element of policy convergence, militant republicanism was also able to rely on a supportive ideology propagated by the state itself. This was not simply a product of Fianna Fáil's nationalism; during the only two periods between 1932 and 1973 when the party was out of office (1948–51 and 1954–7), Fine Gael-led coalition governments followed a similar line. This rested on a distinctive foundation myth of the state. According to the official versions of state history, as reflected in national commemorations and as taught in the schools, the state owed its existence to a glorious armed rebellion in 1916; the ideals of this rebellion had been partly fulfilled with the creation of the state following a further war in 1922; but the victory of 1922 had been incomplete, as the British had remained in occupation of part of the island. The interpretation of Irish history that gave a central place to military endeavour was inscribed in the song that was eventually adopted, in 1926, as the national anthem of the new state:

> We'll sing a song, a soldier's song
> With cheering, rousing chorus
> As round our blazing fires we throng,
> The starry heavens o'er us;
> Impatient for the coming fight,
> And as we wait the morning's light
> here in the silence of the night
> We'll sing a soldier's song (Kearney, 1928).[5]

These values were written into the new constitution in 1937 – not just in the case of articles 2 and 3 and their reference to the 'national territory', but in the preamble to the constitution itself. This runs: 'We, the people of Éire, humbly acknowledging all our obligations to our Divine Lord, Jesus Christ, who sustained our fathers through centuries of trial, gratefully remembering their heroic and unremitting struggle to regain the rightful independence of our nation', and refers to the aim of having 'the unity of our country restored'.

This official position buttressed militant nationalism not only in the south but also in Northern Ireland, where republican ideology helped to sustain an image of deprivation and victimisation (see Arthur, 1997). But in Northern Ireland the Catholic minority was confronted by more substantial obstacles. As Joseph Ruane points out in chapter 8, a long historical legacy of socio-economic and political disadvantage continued among Northern Ireland Catholics. As the demographic and organisational resources of this minority grew in the second half of the twentieth century, however, the imbalance between these 'structural' factors and a major 'institutional' circumstance – the political exclusion of the Catholic community – became more marked. The outcome, Ruane argues, was a struggle to resolve the tension between these two dimensions – to endow Catholics with a share of political power commensurate with their structural resources. The rise of militant republicanism may thus be seen precisely as a response to this contradiction in Northern Ireland society.

But republicanism was not the only militant tradition that drew lessons from its interpretation of the past. If Irish nationalists had rediscovered violence as a weapon in establishing at least partial independence, unionists, too, had learned that violence pays – the threat of violence had, as they saw it, delivered them from their enemies, securing their exclusion from the Irish Free State. Thus, as Alvin Jackson shows in chapter 7, the events of 1912–14 entered unionist folklore, becoming a communal foundation myth. Unionist leaders perpetuated the memory of this period by a range of means, including ceremonial ones, as the occasion arose; for example, in 1964 there were commemorations of the fiftieth anniversary of the Larne gunrunning. Indeed, as Jackson argues, the image of 1912–14 was used extensively in mobilising unionist opinion against the Anglo-Irish Agreement of 1985, with mass demonstrations and references to Carson evoking memories of events more than 70 years earlier and helping to legitimise the actions of leaders in the contemporary period.

That unionist leaders might have needed such legitimation becomes clear from Paul Dixon's exploration of the character of contemporary unionism in chapter 9. As British governments appeared to sit on the fence in terms of their attitude towards the union, unionist insecurity tended to grow; and when the union was perceived as being under immediate threat (as in the early 1970s and after the Anglo-Irish Agreement in 1985) these anxieties tended to be expressed through paramilitary activity. This form of violence can, Dixon argues, have a considerable impact on government policy, and is not necessarily simply an irrational reaction to externally imposed change.

Political violence in Ireland: the balance sheet

In looking at the competition between constitutional and militant approaches to political change in Ireland, then, it is worth taking stock of the long-term perspective. As we have seen, the notion that the independent Irish state had been brought into existence by armed struggle became deeply embedded in

Irish political culture, and the ideologically dominant strand in the new state emphasised the extent to which this outcome had been purchased at the barrel of a gun. The founding myth of Northern Ireland, similarly, paid tribute to the role of the threat of armed resistance in securing the partition of the island.

How central, in fact, has the role of political violence been? If we exclude the seventeenth-century wars – hugely important politically, but not part of the path to political modernisation that began in the 1820s – and the 1798 rebellion, we encounter a nineteenth century that was relatively peaceful. The casualties of 1798 had been huge – an estimated 25,000 rebels and civilians killed, together with a few hundred soldiers (Bartlett, 1996: 287) – and a handful had been killed in the rebellion's aftershock when Robert Emmet attempted an insurrection in 1803 (Geoghegan, 2002: 154–200). By this standard, the numbers of deaths in 1848 (two) and 1867 (about a dozen) were paltry. Of course, this assessment means ignoring the large number of assassinations and murders that arose from agrarian insurgency and isolated incidents in the countryside; but agrarian 'outrages' showed a pattern of steady decline in the four decades after 1880, a belated peak in 1906–10 notwithstanding (Garvin, 1981: 75). It also means ignoring the sectarian clashes that took place in rural Ulster from the 1780s (with the Battle of the Diamond in 1795 and Dolly's Brae in 1847 as high points) and in Belfast from 1812 to the present (with particularly notable eruptions in 1857 and 1886; see Stewart, 1977: 128–42).[6]

In this context, the rise of militarism in the early twentieth century was startling. No fewer than four such episodes may be identified between 1916 and 1923, though drawing a rigid boundary between all of them is not easy:

- The 1916 rising, with an estimated 80 rebel, 132 security force and 300 civilian fatalities

- The War of Independence of 1919–21, with an estimated 600 IRA, 550 security force and 200 civilian deaths

- The Civil War in the south, 1922–3, with an estimated 400 IRA, 500–800 Free State army and an unknown number of civilian deaths (estimates range as high as 5,000)

- The conflict in Northern Ireland, 1920–3, related to events in the south but with a central dimension of communal conflict, with an estimated 50 IRA, 37 security force and 370 civilian deaths.[7]

It appeared, however, as if the terrible experiences of these years had been followed by the victory of conventional politics. In the south, the pro-Treaty IRA formed the core of the new national army, and by 1932 it was clear that its political arm, organised first as Cumann na nGaedheal and after 1933 as Fine Gael, was disposed to accept fully the verdict of the ballot box. Most of those who had not accepted the implications of a pro-Treaty majority in the 1922 general election and who fought a civil war against the new state followed de Valera into his new Fianna Fáil party after 1926, and, after a transitional 'semi-constitutional' stage of indefinite duration, this was clearly in the camp of the democrats by the 1930s. The origins of the new Northern Ireland administration were more obviously 'legal' in a formal sense, but there, too, the very existence of a unionist government had, of course, arisen from the paramilitary organisation that was launched in 1912 and from the related proposal for the establishment of a provisional government that would seize control of the administration of Ulster were home rule to take effect in 1914.[8]

Notwithstanding the south's implicit – and at times vocal – claim to rule over the Protestant north, and the northern government's actual rule over the Catholic third of its population, conventional politics seemed, then, eventually to triumph in both parts of Ireland. The IRA campaign of 1956-62 had fizzled out with a formal acknowledgement by the IRA leadership that support for the campaign among northern nationalists was lacking. As the statement announcing the end of the campaign put it:

> The decision to end the Resistance Campaign has been taken in view of the general situation. Foremost among the factors motivating this course of action has been the attitude of the general public whose minds have been deliberately distracted from the supreme issue facing the Irish people – the unity and freedom of Ireland (cited in Bell, 1997: 334).

By 1965, the Nationalist Party in Northern Ireland had recognised the constitutional status quo to the extent of accepting the position of official parliamentary opposition. There had, it is true, been moments of armed violence – in a scattered way during the Second World War, and more deliberately during the IRA campaign of 1956–62 – but by the late 1960s it seemed as if the 'politics of the streets' was as far as nationalists were prepared to deviate from the politics of parliament; the gun appeared to have been buried.

The circumstances associated with the growth of politically motivated violence in Northern Ireland have already been explored in other contributions in this book. But it is worth looking in greater detail at the character of this violence. Its overall effect has been virtually unmeasurable. We need to take account not only of social and economic costs, but also of physical and environmental ones; and the personal costs are the most obvious of all. In terms of its toll on individuals, the dimensions of damage are also complex: loss of freedom, degradation of quality of life, psychological trauma, pain of bereavement, and physical injury, often of a most debilitating kind (see

O'Leary and McGarry, 1996: 40–50; Fay, Morrissey and Smyth, 1999; McKittrick et al. 1999: 14–15). Over the period 1971–96, more than 37,000 people were injured in incidents related to the civil unrest (Fay, Morrissey and Smyth, 1999: 160). For present purposes, though, data permit us to focus on the ultimate personal injury – death. By the end of 2002, a total of 3,536 people had died in incidents related to the civil unrest (most but not all of them within Northern Ireland). It is worth looking at some of the characteristics of this experience, and in particular at the conflict between paramilitary groups and security forces that lay at its core.[9]

Figure 11.1 reminds us of the sheer degree of suffering. The number of deaths per annum climbed rapidly from 16 in 1969, to 26 in 1970, and then to 171 in 1971; it peaked at 479 in 1972. For the following four years (1973–6) it averaged 276 annually, before dropping to an average of 89 for the 17 years 1977–93. The effect of the 1994 ceasefires was obvious, with 61 deaths in the first two thirds of that year but only three after 31 August, the date of the IRA ceasefire. Since then, though, over the eight years 1995–2002, the average has

Figure 11.1. **Deaths related to civil unrest in Northern Ireland by category of victim, 1969–2002**

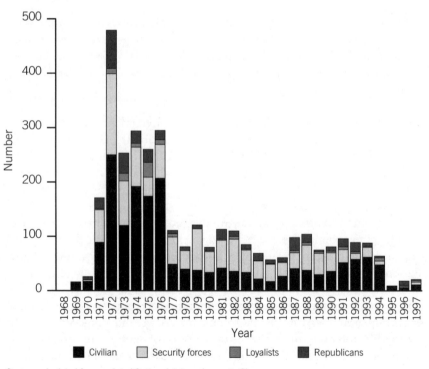

Source: calculated from updated Sutton database (see note 9)

been 20 (or 16 if the 29 deaths in the Omagh bombing of 15 August 1998 are excluded). The brunt of the violence over the whole period has been borne by the civilian population, which accounted for 53 per cent of the deaths (of these, 60 per cent were Catholic, 31 per cent Protestant and 9 per cent from outside Northern Ireland); 32 per cent of those who died were members of the security forces, 11 per cent were republican paramilitaries and 4 per cent were loyalist paramilitaries.

Figure 11.2 looks at the same data from a different perspective: the group responsible for the deaths (in 81 cases it was not possible to assign this to any group, or even to such broad categories as 'other loyalist' or 'other republican'). Here three patterns are obvious: the steady decline in the number of deaths caused by the security forces, which had peaked in 1972; the maintenance of a high level of casualties inflicted by the IRA until the 1994 ceasefire; and a tendency for loyalist violence to peak during two periods: 1972–6, and a nine-year period after the Anglo-Irish Agreement of 1985 (a pattern whose roots are explored in some detail by Paul Dixon in chapter 9). Some further details on

Figure 11.2. **Deaths related to civil unrest in Northern Ireland by group responsible, 1969–2002**

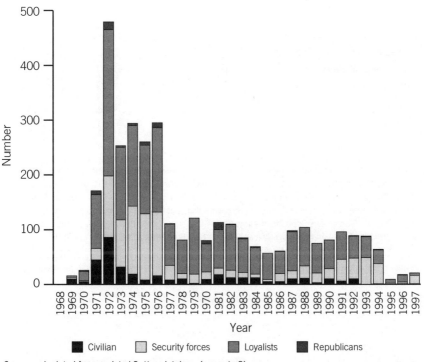

Source: calculated from updated Sutton database (see note 9)

Table 11.1 **Deaths related to civil unrest in Northern Ireland by period and by body responsible, 1969–2002**

Group	1969–76	1977–94	1994–2002	1969–2002
Security forces:				
British Army	196	101	0	297
Royal Ulster Constabulary	19	36	0	55
Other security forces	6	7	3	16
Total	221	144	3	368
Loyalists:				
Ulster Volunteer Force	286	178	19	483
Ulster Defence Association	101	144	20	265
Loyalist Volunteer Force	0	0	18	18
Other loyalists	198	45	19	262
Total	585	367	76	1,028
Republicans:				
Irish Republican Army	807	908	20	1,735
Official Irish Republican Army	47	5	0	52
Irish National Liberation Army	18	88	14	120
Irish People's Liberation Organisation	0	27	0	27
Real Irish Republican Army	0	0	30	30
Other republicans	71	10	10	91
Total	943	1,038	74	2,055
General total	1,749	1,549	153	3,451

Note: 'Other security forces' includes Ulster Special Constabulary, Ulster Defence Regiment and Irish security forces; Ulster Volunteer Force includes Red Hand Commandos, Loyalist Retaliation and Defence Group, Protestant Action Force and Protestant Action Group; Ulster Defence Association includes Ulster Freedom Fighters; other loyalists include Red Hand Defenders; Irish Republican Army includes Direct Action Against Drugs and Republican Action Force; Irish National Liberation Army includes People's Liberation Army and People's Republican Army; Irish People's Liberation Organisation includes the Catholic Reaction Force; and other republicans include Saor Eire. In an additional 85 cases, the identity of the group responsible was not known.

Killings up to the announcement of the IRA ceasefire on 31 August 1994 are included in the second period; those after this date are included in the third period.

Source: calculated from updated Sutton database; see note 9.

the responsibility of the organisations making up these broad groups are given in table 11.1, separately for the three periods into which the civil unrest may be divided. The decline in activity by the mainstream organisations after 1994 is striking; but so, too, is the rise of dissident loyalist and republican groups (and specifically the LVF and the Real IRA) during the same period.

Figure 11.3 **Deaths related to civil unrest in Northern Ireland by group responsible and category of victim, 1969–2002**

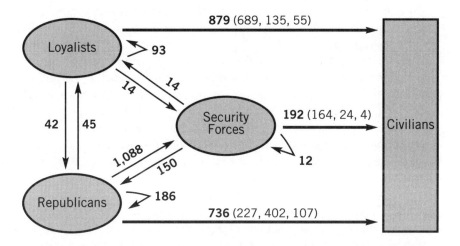

Note: Arrows and associated numbers indicate the number of killings inflicted by each group on the others. Autoreversing arrows indicate killings within the group. In the case of civilian killings, the numbers in brackets refer respectively to Catholics, Protestants and persons who were not from Northern Ireland (this last group comprised 33 civilians killed in Northern Ireland, 59 in the Republic, 68 in Great Britain and six in continental Europe). In an additional 85 cases, the status of the killers was not known.
Source: calculated from updated Sutton database (see note 9, p. 226)

The pattern of inter-group violence over the 1969–89 period has already been analysed in detail by O'Leary and McGarry (1996: 22–40), who demonstrate the complex, multilateral character of the conflict. Their approach is revisited in figure 11.3, which extends the coverage to 2002, using arrows of varying widths to indicate levels of deaths inflicted by each group on the others. The intensity of the confrontation between republicans (and especially the IRA) and the security forces is obvious: republicans killed more than a thousand members of the security forces, at whose hands they suffered 150 fatalities. Notwithstanding the many tense standoffs between the security forces and loyalists, the numbers of deaths that each of these groups inflicted on the other remained small (14 in each case). Neither did republican and loyalist paramilitaries inflict exceptionally heavy casualties on each other; the civilian population suffered much more at the hands of each. Thus republicans killed 736 civilians, but only 45 loyalists; loyalists killed 879 civilians, but only 42 republicans; and even the security forces killed more civilians (192) than they did republicans and loyalists combined (respectively, 150 and 14). It should be noted that each of the groups in combat also inflicted casualties on themselves, sometimes accidentally but, in the case of the paramilitary groups, mainly as a consequence of feuds between rival organisations. These figures do not include the 12 republicans who died on hunger strike in 1974, 1976 and 1981.

In view of the recent history of the conflict, moves to bring paramilitary action to an end not by defeating the paramilitaries but by encouraging them down a political path have acquired particular importance. Even before the 1998 agreement, as John de Chastelain points out in chapter 10, participants in the talks process were required to subscribe to the 'Mitchell principles' of 1996, which included commitments to 'democratic and exclusively peaceful means of resolving political issues' and to 'the total disarmament of all paramilitary organisations'. Republicans had thus locked themselves in to a new approach towards political change even before assenting to the more demanding package contained in the Good Friday Agreement. But, as de Chastelain reminds us, going along with matters of principle is one thing; accepting all of their implications in practice is another, and 'the devil was in the detail'. The data presented in figures 11.1 and 11.2 and in table 11.1 convey a powerful message about the huge changes that have taken place since the ceasefires of 1994; but de Chastelain's account of the painfully slow pace of progress towards decommissioning highlights the failure to achieve a completely satisfactory resolution to this issue, despite the patient diplomacy that he and his colleagues on the Independent International Commission on Decommissioning brought to bear (the commission was established in 1997 in an attempt to separate the issue of decommissioning from other difficult issues, as de Chastelain discusses in chapter 10).

Is the glass of paramilitary weaponry, then, half empty or half full? Unionist critics would probably argue that it is at least three quarters full (and they would object that no-one they trust is allowed to see the glass to verify that it has been even partly emptied). The more pragmatic might respond that, even if this is the case, the contents of the glass have now become redundant, and that with every passing day they become further buried in the mire of inactivity. The gun may not have been taken entirely out of Irish politics at this point, but it could be argued that its value to that group which had argued most persistently for its central role seems to have been fatally undermined.

Political violence: a comparative perspective

Whatever the vicissitudes of the Irish peace process, a glance at the comparative position provides reason for hope. An important recent survey of armed conflicts and self-determination movements concluded that the general pattern was towards a resolution of such conflicts in the 1990s (Gurr, Marshall and Khosla, 2001: 16–18), and a follow-up overview noted that this pattern had continued into the early years of the present century (Quinn and Gurr, 2003: 26). But if establishing the general global position is not difficult, describing it in detail is more challenging. The problem does not lie in any scarcity of easily accessible data; indeed, several major continuing research projects seek systematically to document political (including ethnic) violence and conflict. But these projects have slightly different priorities, resulting in some variation in operational definitions, and they encounter the usual difficulties of measurement, resulting in datasets that differ greatly from each other in terms both of the conflicts they identify as significant and the manner in which they quantify the level of violence in these cases. The extent of these divergences on what might appear at first sight to be 'objective' empirical matters is illustrated in one of the most recent efforts to devise a new dataset covering armed conflict since 1946. This begins by considering a 'candidate list' of more than a dozen existing datasets – but no two of these converge on exactly the same universe of cases (Gleditsch et al., 2002).[10] These comparative initiatives are nevertheless useful in setting two aspects of the Northern Ireland conflict in context: the broad profile of the civil conflict itself, and the political path down which it has been moving.

Political violence in comparative context
It is difficult to rank Northern Ireland in terms of reliable quantitative indicators of levels of civil violence, but one effort to do so has demonstrated just how exceptionally high the level of political violence there has been, relative to population size, by contrast with other liberal democracies – though its profile is less exceptional when one sets it in the context of other countries with a tradition of political violence (O'Leary and McGarry, 1996: 12–20). A less ambitious attempt at comparative analysis is presented in table 11.2, which selects four conflicts from each of five global regions. This list is intended to be illustrative rather than representative. One major region, Latin America, is absent, notwithstanding the many internal wars there (the ethnic dimension to these, when it is present, may easily be overlooked in comparative overviews); and Africa and Asia are clearly underrepresented.

The 20 cases listed in table 11.2 illustrate a very wide range of types of ethnic conflict. In some, the struggle is between two or more groups fighting for control of the state and its resources (Israel / Palestine, Lebanon, Burundi

Table 11.2 **Deaths in selected ethnic conflicts, late twentieth century (estimates)**

Case	Period	Deaths
Western Europe:		
Cyprus	1963–74	1,600–6,000
France (Corsica)	1975–99	50
UK (Northern Ireland)	1968–99	2,700–3,000
Spain (Basque country)	1960–99	500
Former Communist States:		
Bosnia-Herzegovina	1992–94	200,000
Georgia (Abkhasia)	1989–99	19–20
Russia (Chechnia)	1991–99	72,000
Yugoslavia (Kosovo)	1997–99	2,200
Middle East:		
Iraq (Kurds)	1979–86	180,000–200,000
Israel–Palestine	1987–93	1,700
Lebanon	1975–84	8,600
Turkey (Kurds)	1989–99	5,000–9,000
Asia:		
India (Kashmir)	1988–99	15,000–20,000
Indonesia (East Timor)	1976–99	100,000–250,000
Philippines (Moros)	1970–99	100,000–150,000
Sri Lanka (Tamils)	1983–99	32,000–130,000
Africa:		
Burundi	1993–99	100,000
Ethiopia (Eritrea)	1967–93	36,000–2m.
Nigeria (Biafra)	1967–70	1–2m.
Rwanda	1990–4	500,000–1m.

Source: Heidelberg Institute of International Conflict Research, *Kosimo database*, available www.hiik.de/en/kosimo/kosimo_download.htm; see also HIIK, 2002. For rather different estimates, see, for example, Bill Ayres, *Database on violent intrastate nationalist conflicts*, available facstaff.uindy.edu/~bayres/vinc.htm, and Monty G. Marshall, *Database on major episodes of political violence 1946–2002*, available members.aol.com/CSPmgm/warlist.htm.

and Rwanda, for example). In others, there is a powerful separatist movement that wishes to break the state up rather than to seize control over it (the Basques, Chechens, Kurds and Eritreans, for example). In yet others, the location of an international frontier is the issue, with local groups aligning themselves with competing adjacent powers (Northern Ireland, Bosnia and Kashmir, for example). But the various cases fit uneasily into these categories, which in any event are not entirely watertight.

What is immediately striking about table 11.2 is the disparity between levels of fatalities in Northern Ireland and in many other cases of ethnic conflict, especially outside Europe. The intensity of the conflict there pales when it is placed alongside that in, say, Bosnia or Lebanon, not to mention the African cases. But when it is related to population size the picture changes. It is true that one version of this statistic places Northern Ireland well down the list (0.06 deaths per 1,000 population, compared with 9.6 in Cyprus and 94.2 in Bosnia); but this depends on a calculation where the base is the total population of the state. In the case of the Northern Ireland conflict, this base is the total population of the United Kingdom; but if we use instead the population of Northern Ireland – probably a more appropriate one – the rate increases to 2.4 per 1,000 population. Comparisons of this kind illustrate the point that matters might be worse; but this is of course a matter of perspective. The reality is that the conflicts reported in table 11.2 are found in atypical societies, with high levels of ethnic violence; most societies are not internally fractured in this way, and we need to bear in mind the fact that even in multi-ethnic societies ethnic peace rather than ethnic war is the norm.

Paths out of ethnic violence

Any effort to assess the Northern Ireland problem in a broader comparative context must also address a political question that is of central concern in this book: the extent to which violence may have been set aside as a mechanism for achieving political goals (for a valuable set of essays that set the Northern Ireland peace process in such comparative context, see Elliott, 2002). Another recent study has presented a very useful framework for assessing the progress of self-determination movements globally from the 1940s onwards. Based on a very large number of cases of violent conflict (70 of them surviving, though not necessarily in violent form, to 2003), it suggests that such conflicts potentially pass through ten phases as protest escalates progressively, and then de-escalates as the pursuit of a settlement gathers momentum. These phases have been described as follows:

1. Conventional politics: self-determination is sought by conventional political strategies including advocacy, representation of group interests to officials, and electoral politics

2. Militant politics: self-determination is sought by organizing and inciting group members to use disruptive strategies (mass protest, boycotts, resistance to authorities), possibly accompanied by a few symbolic acts of violence

3. Low-level hostilities: self-determination is sought by localized use of violent strategies such as riots, local rebellions, bombings, and armed attacks against the authorities

4. High-level hostilities: self-determination is sought by widespread and organized armed violence against the authorities

5. Talk-fight: group representatives negotiate with the authorities about a settlement and its implementation while substantial armed violence continues; fighting may be done by the principals or by factions that reject efforts at settlement

6. Cessation of open hostilities: most fighting is over but one or more principals are ready to resume armed violence if efforts at settlement fail (international peace-keeping forces may play a role)

7. Contested agreement: an interim or final agreement for group autonomy within an existing state has been negotiated between the principals but some parties, within the group or the government or both, reject and attempt to subvert it

8. Uncontested agreement: a final agreement for group autonomy is in place, is accepted in principle by all parties, and is being implemented

9. Implemented agreement: a final settlement or agreement for group autonomy has been largely or fully implemented

10. Independence: the group has its own internationally recognized state (Quinn and Gurr, 2003: 27–8).

This is a singularly appropriate framework for describing the unfolding of events in Northern Ireland (removing the recent conflict, for present purposes, from its broader setting in the past two centuries of Irish history). Looked at from the perspective of the Catholic minority, it is easy to identify the first phase, of conventional politics, which lasted for several decades up to 1968: Catholic voters supported the Nationalist Party, which in 1965 signalled its full acceptance of conventional politics by becoming the official opposition in the Northern Ireland parliament.[11] The beginning of the second phase, militant politics, was marked by the birth of the civil rights movement and by the campaign of marching and civil disobedience that began in 1968 (though the formal objectives of the movement made no mention of the issue of self-determination). The third phase, low-level hostilities, was under way by 1970, as the newly born Provisional IRA began to have an impact. The date by which a transition to high-level hostilities had taken place is unclear, but this had certainly occurred by late 1971. The fifth 'talk-fight' phase took place discreetly in 1972, to be followed by a cessation of hostilities in 1975; but this petered out in the absence of agreement, and hostilities resumed. Again in the early 1990s, though, the IRA moved towards acceptance of a renewed 'talk-fight' phase, and this was followed in 1994 by the sixth phase, cessation of hostilities. The Good Friday Agreement of 1998 marked the beginning of the seventh phase, the reaching of a contested agreement. Since then, there has been only limited progress beyond this phase. The agreement continues to be contested; if anything, unionist scepticism about it has grown. Movement towards implementation has also been slow, and has been anything but unidirectional.

Three general points may be made about this comparative interpretation of the Northern Ireland conflict. First, it is clear that not all ten phases discussed above are necessarily relevant, or applicable. Thus, the last phase described above, independence, is central to the formal goals of the IRA, and has formed a core principle in Irish republican ideology for almost a century and a half: the stated goal has always been to establish the full independence of the island of Ireland from Great Britain. It may indeed be the case that in the broad sweep of history over the centuries we will be able to see the conflict precisely as being dominated by such a simple, bilateral struggle. But when the focus narrows to the last decades of the twentieth century this simple picture is disrupted by the intrusion of other realities. The IRA struggle has had to take account not just of its formally defined enemy, the British military presence in Ireland, but also of two other major forces: the hostile Protestant population within which it is embedded in Northern Ireland, and an unevenly sympathetic population in the Republic of Ireland. The republican movement is, then, confronted with a need to address tensions not with one but with three other sets of forces: first, that which it has always acknowledged, the British; second, that which it has recognised more recently, the unionist population within Northern Ireland; and third, the southern state, which has for long shown itself to be prepared to accept partition and the constitutional status quo. The question is not a simple one of managing the departure of Northern Ireland from the United Kingdom; securing its admission to a united Ireland constitutes a second significant challenge. Indeed, the international experiences show that, leaving aside the relatively peaceful disintegration of the former Soviet Union and Czechoslovakia, only five internationally recognised states came into existence in the past 40 years as a consequence of an armed separatist conflict: Bangladesh in 1971, Slovenia and Croatia in 1991, Eritrea in 1993 and East Timor in 2002 (Quinn and Gurr, 2003: 29).

Second, we should note a closely related point: as figure 11.3 shows, the Northern Ireland conflict is not just one between the security forces and republicans. The military capacity of the loyalist paramilitaries is considerable. This has been directed overwhelmingly not against republican paramilitaries but against the Catholic population, as a larger and more easily identifiable target. Paul Dixon has argued in chapter 9 that loyalist violence, at least up to this point, has had the capacity to secure continued British commitment to the union; whether or not this is the case, it probably does have the capacity to secure continued southern Irish reluctance to become too deeply involved in the internal affairs of Northern Ireland. In this respect, it mirrors the position of republican paramilitaries, who may well have underestimated their capacity to unite Northern Ireland with the Republic – a possibly more daunting task than merely forcing the British to withdraw.

Third, it is clear from the evidence of other conflicts, and indeed from Irish history, that movement from phase to phase in the framework described above is not necessarily unidirectional; it is reversible. Contested agreements are potentially unstable. As the comparative evidence shows,

> Some rebel factions may continue fighting either to cut a better deal, like the Abu Sayaf faction of Philippine Moros, or because they reject any compromise, like Chechen Islamicists who mounted a jihad against Russian influence in the Caucasus after the first Chechen war ended in a Russian withdrawal. On the other side, political opponents of a government may try to subvert an agreement between authorities and an autonomy movement. They may use legislative means to block implementation or stage provocative actions, like Likud leader Ariel Sharon's visit in the company of armed police to Jerusalem's Temple Mount in September 2000 (Quinn and Gurr, 2003: 32).

The Irish conflict offers several instances of such efforts to subvert inter-ethnic agreements. From the side of those for whom the settlement is not enough, examples include the radical republicans of the IRB in 1916 in attempting to overturn the home rule settlement of 1914, the IRA in 1974 in attempting to overthrow the Sunningdale Agreement,[12] and the Real IRA in attempting to undermine the Good Friday Agreement. From the other side, the British Tories and Ulster Unionists in 1912–14, the loyalist paramilitaries in 1974 in securing the collapse of the institutions established under the Sunningdale Agreement, and militant unionists in the 1990s opposed to the Good Friday Agreement represent the position of those for whom the settlement has conceded too much. Seeking to present an agreement that in reality is a compromise as a victory for all sides is a considerable challenge, but it can be attempted with some success (see Hartman, 2003). However, it is clear that unionist perceptions of the 1998 agreement are becoming more negative, while on the militant nationalist side the current perception that the agreement represents an honourable compromise rather than a defeat will not necessarily survive indefinitely. In this context, the issue of decommissioning acquires a particular salience. As Joseph Ruane warns in chapter 8, the premise on which the Good Friday Agreement was reached was one in which the British and Irish governments had accepted that the IRA campaign was a war, not terrorism, and in wars 'undefeated enemies do not surrender their weapons before peace negotiations begin, and may not need to do so afterwards'. The challenge, on the nationalist side, he argues, is to ensure that disappointment with the outcome does not lead another generation to revert to violence.

Conclusion

In 1920, as he planned the implementation of the partition of Ireland, British Prime Minister David Lloyd George expressed the view that the union with Ireland was maintained essentially by force, rather than by any ties of emotion or interest. Ireland thus deserved to be treated differently from other parts of the United Kingdom: 'There is union between Scotland, England and Wales. This is a union that bears the test of death. There is no union with Ireland. A grappling hook is not a union' (Fanning, 1989: 119). The history of the decades immediately before he spoke might not have offered unambiguous support for that perspective, but later decades offered more convincing evidence in support of Lloyd George's view, at least as far as Catholic Ireland was concerned.

According to a popular view of Irish history, the Irish alternately sought to deal with the British grappling hook in two ways: by persuading the British to remove it by means of agitation in the British parliament, and by seeking to cast it off by force through armed action in Ireland. This book has concerned itself with the tension between these two approaches to political change, viewed as ideal types. Of course, reality can never be forced to conform to ideal types of this kind. It is not possible to place parties, movements, groups or even most individuals clearly in one category or the other. Paul Dixon has drawn attention in chapter 9 to the absence of a clear-cut distinction between constitutional and unconstitutional unionism: individuals and groups may veer from one extreme to the other, depending on context. This ambiguity has for long also been recognised on the nationalist side, too, and F. S. L. Lyons's summary of the motor force of political change in pre-independence Ireland probably applies also to the Northern Ireland conflict in the last three decades of the twentieth century:

> If there is any single generalisation that is valid for the whole period 1798 to 1921 it is surely this – that no substantial gains were made by Irish nationalism without powerful and sustained pressure. It is, however, a very inadequate definition which identifies pressure with violence and reserves a monopoly of it to the

exponents of physical force. On the contrary, those constitutional movements which have been most formidable in our history are precisely the movements which have combined action in parliament with the mobilisation of extra-parliamentary agitation. Such movements, in short, have been Janus-faced, one face looking towards Westminster, the other looking towards Ireland (Lyons, 1969: 103).

The existence of this intermediate category of 'militant politics' in between conventional politics and violence is, of course, widely acknowledged, as discussed above; and it has been analysed in the Northern Irish case (Irvin, 1999). It is as yet too early to assess the long-term probability that the new path of conventional politics down which the competing traditions in Ireland have gone will in future be reinforced by military or by merely militant tactics. But, in the shorter term, there are grounds for believing that the patient diplomacy that has been a hallmark of the peace process for more than a decade may well have paid dividends, and that a larger portion of the population of the island of Ireland now reject political violence than at any time since the early decades of the twentieth century.

Appendices

Appendix 1

Selected paramilitary and parapolitical organisations in Ireland

Ancient Order of Hibernians. Catholic activist organisation dating from the 1830s, evolving separately in Ireland and America. Said to be descended from earlier Catholic and agrarian societies, it was close to Fenianism in the middle of the nineteenth century but later developed strong links to constitutional nationalism. In the twentieth century it became increasingly concentrated in Ulster, and evolved into a 'friendly society' rather than a political organisation.

Clan na Gael. American-based secret society founded in New York in 1867. It was active in all aspects of Irish militant nationalist politics, and its membership overlapped with that of the IRB. It split over the issue of the Anglo-Irish Treaty of 1921 and it had ceased to play any active political role by the 1940s.

Continuity IRA. Dissident republican paramilitary group, active since 1996, said to share the perspective of Republican Sinn Féin, a body whose members seceded from Sinn Féin in 1986.

Defenders. Catholic secret society formed in Armagh in the mid-1780s, in part as a reaction to the Protestant Peep of Day Boys, and later spreading throughout the northern part of Ireland. It targeted high rents and tithes and, at a time when high emigration from Ulster and the repeal of the penal laws were giving Catholics new opportunities to acquire land, it also caused insecurities among Protestants. Organisationally, the movement was cell-based, and was tighter and more secretive than the Whiteboys. During the mid- and late 1790s it co-operated closely with the United Irishmen in pursuit of political reform.

Fenians. See Irish Republican Brotherhood.

Irish National Liberation Army (INLA). Militant group that seceded in 1974 from the 'Official' IRA, and seen as the military equivalent of the Irish Republican Socialist Party which split with 'Official' Sinn Féin at the same time. One of the most uncompromising and fractious paramilitary bodies, it was subject to several internal feuds. Its military campaign was formally called off only in 1998.

Irish Republican Army (IRA) (1). Name used from 1918 onwards to describe the Irish Volunteers (an open paramilitary organisation founded in 1913 to support the cause of home rule, but which split in 1914 on the outbreak of war). Following its struggle against the British in 1919–21, it split over the issue of the Anglo-Irish Treaty of 1921. Many of its members went on to join the army of the Irish Free State, while others regrouped in opposition. Following the Civil War of 1922–3, the position of the anti-Treaty group became progressively weakened, though it engaged in sporadic military activities (notably in Northern Ireland in 1956–62).

Irish Republican Army (IRA) (2). Paramilitary organisation that broke with the 'Official' IRA in December 1969, anticipating a parallel split in Sinn Féin in Janurary 1970, and known originally as the 'Provisional' IRA. The 'Official' IRA faded away eventually; it had declared a ceasefire in 1972. The (Provisional) IRA campaign that began in 1970 was formally ended only in August 1994, though there had been earlier ceasefires (June–July 1972 and December 1974–February 1976) and a later prolonged abandonment of the 1994 ceasefire (February 1996–July 1997).

Irish Republican Brotherhood. Secret, oathbound society founded in 1858 in Dublin. In its early years its members were commonly known as 'Fenians' (a name used for a similar organisation established in New York in 1858). Its military activities included an attempted rebellion in 1867. Its constitution (1873) committed it to a revolutionary, separatist path, and it was a significant if invisible force in the leadership of the Irish Volunteers and in planning the 1916 rising. Michael Collins's influence caused the IRB leadership to support the 1921 treaty. The body came to an effective end following the 'army mutiny' of 1924, in which its members were involved, but it seems to have maintained a paper existence for some decades after this.

Loyalist Volunteer Force (LVF). Loyalist paramilitary group founded in 1996 by former members of the Ulster Volunteer Force and responsible for a number of killings.

Oakboys (Hearts of Oak). Agrarian protest movement originating in Armagh in 1762 and active in mid-Ulster before its supression in 1766. Its grievances included rising tithes and rents.

Orange Order. Protestant society founded in 1795 in an atmosphere of sectarian tension in south Ulster. Though central organisation was lacking in the middle decades of the nineteenth century, especially after a brief suppression of the order in 1825, individual lodges continued in existence, and a revival took place when the issue of home rule arose in 1886. The order played a major role in establishing the Ulster Unionist Council in 1905, and continues to enjoy substantial representation in that body. It possessed great influence in Northern Ireland after 1921, when almost all Unionists ministers and MPs were members of the order; and its continuing popularity is attested to by the numbers that attend its marches commemorating the major events of Ulster Protestant history.

Peep of Day Boys. Protestant movement active in South Ulster from the mid-1780s. One of its objectives was to protect the interests of Protestant farmers; the movement was substantially superseded by the Orange Order in 1795.

Real IRA. Dissident republican paramilitary group founded in 1997 by former IRA members, said to share the perspective of the Thirty-Two County Sovereignty Committee. It admitted responsibility for the Omagh bomb in August 1998 that killed 29 people.

Ribbonmen. The most important popular protest movement in Ireland during the first half of the nineteenth century. It grew out of Defenderism and developed a very effective organisation, especially in Leinster, adopting an uncompromising position on tithes. It was active in the 'tithe war' of the early 1830s, which witnessed violent confrontations both with the military and with those involved in the collection of tithes. It was revived after the famine of the 1840s and, in one guise or another, continued to agitate for agrarian reform until the 1870s.

Rightboys. Agrarian protest movement originating in Cork in the early 1780s and spreading throughout Munster and adjoining counties. Rightboys were named for the 'righteousness' of their cause, and conducted a vigorous campaign against tithes. More co-ordinated and better organised than the Whiteboys, they also sought to regulate the dues which were paid to the Catholic clergy. Promises to enquire into their grievances and more active military and judicial intervention caused the movement to peter out in 1789.

Rockites. Agrarian protest movement in the tradition of the Whiteboys and Rightboys in west Munster during the early 1820s. The movement was influenced by millenarianism and saw itself as a means blessed by Providence to restore 'the true religion' (Catholicism), giving it an appeal to all classes of Catholics.

Steelboys (Hearts of Steel). Agrarian protest movement active during the late 1760s and early 1770s in south-east Ulster. Though composed mainly of Protestant tenants, it was concerned with the same issues as the Whiteboys, especially rents, tithes, other taxes and evictions.

Ulster Defence Association (UDA). Loyalist paramilitary organisation founded in 1971 by bringing together a number of existing local groups. It was largely responsible for the May 1974 strike that brought the institutions established by the Sunningdale Agreement to an end. It sometimes used the cover name 'Ulster Freedom Fighters' for its activities. It declared a ceasefire in October 1994.

Ulster Freedom Fighters (UFF). See Ulster Defence Association.

Ulster Volunteer Force (UVF) (1). Loyalist paramilitary organisation founded in 1913 to oppose the implementation of home rule. Many volunteers joined the army on the outbreak of war in 1914, and the organisation was disbanded following the establishment of the Ulster Special Constabulary (in which many UVF members enlisted) in 1920.

Ulster Volunteer Force (UVF) (2). Loyalist paramilitary organisation founded in 1966 in opposition to the liberal policies of the O'Neill government. It pursued an armed campaign from 1969 onwards, overshadowing the activities of the larger UDA. It declared a ceasefire in October 1994.

United Irishmen. Reformist society established in 1791, later (1795) becoming a secret revolutionary organisation committed to overthrowing the political establishment. Though managing to recruit thousands of supporters from all religions, its rebellion in 1798 was unsuccessful and it faded away following a smaller rebellion in 1803.

Whiteboys. Agrarian protest movement originating in Tipperary in 1761 and later spreading throughout Munster and adjoining counties. Its name derived from the white tunics which its members sometimes wore over their clothes. Initially protesting against the enclosure of common lands and tithes, it later attacked rising rents and tackled other agrarian grievances. The movement remained active until the 1840s, especially in Munster.

Young Ireland. Nationalist movement dating from 1842 and operating initially under the umbrella of O'Connell's Repeal Association. It broke with the Association in 1846 and embarked on an unsuccessful attempt at rebellion in 1848.

Appendix 2

The beginning and end of political violence in Ireland? Selected documents

2.1 Ulster's Solemn League and Covenant, 1912

Drafted by the Ulster unionist leadership and based on the Scottish Solemn League and Covenant (a Scottish–English agreement of 1643 designed to defend Protestantism), the covenant was signed by 471,414 persons in Ulster, or of Ulster birth, in a single day, 28 September 1912; it achieved iconic status within the Ulster unionist community.

> Being convinced in our consciences that Home Rule would be disastrous to the material well-being of Ulster as well as of the whole of Ireland, subversive of our civil and religious freedom, destructive of our citizenship and perilous to the unity of the Empire, we, whose names are underwritten, men of Ulster, loyal subjects of his Gracious Majesty King George V., humbly relying on the God whom our fathers in days of stress and trial confidently trusted, do hereby pledge ourselves in solemn Covenant throughout this our time of threatened calamity to stand by one another in defending for ourselves and our children our cherished position of equal citizenship in the United Kingdom and in using all means which may be found necessary to defeat the present conspiracy to set up a Home Rule Parliament in Ireland. And in the event of such a parliament being forced upon us we further solemnly and mutually pledge ourselves to refuse to recognise its authority. In sure confidence that God will defend the right we hereto subscribe our names. And further, we individually declare that we have not already signed this Covenant.
>
> The above was signed by me at _____
>
> 'Ulster Day', Saturday, 28th September, 1912.
>
> GOD SAVE THE KING

2.2 Proclamation of 1916

Drafted by the IRB leadership and read by Pádraic Pearse to a crowd outside Dublin's General Post Office, headquarters of the 1916 rebels, on 24 April 1916; it later became regarded as the foundation document of the independent Irish state.

POBLACHT NA H EIREANN

THE PROVISIONAL GOVERNMENT OF THE IRISH REPUBLIC

TO THE PEOPLE OF IRELAND

IRISHMEN AND IRISHWOMEN: In the name of God and of the dead generations from which she receives her old tradition of nationhood, Ireland, through us, summons her children to her flag and strikes for her freedom.

Having organised and trained her manhood through her secret revolutionary organisation, the Irish Republican Brotherhood, and through her open military organisations, the Irish Volunteers and the Irish Citizen Army, having patiently perfected her discipline, having resolutely waited for the right moment to reveal itself, she now seizes that moment, and, supported by her exiled children in America and by gallant allies in Europe, but relying in the first on her own strength, she strikes in full confidence of victory.

We declare the right of the people of Ireland to the ownership of Ireland, and to the unfettered control of Irish destinies, to be sovereign and indefeasible. The long usurpation of that right by a foreign people and government has not extinguished the right, nor can it ever be extinguished except by the destruction of the Irish people. In every generation the Irish people have asserted their right to national freedom and sovereignty; six times during the past three hundred years they have asserted it in arms. Standing on that fundamental right and again asserting it in arms in the face of the world, we hereby proclaim the Irish Republic as a Sovereign Independent State, and we pledge our lives and the lives of our comrades-in-arms to the cause of its freedom, of its welfare, and of its exaltation among the nations.

The Irish Republic is entitled to, and hereby claims, the allegiance of every Irishman and Irishwoman. The Republic guarantees religious and civil liberty, equal rights and equal opportunities to all its citizens, and declares its resolve to pursue the happiness and prosperity of the whole nation and of all its parts, cherishing all the children of the nation equally and oblivious of the differences carefully fostered by an alien government, which have divided a minority from the majority in the past.

Until our arms have brought the opportune moment for the establishment of a permanent National Government, representative of the whole people of Ireland and elected by the suffrages of all her men and women, the Provisional Government, hereby constituted, will administer the civil and military affairs of the Republic in trust for the people.

We place the cause of the Irish Republic under the protection of the Most High God, Whose blessing we invoke upon our arms, and we pray that no one who serves that cause will dishonour it by cowardice, inhumanity, or rapine. In this supreme hour the Irish nation must, by its valour and discipline and by the readiness of its children to sacrifice themselves for the common good, prove itself worthy of the august destiny to which it is called.

Signed on Behalf of the Provisional Government.

THOMAS J. CLARKE.

SEAN MAC DIARMADA. THOMAS MACDONAGH.

P. H. PEARSE. EAMONN CEANNT.

JAMES CONNOLLY. JOSEPH PLUNKETT.

2.3 Mitchell principles, 1996

The establishment of the International Body on Arms Decommissioning was announced by the British and Irish governments on 28 November 1995, and it produced its report two months later. Acceptance of the principles it incorporated, which became known as the 'Mitchell principles', became a requirement for participation in the talks that led to the Good Friday Agreement.

Report of The International Body on Arms Decommissioning (extract)

III. RECOMMENDATIONS: PRINCIPLES OF DEMOCRACY AND NON-VIOLENCE

19. To reach an agreed political settlement and to take the gun out of Irish politics, there must be commitment and adherence to fundamental principles of democracy and non-violence. Participants in all-party negotiations should affirm their commitment to such principles.

20. Accordingly, we recommend that the parties to such negotiations affirm their total and absolute commitment:

    a   To democratic and exclusively peaceful means of resolving political issues;

    b   To the total disarmament of all paramilitary organisations;

    c   To agree that such disarmament must be verifiable to the satisfaction of an independent commission;

    d   To renounce for themselves, and to oppose any effort by others, to use force, or threaten to use force, to influence the course or the outcome of all-party negotiations;

    e   To agree to abide by the terms of any agreement reached in all-party negotiations and to resort to democratic and exclusively peaceful methods in trying to alter any aspect of that outcome with which they may disagree; and,

f   To urge that 'punishment' killings and beatings stop and to take effective steps to prevent such actions.

21. We join the Governments, religious leaders and many others in condemning 'punishment' killings and beatings. They contribute to the fear that those who have used violence to pursue political objectives in the past will do so again in the future. Such actions have no place in a lawful society.

22. Those who demand decommissioning prior to all-party negotiations do so out of concern that the paramilitaries will use force, [or] threaten to use force, to influence the negotiations, or to change any aspect of the outcome of negotiations with which they disagree.
    Given the history of Northern Ireland, this is not an unreasonable concern. The principles we recommend address those concerns directly.

23. These commitments, when made and honoured, would remove the threat of force before, during and after all-party negotiations. They would focus all concerned on what is ultimately essential if the gun is to be taken out of Irish politics: an agreed political settlement and the total and verifiable disarmament of all paramilitary organisations. That should encourage the belief that the peace process will truly be an exercise in democracy, not one influenced by the threat of violence.

George J. Mitchell; John de Chastelain; Harri Holkeri.

January 22nd, 1996

2.4. Good Friday Agreement, 1998: declaration of support
The agreement arose from multi-party talks that began in 1996 and was ultimately assented to by eight parties as well as the British and Irish governments. The parties were the Alliance Party, Labour (a small Northern Ireland group), Northern Ireland Women's Coalition, the Progressive Unionist Party, the Social Democratic and Labour Party, Sinn Féin, the Ulster Democratic Party and the Ulster Unionist Party. The 'declaration of support' formed a preamble to the main document.

DECLARATION OF SUPPORT

1. We, the participants in the multi-party negotiations, believe that the agreement we have negotiated offers a truly historic opportunity for a new beginning.

2. The tragedies of the past have left a deep and profoundly regrettable legacy of suffering. We must never forget those who have died or been injured, and

their families. But we can best honour them through a fresh start, in which we firmly dedicate ourselves to the achievement of reconciliation, tolerance, and mutual trust, and to the protection and vindication of the human rights of all.

3. We are committed to partnership, equality and mutual respect as the basis of relationships within Northern Ireland, between North and South, and between these islands.

4. We reaffirm our total and absolute commitment to exclusively democratic and peaceful means of resolving differences on political issues, and our opposition to any use or threat of force by others for any political purpose, whether in regard to this agreement or otherwise.

5. We acknowledge the substantial differences between our continuing, and equally legitimate, political aspirations. However, we will endeavour to strive in every practical way towards reconciliation and rapprochement within the framework of democratic and agreed arrangements. We pledge that we will, in good faith, work to ensure the success of each and every one of the arrangements to be established under this agreement. It is accepted that all of the institutional and constitutional arrangements – an Assembly in Northern Ireland, a North/South Ministerial Council, implementation bodies, a British–Irish Council and a British–Irish Intergovernmental Conference and any amendments to British Acts of Parliament and the Constitution of Ireland – are interlocking and interdependent and that in particular the functioning of the Assembly and the North/South Council are so closely inter-related that the success of each depends on that of the other.

6. Accordingly, in a spirit of concord, we strongly commend this agreement to the people, North and South, for their approval.

Notes

Chapter One   The roots of militant politics in Ireland

1   John Whyte (1990: 4–5) made the point that 'Northern Ireland people express more moderate views than they really hold' on the basis of survey evidence up to 1989 that showed Alliance Party support being consistently over-reported in opinion polls, and Sinn Féin support being under-reported. Subsequent evidence gives us no reason to doubt this judgement.

2   Unionists and nationalists were defined by their response to the question 'Generally speaking, do you think of yourself as a unionist, a nationalist or neither?'; attitudes to the agreement were derived from the questions 'If a vote on the Good Friday Agreement was held again to-day, how would you vote?', and 'How did you vote in 1998 when the referendum was held?' For a description of the survey, a copy of the questionnaire and access to the data, see http://www.ark.ac.uk/nilt/.

3   The fact that 28 per cent of SDLP respondents and nine per cent of Sinn Féin respondents claimed that their preferred long-term solution was maintenance of the union with Great Britain is compatible with other Northern Ireland survey data over the years.

4   It is worth noting that only 37 per cent believed that a united Ireland was likely within the next 20 years; there was almost no difference between the unionist parties (39 per cent), but only 20 per cent of SDLP supporters believed a united Ireland was likely, as opposed to 53 per cent of Sinn Féin supporters.

5   'Captain Moonlight' symbolised agrarian protest in nineteenth-century Ireland; 'P. O'Neill' is the signature that appears on IRA statements; and 'Captain William Johnston' is his UVF counterpart.

Chapter Two   The invention and reinvention of public protest in Ireland, 1760–1900

Acknowledgement: For their comments on an earlier draft of this paper, the author is grateful to Vincent Comerford, Tom Garvin, Alvin Jackson and Tim P. O'Neill.

1   For the background to the notion of the organic polity, see Bric, 2003: 134–6.

2   'Patriotism' is a contemporary term which was usually applied to those who wanted to reform the eighteenth century Irish polity and, in particular, the Irish parliament and its relationship with the executive; McDowell, 1979.

3   *Freeman's Journal,* 1 August 1786.

4   Quoted of the MP for Dublin, Sir Edward Newenham, in *The Parliamentary Register: or, History of the Proceedings and Debates of the House of Commons.* Dublin: Byrne & Porter, 1787, vii, 13 Mar. 1787.

5   For the considerable emigration from contemporary Ulster, see Dickson, 1966.

6   The 'battle of Carrickshock' took place in December 1831 when some 500 people attacked a police escort which was protecting a process server. As a result, the local chief constable, 11

of his men, and three local men were killed, and several others were seriously injured; O'Hanrahan, 1990.

7 'Captain Moonlight' was one of the names used by popular protest movements to sign threatening or public letters which these movements issued from time to time.

8 William Allen, Michael Larkin and Michael O'Brien were arrested following the rescue of two Fenian prisoners who were being returned from a court appearance in Manchester in September 1867. During this attack, one of the unarmed police escort was killed and the three 'Manchester martyrs' were hanged as a result.

9 Tim P. O'Neill (2000) makes a similar point about the impact which half a million evictions between 1846 and 1854 had on the relationship between landlord and tenant; he sees these as breaking a social compact between landlord and tenant, and therefore compromising the conventional patterns of deference and authority which had existed within the village world.

10 *Freeman's Journal*, 10 March 1867.

11 JKL was the pen name of Dr James Doyle, bishop of the much-disturbed diocese of Kildare and Leighlin (1819–34). Doyle took a relatively sympathetic view of the anti-tithe movement and defended the right of every individual to oppose what was unjust and excessive. As such, he was often taken as supporting, if not encouraging, the popular campaign against tithes; McGrath, 1999.

12 The 'three Fs', fixity of tenure, fair rent and free sale (the freedom of a tenant to sell his interest in his holding) were central to the land agitation of the 1870s and were recognised in the provisions of the Land Act of 1881.

13 *Freeman's Journal*, 20 September 1880.

14 The 'manifesto' was launched in October 1881 and was intended as a popular campaign to compel landlords to accept only a certain level of rents (Geary, 1986).

15 Salisbury was prime minister between 1886 and 1892, and between 1895 and 1902, the year in which his nephew, Arthur Balfour, succeeded him. Balfour had been chief secretary of Ireland between 1887 and 1891.

Chapter Three *The home rule crisis of 1912–14*

1 Austen Chamberlain to Mary Chamberlain, 31 March 1910, Austen Chamberlain Papers, Birmingham University Library, AC 4/1/256.

2 The play was revived three times in 1905 and a special performance was arranged for King Edward VII, who laughed so heartily that he broke the special chair hired for the evening by the theatre manager and, 'in falling, flung Shaw's reputation high in the air . . . The Prime Minister had told the King, and the King had told his countrymen, and now they were all telling the world that GBS was the funniest of Irishmen' (Holroyd, 1988–92, II: 99). Shaw later wrote, in a 'Preface for politicians', of having so 'delighted and flattered English audiences' that they 'very naturally swallowed it eagerly and smacked their lips over it, laughing all the more heartily because that they felt that they were taking a caricature of themselves with the most tolerant and largeminded goodhumour. They were perfectly willing to allow me to represent Tom Broadbent as infatuated in politics, hypnotised by his newspaper leader-writers and

parliamentary orators into an utter paralysis of his common sense, without moral delicacy or social tact, provided I made him cheerful, robust, goodnatured, free from envy, and above all, a successful muddler-through in business and love' (Shaw, 1907: v–vi).

3   See also *Annual register* 1908, 195–7, where it was reported that the procession took place 'shorn of much of its splendour' but watched by 'dense and sympathetic crowds, who were by no means all Roman Catholics'. Members of religious orders carried their vestments instead of wearing them. Bishops wore court dress and Cardinals scarlet. One immediate consequence was that the Irish vote in the Newcastle-on-Tyne by-election on 24 September went Unionist and lost the seat for the Liberals.

4   Asquith to Crewe, 10 Sept. 1908, Asquith Papers, Bodleian Library, Oxford, MS Asquith 46 f. 169.

5   House of Commons, *Debates*, 4th ser., vol. 174, cols. 317–18. Redmond (John's brother, who was killed in Flanders in 1917) and Talbot were united in religion but opposed in politics. Edmund FitzAlan Howard (known as Lord Edmund Talbot, 1876–1921, Conservative MP since 1894 and Chief Whip 1913–21) became the first Viscount FitzAlan of Derwent and the last Viceroy of Ireland in 1921. The first Catholic Viceroy since the reign of James II, he instructed that the Chapel Royal at Dublin Castle be restored and it was decided to hang a suitable picture of the Madonna, Joseph and the infant Jesus above the altar. When Lord and Lady FitzAlan inspected the chapel they were greeted by a picture of Charles II, Lady Castlemaine and their baby! (Jones, 1971: 99).

6   Churchill, 1969: 1089, 5 Jun. 1911. The page-heading chosen by Churchill's biographer-son for this letter more than fifty years later is also instructive: 'THE CURSE OF CATHOLICISM'.

7   The memorandum (LGP C/16/9/1) has been published in Petrie, 1939–40, 1: 381–8.

8   Birrell to Churchill, 26 Aug. 1911; quoted in Jalland, 1980: 58–9.

9   His luncheon companions were M'Kinnon Wood, the Financial Secretary to the Treasury who became Secretary for Scotland with a seat in the cabinet on 13 February 1912, and Richard Holt, a Liberal backbencher; see Holt's diary entry for 5 Feb. 1912 (Jalland, 1980: 61).

10   This was a classic example of the style so well described by Charles Hobhouse: 'Asquith, the Prime Minister, carries naturally great weight, and everybody likes him, and has great admiration for his intellect and for the ease and rapidity of transacting business, and extraordinary quickness in seizing the right point in any case. On the other hand he has little courage; he will adopt the views of A with apparent conviction and enthusiasm, but if the drift of opinion is against A he will find an easy method of throwing him over. He is nearly always in favour of the last speaker, and I have never seen him put his back to the wall' (Hobhouse, 1977: 120, 13 Aug. 1912).

11   Asquith to Churchill, 19 Sept. 1913; see Churchill, 1969: 1400.

12   C. P. Scott's diary, 2 Feb. 1911, Scott papers, British Library Add. MS 50901, f. 2.

13   An apprehensive Redmond, already fearful about 'Asquith's overpowering love of compromise' and mistrustful of Churchill, 'had counted upon Loreburn and Morley as the most reliable Home Rulers in the Cabinet'; see Gwynn, 1932: 227–8.

14   The memorandum is published in full in Jenkins, 1964: 545–9.

15   Redmond's note of his interview with Lloyd George on 25 November indicates that Lloyd George told him of the proclamation but placed it in an exclusively Ulster context. 'He informed me that the Government had discovered ninety-five thousand rounds of ammunition in Belfast, and that they had made up their minds at once to issue a proclamation and to seize

the entire of this. He further informed me that they had reason to believe that the next move of Sir Edward Carson would be to hold a review of armed men, and that the Government were determined at any cost to suppress this, and that they would issue any necessary proclamation and use any force necessary for the purpose' (Gwynn, 1932: 237).

16   Compare Jackson, 1998: esp. 193–4, where it is argued that 'Asquith and other members of his Cabinet were in fact convinced of the probable need to deal separately with Ulster'.

Chapter Four *Republicanism in the revolutionary decade*

1   *Hansard,* 5th ser., 37, col. 1702, 30 Apr. 1912.
2   *Irish Freedom,* Jul. 1912.
3   *Irish Freedom,* Oct. 1911.
4   Barton to Archbishop Mannix, n.d. [1921/1922], de Valera papers, University College Dublin (UCD) Archives, P150/568.
5   *Private Sessions of Second Dáil* (Dublin, 1972), p. 255 (17 Dec. 1921).
6   M. W. [?] to Michael Hayes, 7 July 1921, Hayes MSS, UCD Archives, P53/100.
7   John Dillon, diary, 27 Mar. 1922, Dillon papers, Trinity College, Dublin (TCD) Library, MS 6582, p. 181.

Chapter Five *Moderate nationalism, 1918–23*

1   An earlier version of this chapter appeared as 'Moderate nationalism and the Irish revolution 1916–23' in *Historical journal* 42 (3) 1999: 729–49.
2   *Observer,* 18 Mar. 1923, 'The Redmonds' Ireland'.
3   *Observer,* 24 Apr. 1926.
4   *The Irish Times,* 18 Mar. 1916.
5   *Observer,* 26 Apr. 1926.
6   *Weekly Freeman,* 13 Dec. 1919; for Harrison see *The Irish Statesman,* 13 Dec. 1919.
7   *The Witness,* 19 Jun. 1914; Rentoul, 1921: 237.
8   *Weekly Freeman,* 28 Sept. 1917.
9   Phoenix, 1994: 23–7; *Weekly Freeman,* 28 Sept. 1917.
10   *Roscommon Messenger,* 5 Aug. 1921, 'The Peace Movement'. The editorial continues with a phrase which has a precise resonance in the language of the Downing Street Declaration of 1993: 'It was with the false cry of partition that the ferocity of the attack on the Irish Party grew. Partition in real earnest and full operation must now be faced. It is evident from his pronouncements that Mr de Valera is quite prepared to accept it in principle, provided that it comes from an Irish not a British authority.'
11   *Weekly Freeman,* 28 Sept. 1917.
12   Ackerman, 1922a: 437. The material in these articles is broadly confirmed by the notes in Ackerman's diaries held in the Library of Congress, Washington.
13   *Weekly Freeman,* 26 Mar. 1921. The best treatment is Bowman, 1982.

14 *Weekly Freeman,* 19 Jun. 1916; for another prominent Sinn Féin heretic on the partition issue, see Maume, 1998.

15 *Fermanagh Herald,* 8 Sept. 1917.

16 Coogan, 1991: 67. Coogan's account is unsubstantiated in this form elsewhere. Good (1996: 109) does, however, describe the need for a 'recount'. Gearty (1998: 41) acknowledges that 'vote early, vote often' was the Sinn Féin watchword in the election.

17 Colonial Office etc. papers, Public Record Office (PRO), CO 904/24/1. This is the most recently released file on the government's decision-making process.

18 *The Irish Times,* 30 Dec. 1918.

19 *Mayo News,* 4 Jan. 1919.

20 *The Irish Times,* 30 Dec. 1918.

21 *Weekly Freeman's Journal,* 4 Jan. 1919.

22 *Roscommon Herald,* 19 May 1923.

23 *The Irish Times,* 30 Dec. 1918.

24 *Killarney Echo,* 29 Mar. 1919.

25 *Weekly Freeman,* 4 Jan. 1919.

26 *Cork County Eagle,* 4 Jan. 1919.

27 *Weekly Freeman,* 4 Jan. 1919; Carroll, 1993: 98–9.

28 Quoted in *Freeman's Journal,* 18 Jan. 1919.

29 Ibid.

30 For a more evasive analysis see Flynn, 1997. More realistically, see Breen's own account in Younger, 1968: 86: 'The gelignite was only coincidental. We were surprised there were only two of them – we hoped we could take on ten.'

31 *Cork County Eagle* and *Munster Advertiser,* 1 Feb. 1919.

32 *Tipperary Star,* 1 Feb. 1919.

33 *Killarney Echo,* 8 Feb. 1919. But as Foster (1995) points out, this was a controversial claim. Sullivan's father, upon greater acquaintance in later life with the English, regretted his earlier extreme Anglophobic language.

34 Sullivan, 1927: 279–81; *Weekly Freeman,* 17 Jan. 1920, 'Attempt on life of eminent Irish KC: Serjeant Sullivan: Escape'.

35 *Weekly Freeman,* 24 Mar. 1919.

36 Ibid., 29 Mar. 1919.

37 Colonial Office etc. Papers, PRO, CO 904/23/948.

38 Padraig Ó Súilleabháin, *Irish Independent,* 24 Aug. 1922; Stewart, 1997: 102–7, confirms the point.

39 Fanning, 1998: 202–10. This is the conventional wisdom; see Hopkinson, 2002: 178–9, and Costello, 2003. Costello does, however, face up to the negative northern side of the story. For a powerful critique, see Kennedy, 2002.

40 *Western News,* 24 Jan. 1920.

41 Winter, 1955: 301; Colonial Office etc. Papers, PRO, CO 904/156/24.

42 For these events, see *Plain English,* 10 Sept. 1921: 729, and 27 Aug. 1921; *Roscommon Herald,* 30 Apr. 1921; *Plain English,* 27 Aug. 1921: 687; and *Western News,* 18 Jun. 1921.

43 *Weekly Freeman,* 5 Oct. 1920.

44 Healy, 1928, vol. II: 629; F. Daly to Kitty Kiernan, 24 Dec. 1920, in Ó Broin, 1996: 12.

45 *Roscommon Herald,* 11 Sept. 1920.

46 *Weekly Freeman*, 26 Mar. 1921; *Enniscorthy Guardian*, 26 Mar. 1921; McDowell, 1997: 96. In a private communication, Dr Conor Cruise O'Brien has told me that he thinks O'Dempsey may well have been the best man at his parents' wedding.

47 *Roscommon Herald*, 6 Aug. 1921, 'Ireland's parliament, described by a recognised historian'. For a more general account see Kotsonouris, 1994.

48 *Blackwood's Magazine*, 210, 21 Nov. 1921: 623.

49 *The Nation*, 1 May 1920.

50 *The Times*, 7 Jul. 1920.

51 Campbell, 1997: 198. But note Duffy's last hurrah; he was elected to the Dáil in 1927 when Dan Breen, the hero of the revolution, was rejected by the electorate, a fact maliciously noted by Stephen Gwynn; *The Observer*, 19 Jun. 1927.

52 *Young Ireland*, 14 Aug. 1920.

53 *The Irish Statesman*, 1 May 1920 (Taylor, interestingly, was believed to be Catholic by this source); *Weekly Freeman*, 10 Apr. 1920; G. C. Duggan's letter in *The Irish Times*, 5 May 1958; Townshend, 1975: 176.

54 *Young Ireland*, 17 July 1920, shows a sharp awareness on the part of Sinn Féin of the significance of developments.

55 Gilbert, 1977: 1149, Hal Fisher diary, 23 Jul. 1920.

56 *Weekly Freeman*, 20 Aug. 1919.

57 *Nenagh Guardian*, 12 May 1919; Gaynor, 1997: 60.

58 Ackerman, 1922b: 803. Ackerman is probably oversimplifying matters here. In fact, in early 1920 de Valera did not have full confidence in Boland's optimistic assessment of American opinion and by May 1921 de Valera had effectively given up hope of American recognition of the Dáil. See Fanning et al., 1998: 120; Maher, 1998: 141.

59 Colonial Office etc. papers, PRO, CO 904/156/53. This report is the work of 'O' – Brigadier Ormond de L'Epée Winter. Eunan O'Halpin observes: 'Winter may be dismissed as a Micawberish figure, but there is other evidence to suggest that, despite personal rivalries and continuing inefficiencies, what might be termed the continuing bureaucratisation of intelligence slowly bore fruit after 1920'; see O'Halpin, 1998: 73.

60 Pottle, 1998: 131; diary entry for 1 Apr. 1921. In public, of course, the *Irish Bulletin* denied that anything of significance had been found at their office. The very full diary of Childers, held at Trinity College, Dublin, breaks at 24 Mar. 1921 and picks up again at 10 May 1921.

61 Tim Healy to Maurice Healy; Healy, 1928, vol. II: 638. For Collins's unconvincing denial of such meetings, and the controversy surrounding it, see Murphy, 1991: 114–29.

62 Colonial Office etc. Papers, PRO, CO 904/23, no. 53/6094. Collins to de Valera, 18 Jun. 1921. Epitome of document seizure, 22 June 1921, seized at Eamon de Valera's Blackrock home.

63 *Kilkenny People*, 30 Jul. 1921, 'Colonel Archer-Shee MP: anti-Irish bearer of two Kilkenny names'.

64 Reprinted in *Roscommon Herald*, 6 Aug. 1922.

65 *Cork County Eagle*, 29 Apr. 1922. Stephen Gwynn agreed: 'In June 1921, the military strength of Great Britain in Ireland was increasing and the IRA were running short of rifles and ammunition. Sinn Féin had strong military reasons for getting what it could while it could' (Gwynn, 1925: 305).

66 *Sinn Féin*, 8 Apr. 1911.

67 *Atlantic Monthly*, Nov. 1922: 695.

68 *Roscommon Herald,* 29 Sept. 1903.

69 Ibid., 19 May 1923.

70 Duffy to Dillon, 24 May 1923, Dillon Papers, TCD Library, MS 6753/400.

71 Plunkett to Dillon, 11 Jan. 1925, Dillon Papers, TCD Library, MS 6798. For a recent analysis of Plunkett's role, very much in the style of D. P. Moran, see Eagleton, 1995: 100–1.

72 *Weekly Freeman's Journal,* 20 Feb. 1923, 'In philosophic mood: Mr Stephen Gwynn's destruction of history'.

73 See the present author's analysis of the Craig–Collins pact in *The Irish Times,* 31 Mar. 1997: 'The 1922 pact had lessons for closer links with the North'. Gwynn was a strong supporter of the pact, which, he felt, displayed a surprising degree of Ulster unionist moderation. For more detail see Bew, 1999.

74 *Observer,* 29 Apr. 1923.

75 Ibid., 23 Oct. 1923. Gwynn is probably reacting in part to the role of Collins's cousin who worked as a spy in Dublin Castle; Irish unionists suspected that Collins murdered Frank Brooke, a cousin of a later Northern Irish Premier and a member of a Dublin Castle advisory committee 'with his own hand'. See Butler, 1995: 589, entry for 27 Aug. 1922. See also *Weekly Freeman,* 7 Aug. 1920. The diaries of Mark Sturgis, a key figure amongst the Dublin Castle conciliators, described on 27 Jul. 1920 the way in which such violence hindered London's ability to arrange a deal with Sinn Féin: 'Yesterday at about 12.30 Frank Brooke was shot dead in his office – a dirty, cold-blooded senseless murder. London will react badly against anything that looks like truckling now and small blame to them. The only line for peace, which is true, is that the gun man element want to *smash* Dominion Home Rule – they want martial law to get a republic out of the ruins'; Hopkinson, 1999: 15.

76 Garvin to Gwynn, 28 Sept. 1922, Gwynn Papers, National Library of Ireland, MS 8600 (5).

Chapter Six The geopolitics of republican diplomacy in the twentieth century

1 See for example Goren, 1984: 171–2, which lies on the boundary between legitimate scholarship and unsubstantiated generalisation.

2 But see the comments of Robert Chapman, a former CIA Latin America specialist, quoted in Godson, 1980: 149–50, where incidental links between a wide range of terrorist groups are construed as evidence of a single Marxist international revolutionary structure ultimately controlled by the Soviet Union.

3 Hankey diary, 22 May 1918, Hankey Papers, Churchill College Cambridge, HNKY 1/5. Sir Maurice Hankey was Secretary to the Cabinet from 1916 to 1938.

4 Long to Reading, and reply, 17 and 20 May 1918, Balfour Papers, British Library, Add. MS 49741/178–9.

5 'The Security Service: its problems and operational adjustments 1908–1945, Vol. 1 (Chapters I to IV)', March 1946, Security Service records, Public Record Office, London (PRO), KV4/1, p. 22.

6 Undated SIS report passed on to MI5, and [author unknown] (MI5) to Vivian (SIS), 8 Aug. 1933, Security Service records, PRO, KV2/819.

7   Undated SIS report passed on to MI5, and [author unknown] (MI5) to Vivian (SIS), 8 Aug. 1933, Security Service records, PRO, KV2/819.

8   Confidential interview with a former British official who worked on countersubversion in India between 1939 and 1941, and subsequently in MI5, Tipperary, Aug. 2000.

9   The decrypted Comintern/CPGB traffic is in Government Communications Headquarters records, PRO, HW17/1 and 2.

10   'Note of the work of the Irish Section of the Security Service September 1939–1945', Jan. 1946, Security Service records, PRO, KV4/9, cited hereafter as 'Irish Section history'. This has now been published as O'Halpin, 2003.

11   Decode of Lodi Fé (Italian Legation, Dublin) to Foreign Ministry, Rome, 9 Dec. 1935, decoded 14 Dec. 1935, Government Communications Headquarters records, PRO, HW12/198. The decoded message included the following: 'to secure that the IRA should carry out suitable action in the United States I have interviewed its leaders here . . . while it was [? Agreed] that action should be carried on in such way as might be considered best in America [? in agreement with] our agents. With this end a —, suitably chosen, may present himself under the name of BREN— to the [? Lawyer] John T. Ryan living in NEW YORK . . . already [? Advised] by telegraph of the visit of [? Our] nominees.' John T. Ryan of the Irish–American secret society Clan na Gael had been involved in IRA gunrunning in Germany in the 1920s (O'Halpin, 1999: 28).

12   Desmond Morton to Churchill, 29 May 1940, Prime Minister's Office records, PRO, PREM 7/4.

13   Amongst these were the maverick Fianna Fáil backbench TD Dan Breen, who 'cried all day' on news of Hitler's death, the leader of the pre-war Blueshirts and would be Irish *Duce* General O'Duffy, who died in 1944, and the former Cumann na nGaedheal minister J. J. Walsh.

14   In a public exchange with the author in the Rosemount Centre in Derry in October 1984.

15   Interview with Dr Cleveland Cram, formerly of the CIA, Washington, Jan. 1998; confidential interview with a former British official, Aug. 2000, as in note 8 above.

16   Slessor to First Sea Lord, Chief of the Imperial General Staff, and Lt Gen Brownjohn, 2 Dec. 1952, PRO, Dominions Office records, DO 35/3935.

17   See Joint Intelligence Committee report JIC (A) (UWG) 29, 18 Aug. 1969, Prime Minister's Office records, PRO, PREM 13/2844.

18   *Irish Independent*, 15 May 2002.

19   For British concerns about IRA activities to mark the 50th anniversary of the Easter rising see the material in Prime Minister's Office records, PRO, PREM 13/980.

20   Statements of 'James' and 'Julian', opened at the Bloody Sunday Inquiry on 14 June 2000, available www.bloody-sunday-inquiry.org.uk.

21   Speaking under Chatham House rules at a seminar of the Study Group on Intelligence, London, 11 Nov. 1997.

22   Confidential interview with a former intelligence analyst with knowledge of the JIC in that era, in Britain, Dec. 1999.

23   Ibid.

24   See Joint Intelligence Committee report JIC (A) (UWG) 29, 18 Aug. 1969, Prime Minister's Office records, PRO, PREM13/2844.

25   Confidential interview, as in note 8 above.

26   http://www.house.gov/king/petework.html [2003-03-22].

Chapter Seven   Modern unionism and the cult of 1912–14

1   An earlier version of this chapter, incorporating acknowledgements, appeared as 'Unionist myths 1912–1985', in *Past and present*, no. 36, 1992, pp. 164–85.

2   Edward Carson (1854–1935) was leader of the Irish unionist movement between 1910 and 1921; the most accessible full biography is Hyde, 1953; see also Jackson, 1993. James Craig, Viscount Craigavon (1871–1940) was Prime Minister of Northern Ireland between 1921 and 1940; the fullest biography is Ervine, 1949; see also Buckland, 1979.

3   For the legacy of Tone, see Elliott, 1989: 409–19; for a discussion of Pearse's posthumous reputation, see Edwards, 1977: 323–44; on the British dimension, see Pocock, 1975.

4   McGuinness, 1986: 36. McWilliams's painting is reproduced on the cover of the paperback edition of Shea, 1983.

5   See the photographs reproduced in *Belfast News Letter,* 22 and 25 Nov. 1985, 17 Nov. 1986; *Orange Standard,* Jan. 1986; *Shankill Bulletin,* 29 Nov. 1985. For the unionist campaign against the Anglo-Irish agreement see Aughey, 1989, and Cochrane, 1997.

6   See Sayer, 1988: 21, and Jackson, 1990b. For the role of women in the UVF, see Orr, 1987: 19.

7   'Diary of the Gunrunning', 27 Mar. 1914, F. H. Crawford papers, Public Record Office of Northern Ireland, Belfast (PRONI), D1700/5/17/2. See also Blake, 1955: 203. For William Bull's involvement, see PRONI, Bull Papers, D3813, Bull's annotated copy of McNeill's *Ulster's stand for union.* Revisiting this, and other evidence (Jackson, 2003: 132–3), I now think it probable that Bonar Law did in fact meet Crawford in March 1914.

8   Some iconoclastic observers have speculated that Carson was in fact rejecting 'not an inch Ulster': Mc Cormack, 1988: 52.

9   *Belfast News Letter,* 25 Nov. 1985.

10   Ervine, 1949: 181; see also *ibid,* pp. 52–4, for Craig's varied business fortunes. For some comments on the importance of political pageantry, see Cannadine, 1987: 19.

11   For comments on the parallels, see Allister, 1986: 12; *Shankill Bulletin,* 29 Nov. 1985; *Ulster,* Dec. 1985–Jan. 1986: 24–5.

12   Craigavon Diary, 1 Sept. 1912, Lady Craigavon Papers, PRONI, D1415/B/38.

13   Leaflet signed by W. C. Trimble, 24 May 1913, Colonial Office etc. papers, Public Record Office (PRO), CO 904/27/1 (microfilm copy in PRONI).

14   Orr (1987: 17) suggests a total of 827 cars in the UVF.

15   Fanning, 1983: 203. Commemorative ware bearing Carson's image is preserved among James Craig's papers: PRONI, Craigavon Papers, D1415/E/35, china beaker with Carson's likeness.

16   Colonial Office etc. Papers, PRO, CO 904/27/2, conference of businessmen to meet Lord [*sic*] Carson, 23 July 1913, for evidence of poor attendance and poor contributions (microfilm copy in PRONI).

17   Rodner, 1982; Murphy, 1986: 222. Distrust was heartily reciprocated; see Lord Claud Hamilton, n.d., in Walter Long Papers, British Library, Add. MS 62416; see also, significantly, F. E. Smith to Theresa Londonderry, 19 Apr. 1914, Lady Londonderry Papers, PRONI, D2846/1/6/19.

18   Foy, 1988: 187; in particular, the Irish material among the Colonial Office papers in the English Public Record Office at Kew has become much more widely available due to its publication in microform; see *The British in Ireland,* ed. Charles Townshend (Harvester Microfilms, n.p., n.d.).

19 Foy, 1988: 59, suggests that the nature of the locality determined the effectiveness of recruitment. See also R. Hall, o/c 2nd Battalion, South Down UVF, on the Kilkeel Volunteers, 23 Jan. 1914, Kilmorey Papers, PRONI, D1268/3/5; Drill Attendance, Dungannon UVF, Jan.–July 1914, Lowry Papers, PRONI, D1132/6/14; Peel to Lonsdale, 27 Nov. 1913, on the flagging morale of the Armagh UVF, Peel Papers, PRONI, D889/4C/4; UVF order no. 48, 9 May 1914, on failure to attend, J. B. Hamilton Papers, PRONI, D1518/13/8–9; Birrell on Ulster, recognising the problems which the UVF faced, Cabinet Office records, PRO, CAB 37/120, no. 70 (microfilm copy in PRONI). See also Bowman, 2002.

20 O/C '5' to the senior officer, '6', 1 Dec. 1913, sending three infantry manuals and Baden-Powell's *Aids to scouting,* Lowry Papers, PRONI, D1132/6/3.

21 *News Letter,* 25, 27 Apr. 1964.

22 The manifesto is widely printed in the literature of the society; see Lucy, 1989: 99. Its monthly journal is *New Ulster.* See also the file of material on the society in the Linenhall Library, Belfast. For what follows see, in addition, Ingram, 1989; Hume, 1989.

23 See Paulin, 1987, for one view of the relationship between the English ministerial cadre and what Paulin cruelly defines as the 'parasitical' loyalist middle class. The sense of rejection experienced by leading unionists such as the late Harold McCusker in the aftermath of Hillsborough may be compared to Carson's response to the Anglo-Irish Treaty of 1921.

24 *Ulster,* Dec. 1985–Jan. 1986, pp. 17, 24–5; ibid., Apr. 1986, pp. 6–7; Trimble, 1988: 12. See also *Ulster Defiant,* no. 5 (1986); *Belfast News Letter,* 27 Apr. 1964.

25 *Ulster,* Feb. 1987, pp. 6–7. See also ibid., Nov. 1987, pp. 12–13; *Shankill Bull.,* 9 Nov. 1985 (Dennis Godfrey on 'the last great rally').

26 *Orange Standard,* Feb. 1989, p. 4; ibid., Apr. 1989, p. 6; ibid., July 1989, p. 10. The Closing of the Gates is the annual re-enactment of an action by Protestant apprentices during the siege of Derry in 1689 – an event made famous by Macaulay's account. The Sham Fight is a mock duel, fought at Scarva, County Down, between two men representing William III and James II. This may have originated as early as 1835. See Dewar, 1956; Paterson, 1975: 165–7.

27 Killen, 1985: 55. The postcard is also reproduced in *Ulster defiant,* no. 7 (1986); Trimble, 1988: cover.

28 See, for example, *British in Ireland,* ed. Townshend, passim, esp. reels for CO 904/27.

29 Patricia Jalland (1980: 245–7, 261–4) argues, convincingly, that Asquith was threatened by disunity among his own supporters – but she perhaps overestimates the unity of his opponents. Even Fred Crawford paid tribute to the effectiveness of government inertia in the aftermath of Larne; see 'Diary of the gunrunning', f. 129, Crawford Papers, PRONI, D1415/B/34. I have expanded this view of Asquith in Jackson, 2003: 131–2, 137–41.

30 Report from Acting Sergeant Edwards regarding a private meeting of the Standing Committee of the Ulster Unionist Council, 16 May 1913, Colonial Office etc. papers, PRO, CO 904/17/1 (microfilm copy in PRONI).

31 'Diary of the Gunrunning', fo. 34, Crawford Papers, PRONI, D1415/B/34. See also Crawford to Craig, 8 Apr. 1911, fos. 933–4, Crawford Papers, D1700/10/1/1.

32 Stewart, 1967: 117; Spender to the Rev. Brett Ingram, n.d. (1959), on divisions regarding the guns and on Crawford's reputation, Spender Papers, PRONI, D1295,12/lb. See also Hyde, 1953: 61.

33 See, for example, Hyde, 1953: 366, for Carson's emollient reply to Churchill in May 1914; Marjoribanks and Colvin, 1932–6, II: 380, 'nobody supposes that at my age I prefer strife to peace'; Stewart, 1981: 83, 92; Orr, 1987: 29.

34 Foy, 1988: 155, makes the point that the gunrunning accelerated membership.

35 See Stewart, 1967: 90, for Crawford's military career; Ervine, 1949: 59–65, for Craig's military career; Townshend, 1983: 250.

36 See, for example, Birrell's impressions of a visit to Ulster, 4/14, Cabinet Office records, PRO, CAB.37/12, no. 70 (microfilm copy in PRONI). See also n. 19 above.

Chapter Eight   Contemporary republicanism and the strategy of armed struggle

1   Given the existence of several competing strands of the IRA, and the possible winding up of the Provisional IRA, it is necessary to specify the strand being referred to. For the 1980s and 1990s the terms 'Sinn Féin' and 'IRA' always referred to the Provisional movement. If not otherwise specified, this is also the usage here.

2   This assumption is made with a certain trepidation. The one constant in the Northern Ireland situation is its capacity to surprise.

3   I concentrate in this chapter on armed republicanism; I deal briefly with armed loyalism at the end.

4   For a description of Ballymurphy during that period, see de Baróid, 1989.

5   A defining moment occurred very early, when, in March 1971, the IRA lured three members of the Royal Highland Fusiliers from a bar in central Belfast, took them to a remote mountain road and shot them dead. The IRA denied its involvement, but they were widely assumed to be the perpetrators. One way or another, the nature of the conflict was becoming clear (see Moloney, 2002: 97).

6   Richard English (2003: 376–8) stresses the rational and strategic nature of the IRA's campaign.

7   This is not usually acknowledged in respect of unionists. In fact, what frequently appear as failures of unionist strategic thinking owe much more to the limited options their situation affords than to a lack of strategic ability.

8   In fact, the gains were considerable, particularly in respect of equality legislation, the involvement of the government of the Republic in the affairs of Northern Ireland, and the willingness of the British government to withstand the pressure of Northern unionists.

9   For contrasting views of changes in republican discourses in the 1990s, see Todd, 1999; McIntyre, 2001; and Bean, 2002.

10 The most sustained and coherent dissent from Sinn Fein's peace strategy is to be found on Anthony McIntyre's website *The Blanket* (http://lark.phoblacht.net/).

11 'History will record the Provos' armed struggle not as a resurgence of traditional republicanism but as a continuation of the civil rights movement by other, angry, inappropriate means' (*Belfast Telegraph*, 14 Feb. 2002); see also *Belfast Telegraph*, 26 Oct. 2001.

12 For a sample of such themes, see the writings of the *Belfast Telegraph* commentator, Steven King.

13 McCann's reduction of the republican movement of the 1970s and 1980s to little more than a civil rights movement is not convincing, but the question remains as to how the leadership managed the transition to a peaceful strategy while retaining the support of both militants and mass following.

14 For examples, see Lapping, 1985.

15 The exact nature of the concessions made in respect of legitimacy is difficult to pin down. Although the principle of consent is enshrined in the Good Friday Agreement, Sinn Féin is clearly uncomfortable with it and ambiguous about it, and the IRA has made clear that it does not accept it. As far as Sinn Féin is concerned, it is a principle that it is *observing* rather than one that it has embraced. An alternative way of viewing this is to see Sinn Féin making no concession at the level of *foundational* legitimacy, but giving the British government the opportunity to establish its *practical* legitimacy by demonstrating its openness to Irish unity and its commitment to equality and fairness for all.

16 On what this entailed, see in particular Bell, 2000.

Chapter Nine *Contemporary unionism and the tactics of resistance*

1 In this paper the term British is used to describe those living in Great Britain rather than Northern Ireland. This should *not* be taken to imply that there are no British people living in Northern Ireland.

Chapter Ten *The Northern Ireland peace process and the impact of decommissioning*

1 On the general background and on the peace process itself, see Bew and Gillespie, 1996, 1999; Coogan, 1996; de Bréadún, 2001; Mallie and McKittrick, 1996, 2001; and McKittrick and McVea, 2000.

2 The background of the various paramilitary groups and to the armed conflict is discussed in Harnden, 2000; Moloney, 2002; and Taylor, 1997, 1999, 2001. For the perspectives of the major figures involved see Adams, 2001; MacIntyre, 1999 (on Mandelson); Major, 1999; Mitchell, 1999a; and Mowlam, 2002.

3 The Body suggested that decommissioning might begin during the talks as confidence and trust grew between the participants. That did not happen.

4 This communique on 28 November 1995 announced a twin-track process and appointed the International Body.

5 Both the Dáil and Parliament enacted decommissioning legislation in February 1997, which gave authority for a decommissioning commission. But it was not until 26 August 1997 that the Commission was brought into being; see United Kingdom, 1997; Ireland, 1997a.

6 The parties, with their relative strengths as indicated by the number of seats they won in the Forum election of 1996 (which was also designed to give parties a mandate to enter talks) were as follows: UUP (30), DUP (24), SDLP (21), Sinn Féin (17), Alliance Party (7), UKUP (3), Labour, NIWC, PUP and UDP (2 seats each). Sinn Féin was excluded from the talks in June 1996 but admitted in September 1997 after the second IRA ceasefire. The DUP and UKUP left the talks in September 1997.

7 As had been the case with the International Body and the Independent Chairmen, the Commissioners were each provided with an assistant from their own country. To demonstrate

the Commission's independence, its administrative staff was also provided by the same three countries.

8 In Article 3 of the 26 August 1997 agreement setting up the Commission (see British and Irish Governments, 1997), the governments called on it to 'facilitate the decommissioning of firearms, ammunition, explosives and explosive substances (hereinafter referred to as "arms") in accordance with the Report of the International Body, and regulations or amendments made under the Decommissioning Act 1997 and any decommissioning schemes within the meaning of section 1 of the Northern Ireland Arms Decommissioning Act 1997'. The wording of the Irish *Regulations* and the British *Scheme* was essentially the same (see Ireland, 1997b; Northern Ireland Office, 1998b).

9 P. O'Neill, IRA statement of 5 May 2000, *An Phoblacht*, 11 May 2000.

10 P. O'Neill, IRA Statement of 25 Oct. 2000, *An Phoblacht*, 26 Oct. 2000.

11 P. O'Neill, IRA Statement of 14 Mar. 2001, *An Phoblacht*, 16 Mar. 2001.

12 Gavin Jennings, *News Letter*, 19 Oct. 2001: 7.

13 P. O'Neill, IRA Statement of 23 Oct. 2001, *An Phoblacht*, 25 Oct. 2001.

14 Under the terms of the 1998 agreement, the First Minister and Deputy First Minister may only be elected with the support of a majority within both the nationalist and the unionist blocs.

15 The name of the Royal Ulster Constabulary (RUC) had been changed to that of the Police Service of Northern Ireland (PSNI) the previous November.

16 Ian Graham, 'IRA denies involvement in Castlereagh security breach', *Irish Examiner*, 22 Apr. 2002.

17 P. O'Neill, IRA Statement of 8 April 2002, *An Phoblacht*, 11 Apr. 2002.

18 Stephen Dempster and Alan Erwin, 'Disband, give up terror and join SF, Trimble tells IRA members', *News Letter*, 23 Sept. 2002.

19 Roy Garland, 'UPRG may hold loyalists key to moving forward', *Irish News*, 31 Mar. 2003.

20 Dan Keenan, Gerry Moriarty and Mark Brennock, 'Blair urges the IRA to call a halt to all its activities', *The Irish Times*, 18 Oct. 2002. Mr Blair said: 'We cannot carry on with the IRA half in, half out of this process. Not just because it isn't right anymore. It won't work anymore.' The way ahead, he said, lay in 'acts of completion by the governments, nationalists, unionists and paramilitaries'. The Taoiseach welcomed the Prime Minister's statement and 'pledged to work closely with him in achieving the quantum leap forward that is now required'. He added that 'it was time to move on acts of completion'.

21 Thomas Harding, 'Bush urges IRA to seize historic chance', *Daily Telegraph*, 9 Apr. 2003.

22 Gerry Moriarty, 'Blair and Ahern to decide on statement by IRA', *The Irish Times*, 14 Apr. 2003.

23 'Blair seeks answers from the IRA', BBC news, UK ed., 23 Apr. 2003; available http://news.bbc.co.uk/1/hi/northern_ireland/2968905.stm [2003–06–08].

24 'More answers needed from the IRA', BBC news, UK ed., 28 Apr. 2003; available http://news.bbc.co.uk/1/hi/northern_ireland/2981907.stm [2003–06–08].

25 Henry McDonald and Martin Bright, 'IRA in fresh blow to Peace', *The Observer*, 20 Apr. 2003.

26 Adams said: 'The IRA leadership is determined that there will be no activities which will undermine in any way the peace process and the Good Friday Agreement'; Thomas Harding, 'Sinn Fein fails again to give clarity on IRA standing down', *Daily Telegraph*, 1 May 2003.

Subsequently on 6 May, in a public statement, the IRA confirmed that Sinn Fein had accurately expressed the IRA's position. It also confirmed that it had met with the IICD several times recently and that it had been on the point of carrying out a third act to put arms beyond use.

27 Para 13 of the Joint Declaration states: 'Paramilitarism and sectarian violence therefore must be brought to an end, from whichever part of the community they come. We need to see an immediate, full and permanent cessation of all paramilitary activity, including military attacks, training, targeting, intelligence gathering, acquisition or development of arms or weapons, other preparations for terrorist campaigns, punishment beatings and attacks and involvement in riots. Moreover, the practice of exiling must come to an end and the exiled must feel free to return in safety. Similarly, sectarian attacks and intimidation directed at vulnerable communities must cease' (British and Irish Governments, 2003).

28 'Blair postpones NI elections', BBC news, UK ed., 1 May 2003; available http://news.bbc. co.uk/1/hi/northern_ireland/2992949.stm [2003–06–08].

Chapter Eleven   The legacy of political violence in Ireland

Acknowledgement: the author is grateful to Paul Dixon, Ronan Fanning, Tom Garvin, Michael Laffan and Eunan O'Halpin for helpful comments on an earlier draft.

1   Agreement reached in the multi-party negotiations [Good Friday Agreement], 'Declaration of support', article 4; for the text of the Ulster Covenant and the 1916 declaration see appendix 1.

2   The main incident in the rebellion took place in Ballingarry, County Tipperary, where rebels surrounded a house in which police had taken refuge; failure to attack the house because of the presence of children there nipped the rebels' plans in the bud, transforming a potential national revolution into 'the battle of Widow MacCormack's cabbage patch'.

3   The Sinn Féin candidate had been returned unopposed as a Nationalist in 1906, but when he resigned and stood for election under the Sinn Féin label he was defeated by the new Nationalist candidate by a margin of almost three to one.

4   This approach was articulated by de Valera in 1938 and later, and by his successor, Sean Lemass; but it should be noted that in 1941 de Valera expressed a clear preference for neutrality over unity.

5   The song was written in 1907, first published in 1912, and became popular as a marching song of the Irish Volunteers, and later of the national army; the Irish translation by Liam Ó Rinn that is used today was first published in 1927 in a volume containing an introduction by Eamon de Valera (Ó Cuív, 1927).

6   The similarity between early patterns of rioting in Belfast and those that began in 1969 is illustrated vividly in Boyd, 1969.

7   The general sources are: for 1916, Hayes-McCoy, 1969: 303; for 1919–22, Townshend, 1975: 214; for 1922–3, Hopkinson, 1988: 272–3 (this source emphasises the uncertainty over the actual number of deaths especially of civilians during the Civil War); for Northern Ireland, Elliott, 2000: 374. IRA fatalities were calculated from National Graves Association, 1985, which give the following approximate figures: 1916 (89) and 1917 (14), mainly linked to the rising; 1918 (10), 1919 (9), 1920 (252), 1921 (322) and 1922 up to May (26), mainly linked to the War of Independence; and 1922 from June (217), 1923 (185) and 1924 (11), mainly linked to the Civil

War. Of these, the numbers taking place in Northern Ireland were 13 in 1920, 15 in 1921 and 8 in 1922 (to May), with a further 12 from June 1922 to 1924. For other estimates, see O'Leary and McGarry, 1996: 21.

8   The evidence suggests that the planned provisional government would possess the economic, military and political resources necessary for a coup of this kind; see Stewart, 1967.

9   The database used here is that of Malcolm Sutton, generously made available as part of the University of Ulster's Conflict Archive on the Internet (CAIN) project; see cain.ulst.ac.uk/sutton/. This updates the original database to the end of 2001. The analysis in this chapter updates this further, to the end of 2002, using a draft list compiled by Martin Melaugh; see cain.ulst.ac.uk/issues/violence/deaths2002draft.htm. An earlier version, and analysis, appeared in 1994 (Sutton, 1994). Another major collection, using a more inclusive defining criterion, lists a slightly greater number of deaths in each year, and provides the fullest available detail on these (McKittrick et al., 1999; see pp. 15–19 for a discussion of the methods used to identify those included). The methodology lying behind the different databases is discussed in Melaugh, 2003. For statistical analyses of data of these kinds, see Fay, Morrissey and Smyth, 1999 and Smyth, 2000. Ní Aoláin, 2000, undertakes a detailed study of a set of these fatalities.

10   Among the major datasets that formed part of the 'candidate list' were the *Correlates of war* project (281 events, covering the period 1816–1992; see Singer and Small, 1982; the current version of the dataset may be downloaded from www.umich.edu/~cowproj/dataset.html) and the *Minorities at risk* dataset (340 groups, covering the period 1940–98; see Gurr et al., 1993; the current version of the dataset may be downloaded from www.cidcm.umd.edu/inscr/mar/ [2002–07–10]). For other overviews, see Eck, 2003; Jongman, 2002; Gurr, Marshall and Khosla, 2001; and HIIK, 2002. The last two of these provide valuable qualitative summaries of the current position case by case; and Balencie and de La Grange (1999) provide much more extensive case descriptions.

11   Catholics were also prepared occasionally to lend their votes to more radical voices, as in the UK general election of 1955, when two Sinn Féin MPs were returned from border constituencies.

12   The agreement reached on 6–9 December 1973 between the British and Irish governments and the parties which had agreed to participate in a new power-sharing executive in Northern Ireland provided for the establishment of a Council of Ireland to link North and South, and was a prerequisite to the assumption of office of the executive on 1 January 1974. Its name derived from the location where the talks took place, at the civil service college in Sunningdale, England.

References

Ackerman, Carl W. (1922a) 'Ireland from a Scotland Yard notebook', *Atlantic monthly*, Apr.: 437.

Ackerman, Carl W. (1922b) 'Janus-headed Ireland', *Atlantic monthly*, June.

Adams, Gerry (1986) *The politics of Irish freedom*. Dingle: Brandon.

Adams, Gerry (2001) *An Irish journal*. Dingle: Brandon.

Adgey, R. J. (n. d.) *Arming the Ulster Volunteers*. Belfast: the author.

Allister, Jim (1986) *Anglo-Irish betrayal: what choice for loyal Ulster?* Carrick: n. p.

Andrew, Christopher and Vasili Mitrovkhin (2000) *The Mitrovkhin archive: the KGB in Europe and the west*. London: Allen Lane.

Andrews, C. S. (1982) *Man of no property: an autobiography*, vol. 2. Dublin: Mercier.

Arthur, Paul (1997) '"Reading" violence: Ireland', pp. 234–91 in David E. Apter (ed.), *The legitimisation of violence*. Basingstoke: Macmillan, in association with UNRISD.

Asquith, H. H. (1982) *Letters to Venetia Stanley*, ed. Michael and Eleanor Brock. Oxford: Oxford University Press.

Aughey, Arthur (1989) *Under siege: Ulster unionism and the Anglo-Irish Agreement*. Belfast: Blackstaff.

Augusteijn, Joost (1996) *From public defiance to guerrilla warfare: the experience of ordinary volunteers in the Irish war of independence*. Dublin: Irish Academic Press.

Augusteijn, Joost, ed. (2002) *The Irish revolution 1913–23*. Basingstoke: Palgrave.

Balencie, Jean-Marc and Arnaud de La Grange (1999) *Mondes rebelles: guerres civiles et violences politiques*. Rev. edn. Paris: Éditions Michalon.

Bardon, Jonathan (1992) *A history of Ulster*. Belfast: Blackstaff.

Bartlett, Thomas (1992) *The fall and rise of the Irish nation: the Catholic question, 1690–1830*. Dublin: Gill & Macmillan.

Bartlett, Thomas (1996) 'Defence, counter-insurgency and rebellion: Ireland, 1792–1803', pp. 247–93 in Bartlett and Jeffery, 1996.

Bartlett, Thomas and Keith Jeffery, eds (1996) *A military history of Ireland*. Cambridge: Cambridge University Press.

Barton, Sir Dunbar Plunket (1933) *Timothy Healy: memories and anecdotes*. Dublin: Talbot Press; London: Faber & Faber.

Beames, M. R. (1987) 'Rural conflict in pre-famine Ireland: peasant assassinations in Tipperary, 1837–1847', in Philpin, 1987: 264–83.

Bean, K. (2002) 'Defining republicanism: shifting discourse of new nationalism and post-republicanism', pp. 129–42 in Elliott, 2002.

Beckett, I. (2001) *The encyclopedia of guerrilla warfare*. New York: Facts on File.

Bell, J. Bowyer (1997) *The secret army: the IRA*. 3rd edn. New Brunswick, NJ: Transaction Publishers.

Bell, J. Bowyer (2000) *The IRA, 1968–2000: analysis of a secret army*. London: Frank Cass.

Bew, Paul (1978) *Land and the national question in Ireland, 1858–82*. Dublin: Gill & Macmillan.

Bew, Paul (1987) *Conflict and conciliation in Ireland, 1890–1910: Parnellites and radical agrarians*. Oxford: Clarendon.

Bew, Paul (1991) 'Parnell and Davitt', in Boyce and O'Day, 1991: 38–51.

Bew, Paul (1994) *Ideology and the Irish question: Ulster unionism and Irish nationalism, 1912–1916*. Oxford: Clarendon.

Bew, Paul (1996) *John Redmond*. Dundalk: Dundalgan Press, for the Historical Association of Ireland.

Bew, Paul (1997) 'Collins and Adams, L. G. and Blair', *The Spectator*, 31 May: 18–20.

Bew, Paul (1999) 'The political history of Northern Ireland since partition: the prospects for North-South cooperation', pp. 401–18 in Anthony F. Heath, Richard Breen and Christopher T. Whelan (eds), *Ireland north and south: perspectives from social science*. Oxford: Oxford University Press for the British Academy.

Bew, Paul and Gordon Gillespie (1996) *The Northern Ireland peace process 1993–1996: a chronology*. London: Serif.

Bew, Paul and Gordon Gillespie (1999) *Northern Ireland: a chronology of the troubles 1968–1999*. Dublin: Gill & Macmillan.

Bew, Paul, Peter Gibbon and Henry Patterson (1979) *The state in Northern Ireland 1921–72: political forces and social classes*. Manchester: Manchester University Press.

Bew, Paul, Peter Gibbon and Henry Patterson (1995) *Northern Ireland 1921–94: political forces and social classes*. London: Serif.

Blake, Robert (1955) *The unknown prime minister: the life and times of Andrew Bonar Law, 1858–1923*. London: Eyre & Spottiswoode.

Bowman, John (1982) *De Valera and the Ulster question, 1917–1973*. Oxford: Clarendon.

Bowman, Timothy (2002) 'The Ulster Volunteers, 1913–1914: force or farce', *History Ireland* 10 (1): 43–7.

Boyce, D. George (1992) *Ireland, 1828–1923: from ascendancy to democracy*. Oxford: Blackwell.

Boyce, D. George and Alan O'Day, eds (1991) *Parnell in perspective*. London and New York: Routledge.

Boyd, Andrew (1969) *Holy war in Belfast*. Tralee: Anvil Books.

Bradshaw, Brendan (1989) 'Nationalism and historical scholarship in modern Ireland', *Irish historical studies* 26 (104): 329–51.

Bric, Maurice J. (1985) 'The Whiteboy movement, 1760–1780', in Nolan and Whelan, 1985: 148–84.

Bric, Maurice J. (1986) 'The tithe system in eighteenth-century Ireland', *Proceedings of the Royal Irish Academy*, C, 86 (7): 271–88.

Bric, Maurice J. (1987) 'Priests, parsons and politics: the Rightboy protest in County Cork, 1785–1788', in Philpin, 1987: 163–90.

Bric, Maurice J. (2003) 'Ireland and colonial America: the viewer and the viewed', pp. 132–54 in Howard Clarke and Judith Devlin (eds), *European encounters*. Dublin: UCD Press.

British and Irish Governments (1995) *Joint communiqué, 28 November 1995. Twin-track process to make parallel progress on decomissioning and all-party negotiations*. London: Downing St; also available http://www.cain.ulst.ac.uk/events/peace/docs/com281195.htm [2003–06–08].

British and Irish Governments (1997) *Agreement between the Government of Ireland and the Government of the United Kingdom establishing the Independent International Commission on Decommissioning, 26 August 1997*. Belfast: Northern Ireland Office; Dublin: Department of Foreign Affairs; also available http://www.irlgov.ie/iveagh/information/display. asp?ID=302 [2003–06–08].

British and Irish Governments (2001) *Implementation of the Good Friday agreement* [Weston Park document; letter to party leaders, 1 August 2001, containing 'Proposals by the two governments']. Belfast: Northern Ireland Office; Dublin: Department of Foreign Affairs; also available http://www.nio.gov.uk/pdf/proposals0108.pdf [2003–06–08].

British and Irish Governments (2003) *Joint declaration by the British and Irish governments, April 2003.* Belfast: Northern Ireland Office; Dublin: Department of Foreign Affairs; also available http://www.nio.gov.uk/pdf/joint2003.pdf [2003–06–08].

Brown, Terence (1988) *Ireland's literature: selected essays.* Mullingar: Lilliput.

Brown, Thomas N. (1966) *Irish-American nationalism.* Philadelphia and New York: Lippincott.

Bruce, Steve (1986) *God Save Ulster: the religion and politics of Paisleyism.* Oxford: Oxford University Press.

Bruce, Steve (1994) *The edge of the union: the Ulster loyalist political vision.* Oxford: Oxford University Press.

Buckland, Patrick (1973) *Irish unionism: two: Ulster unionism and the origins of Northern Ireland, 1886–1922.* Dublin: Gill & Macmillan.

Buckland, Patrick (1979) *The factory of grievances: devolved government in Northern Ireland, 1921–1939.* Dublin: Gill & Macmillan.

Butler, John, ed. (1995) 'Lord Oranmore's journal', *Irish historical studies* 29 (116): 553–93.

Cairns, David and Shaun Richards (1988) *Writing Ireland: colonialism, nationalism and culture.* Manchester: Manchester University Press.

Callanan, Frank (1996) *T. M. Healy.* Cork: Cork University Press.

Campbell, Fergus (1997) 'Land and politics in the west of Ireland, 1898–1909'. PhD thesis, University of Bristol.

Campbell, Keith (1986) *ANC: a Soviet task force?* London: Institute for the Study of Terrorism.

Cannadine, David (1987) 'Introduction: divine rites of kings', pp. 1–19 in David Cannadine and Simon Price (eds), *Rituals of royalty: power and ceremonial in traditional societies.* Cambridge: Cambridge University Press.

Canny, Nicholas (2001) *Making Ireland British 1580–1650.* Oxford: Oxford University Press.

Carroll, Dennis (1993) *They have fooled you again: Michael O'Flanagan, 1876–1942: priest, republican, social critic.* Blackrock: Columba.

Churchill, Randolph S. (1966) *Winston S. Churchill – vol. 1: youth.* London: Heinemann.

Churchill, Randolph S. (1969) *Winston S. Churchill – vol. 2: companion, part 3.* London: Heinemann.

Churchill, Winston S. (1907) *Lord Randolph Churchill.* London: Macmillan.

Coakley, John (2002) 'Conclusion: new strains of unionism and nationalism', pp. 132–54 in John Coakley (ed.), *Changing shades of orange and green: redefining the union and the nation in contemporary Ireland.* Dublin: UCD Press.

Cochrane, Feargal (1997) *Unionist politics and the politics of unionism since the Anglo-Irish agreement.* Cork: Cork University Press.

Comerford, R. V. (1985) *The Fenians in context: Irish politics and society, 1848–1882.* Dublin: Wolfhound.

Comerford, R. V. (2003) 'Republicans and democracy in modern Irish politics', in McGarry, 2003: 8–22.

Coogan, Tim Pat (1991) *Michael Collins: a biography.* London: Arrow.

Coogan, Tim Pat (1996) *The troubles: Ireland's ordeal 1966–1996 and the search for peace.* New edn. London: Arrow.

Cooke, Alistair B. and John Vincent (1974) *The governing passion: cabinet government and party politics in Britain, 1885–86*. Brighton: Harvester.

Costello, Francis J. (2003) *The Irish revolution and its aftermath 1916–23*. Dublin: Irish Academic Press.

Costello, Francis J., ed. (1997) *Michael Collins in his own words*. Dublin: Gill & Macmillan.

Cox, Michael, Adrian Guelke and Fiona Stephen, eds (2000) *A farewell to arms? From "long war" to long peace in Northern Ireland*. Manchester: Manchester University Press.

Crawford, F. H. (1947) *Guns for Ulster*. Belfast: Graham & Heslip.

Crossman, Virginia (1996) *Politics, law and order in nineteenth-century Ireland*. Dublin: Gill & Macmillan.

Curtin, Nancy (1994) *The United Irishmen: popular politics in Ulster and Dublin, 1791–1798*. Oxford: Clarendon.

Curtis, L. P. (1963) *Coercion and conciliation in Ireland, 1880–92: a study in conservative unionism*. Princeton: Princeton University Press.

Dangerfield, George (1966) *The strange death of liberal England*. London: Macgibbon & Kee [first edn 1935].

Davis, Richard P. (1987) *The Young Ireland movement*. Dublin: Gill & Macmillan.

Dawe, Gerald (1985) *The Lundys letter*. Dublin: Gallery Press.

De Baróid, Ciarán (1989) *Ballymurphy and the Irish war*. Dublin: Aisling.

De Bréadún, Deaglán (2001) *The far side of revenge*. Cork: Collins Press.

De Búrca, Marcus (1980) *The GAA: a history*. Dublin: Cumann Lúthchleas Gael.

Dewar, M. (1956) *The Scarva story*. Portadown: Portadown News.

Dickson, David, Dáire Keogh and Kevin Whelan, eds (1993) *The United Irishmen: republicanism, radicalism and rebellion*. Dublin: Lilliput.

Dickson, R. J. (1966) *Ulster emigration to colonial America, 1718–1875*. London: Routledge & Kegan Paul.

Dixon, Paul (1995a) '"A house divided cannot stand": Britain, bipartisanship and Northern Ireland', *Contemporary record* 9 (1): 147–87.

Dixon, Paul (1995b) 'Internationalization and unionist isolation: a response to Feargal Cochrane', *Political studies* 43 (3): 497–505.

Dixon, Paul (1996) 'The politics of antagonism: explaining McGarry and O'Leary', *Irish political studies* 11: 130–41.

Dixon, Paul (2001a) 'British policy towards Northern Ireland 1969–2000: continuity, tactical adjustment and consistent "inconsistencies"', *British journal of politics and international relations* 3 (3): 340–68.

Dixon, Paul (2001b) *Northern Ireland: the politics of war and peace*. Basingstoke: Palgrave .

Dixon, Paul (2002a) 'Northern Ireland and the international dimension: the end of the cold war, the USA and European integration', *Irish studies in international affairs* 13: 105–20.

Dixon, Paul (2002b) 'Political skills or lying and manipulation? The choreography of the Northern Ireland peace process', *Political studies* 50 (3): 725–41.

Dixon, Paul (2004) '"Peace within the realms of the possible?" David Trimble, unionist idology and theatrical politics', *Terrorism and political violence* 15(3).

Doherty, Gabriel, and Dermot Keogh, eds (1998) *Michael Collins and the making of the Irish state*. Cork: Mercier.

Donnelly, James S., Jr (1983), 'Pastorini and Captain Rock: millenarianism and sectarianism in the Rockite movement of 1821–4', pp. 102–42 in Samuel Clark and James S. Donnelly, Jr (eds), *Irish peasants: violence and political unrest, 1780–1914*. Madison: University of Wisconsin Press.

Dumbrell, John (2000) 'Hope and history: the US and peace in Northern Ireland', pp. 214–22 in Cox, Guelke and Stephens, 2000.

Eagleton, Terry (1995) 'Ascendancy and hegemony', pp. 27–103 in *Heathcliff and the great hunger: studies in Irish culture*. London: Verso.

Eck, Kristine (2003) Conflict dataset catalog. Uppsala: Department of Peace and Conflict Research, University of Uppsala; available www.pcr.uu.se/pdf/conflictdataset2.pdf [2003–05–27].

Edwards, Ruth Dudley (1977) *Patrick Pearse: the triumph of failure*. London: Victor Gollancz.

Elliott, Marianne (1989) *Wolfe Tone: prophet of Irish independence*. New Haven, CT: Yale University Press.

Elliott, Marianne (2000) *The Catholics of Ulster: a history*. London: Penguin.

Elliott, Marianne, ed. (2002) *The long road to peace in Northern Ireland: peace lectures from the Institute of Irish Studies at Liverpool University*. Liverpool: Liverpool University Press.

Elliott, Sydney and W. D. Flackes (1999) *Northern Ireland: a political directory 1968–99*. Belfast: Blackstaff.

Emmet, Thomas Addis (1915) *Memoir of Thomas Addis and Robert Emmet*. 2 vols. New York: Emmet Press.

English, Richard (2003) *Armed struggle: the history of the IRA*. London: Macmillan.

Ensor, R. C. K. (1936) *England 1870–1914*. Oxford: Clarendon.

Ervine, St John G. (1949) *Craigavon: Ulsterman*. London: Allen & Unwin.

Esher, Oliver, Viscount, ed. (1938) *Journals and letters of Reginald Viscount Esher: Vol. 3 1910–1913*. London: Nicholson & Watson.

Fanning, Ronan (1979) 'The Irish policy of Asquith's government and the cabinet crisis of 1910', pp. 279–303 in Art Cosgrove and Donal McCartney (eds), *Studies in Irish history presented to R. Dudley Edwards*. Dublin: University College Dublin.

Fanning, Ronan (1983) *Independent Ireland*. Dublin: Helicon.

Fanning, Ronan (1989) 'Britain, Ireland and the end of the union', pp. 105–20 in *Ireland after the Union: proceedings of the second joint meeting of the Royal Irish Academy and the British Academy*. Oxford: Oxford University Press.

Fanning, Ronan (1998) 'Michael Collins: an overview', pp. 202–10 in Doherty and Keogh, 1998.

Fanning, Ronan, Michael Kennedy, Dermot Keogh and Eunan O'Halpin, eds (1998) *Documents on Irish foreign policy volume I: 1919–1922*. Dublin: Royal Irish Academy.

Farrell, Michael (1976) *Northern Ireland: the orange state*. London: Pluto.

Farren, Sean and Robert F. Mulvihill (2000) *Paths to a settlement in Northern Ireland*. Gerrards Cross: Colin Smythe.

Fay, Marie-Therese, Mike Morrissey and Marie Smyth (1999) *Northern Ireland's troubles: the human costs*. London: Pluto.

Feeney, B. (2002) *Sinn Féin: a hundred turbulent years*. Dublin: O'Brien.

Fitzpatrick, David (1996) 'Militarism in Ireland, 1900–1922', pp. 379–406 in Bartlett and Jeffery, 1996.

Flynn, Kevin Haddick (1997) 'Soloheadbeg: what really happened?', *History Ireland* 5 (1): 43–6.

Foster, Roy (1995) *The story of Ireland: an inaugural lecture delivered before the University of Oxford on 1 December 1994.* Oxford: Clarendon.

Foy, Michael (1988) 'The Ulster Volunteer Force: its domestic development and political importance in the period 1913–20'. PhD thesis, Queen's University, Belfast.

Froude, James Anthony (1872–4) *The English in Ireland in the eighteenth century.* 3 vols. London: Longmans.

Garvin, Tom (1981) *The evolution of Irish nationalist politics.* Dublin: Gill & Macmillan.

Garvin, Tom (1987), 'Defenders, Ribbonmen and others: underground political networks in pre-famine Ireland', in Philpin, 1987: 219–44.

Garvin, Tom (1996) *1922: the birth of Irish democracy.* Dublin: Gill & Macmillan.

Gaynor, Rev Patrick (1997) 'The Sinn Féin ard fheis of 1917: a North Tipperary priest's account', *Tipperary historical journal* 10: 60–4.

Gearty, Margot (1998) 'Michael Collins: the Granard connection', pp. 38–44 in Doherty and Keogh, 1998.

Geary, Lawrence M. (1986), *The Plan of Campaign, 1886–1891.* Cork: Cork University Press.

Geoghegan, Patrick M. (2002) *Robert Emmet: a life.* Dublin: Gill & Macmillan.

Gilbert, Martin (1977) *Winston S. Churchill: vol. 4: companion, part 2: documents July 1919 – March 1921.* London: Heinemann.

Gleditsch, Nils Petter, Peter Wallensteen, Mikael Eriksson, Margareta Sollenberg and Håvard Strand (2002) 'Armed conflict 1946–2001: a new dataset', *Journal of peace research* 39 (5): 615–37.

Godson, Roy, ed. (1980) *Intelligence requirements for the 1980s: counterintelligence.* Lexington, MA: Lexington Books.

Good, Joe (1996) *Enchanted by dreams: the journal of a revolutionary*, ed. Maurice Good. Dingle: Brandon.

Gordon, David (1989) *The O'Neill years: unionist politics, 1963–1969.* Belfast: Athol Books.

Goren, Roberta (1984) *The Soviet Union and terrorism.* London: Allen & Unwin.

Grigg, John (1978) *Lloyd George: the people's champion, 1902–1911.* London: Eyre Methuen.

Grote, Georg (1994) *Torn between politics and culture: the Gaelic League 1893–1993.* Münster and New York: Waxmann.

Gurr, Ted Robert, Monty G. Marshall and Deepa Khosla (2001) *Peace and conflict 2001: a global survey of armed conflicts, self-determination movements, and democracy.* College Park, MD: Center for International Development and Conflict Management.

Gurr, Ted Robert, with Barbara Harff, Monty G. Marshall and James R. Scarritt (1993) *Minorities at risk: a global view of ethnopolitical conflicts.* Washington, DC: United States Institute of Peace.

Gwynn, Denis (1932) *The life of John Redmond.* London: G. G. Harrap.

Gwynn, Stephen (1911) *The case for home rule.* Dublin: Maunsel.

Gwynn, Stephen (1919) *John Redmond's last years.* London: Edward Arnold.

Gwynn, Stephen (1921) *The Irish situation.* London: Jonathan Cape.

Gwynn, Stephen (1925) *A student's history of Ireland.* Dublin and Cork: Talbot Press.

Haines, Joe (1977) *The politics of power.* London: Jonathan Cape.

Hamill, Desmond (1985) *Pig in the middle: the army in Northern Ireland 1969–84.* London: Methuen.

Hanley, Brian (2002) *The IRA, 1926–1936*. Dublin: Four Courts Press.

Harnden, Toby (2000) *Bandit country: the IRA and South Armagh*. London. Hodder & Stoughton.

Harrison, Richard S. (1993) *Richard Davis Webb: Dublin Quaker printer (1805–72)*. Skibbereen: the author.

Hart, Peter (1996) 'The Protestant experience of revolution in southern Ireland', pp. 81–98 in Richard English and Graham Walker, eds, *Unionism in modern Ireland: new perspectives on politics and culture*. London: Macmillan.

Hart, Peter (1997) 'The geography of revolution in Ireland, 1917–23', *Past and present* 155: 142–76.

Hart, Peter, ed. (2002) *British intelligence in Ireland*. Cork: Cork University Press.

Hart, Peter (2003) 'Paramilitary politics and the Irish revolution', in McGarry, 2003: 23–41.

Hartman, Todd (2003) 'Taking the gun out of Irish politics: framing the peace process'. Paper presented at the 44th annual International Studies Association convention, Portland, OR, 25 Feb.–1 Mar.

Hayes-McCoy, G. A. (1969) 'A military history of the 1916 rising', pp. 255–338 in Nowlan, 1969.

Headlam, M. (1947) *Irish reminiscences*. London: Robert Hale.

Healy, Tim (1928) *Letters and leaders of my day*. London: Thornton Butterworth.

Hepburn, A. C., ed. (1998) *Ireland, 1905–25: vol. 2: documents and analysis*. Newtownards: Colourpoint Books.

HIIK (2002) *Conflict barometer 2002: 11th annual conflict analysis*. Heidelberg: Heidelberg Institute on International Conflict Research, University of Heidelberg; available www. hiik.de/en/conflictbarometer_2002. pdf [2003–05–28].

Hobhouse, Charles (1977) *Inside Asquith's cabinet: from the diaries of Charles Hobhouse*, ed. Edward David Hobhouse. London: J. Murray.

Hobsbawm, Eric (1983a) 'Introduction', pp. 1–14 in Hobsbawm and Ranger, 1983c.

Hobsbawm, Eric (1983b) 'Mass-producing tradition: Europe, 1870–1914', pp. 263–307 in Hobsbawm and Ranger, 1983c.

Hobsbawm, Eric (1997) *On history*. London: Weidenfeld & Nicolson.

Hobsbawm, Eric and Terence Ranger, eds (1983) *The invention of tradition*. Cambridge: Cambridge University Press.

Hogan, Robert (1996) *Dictionary of Irish literature*. Rev. edn. Westport, CT: Greenwood.

Holroyd, Michael (1988–92) *Bernard Shaw*. 5 vols. London: Chatto & Windus.

Hopkinson, Michael (1988) *Green against green: the Irish civil war*. Dublin: Gill & Macmillan.

Hopkinson, Michael (2002) *The Irish war of independence*. Dublin: Gill & Macmillan.

Hopkinson, Michael, ed. (1999) *The last days of Dublin Castle: the Mark Sturgis diaries*. Dublin: Irish Academic Press.

Hume, David (1989) *'For Ulster and her freedom': the story of the April 1914 gunrunning*. Lurgan: Ulster Society.

Hyde, H. Montgomery (1953) *Carson: the life of Sir Edward Carson, Lord Carson of Duncairn*. London: Heinemann.

IBDA (International Body on the Decommissioning of Arms) (1996) *Report of the International Body 22 January 1996 [Mitchell report]*. Belfast; Dublin: The International Body; also available http://www.nio.gov.uk/issues/agreelinks/ptalks/mitchrpt.htm [2003–06–08].

IICD (Independent International Commission on Decommissioning) (1999–2003) *Reports* [to the British and Irish Governments]. Belfast, Dublin: IICD, various dates; also available http://www.nio.gov.uk/azlist.htm [2003–06–08].

Ingram, Brett (1989) *Covenant and challenge: reflections on Ulster's identity*. Lurgan: New Ulster on behalf of the Ulster Historical Society.

Ireland (1997a) *Decommissioning Act 1997, Number 3 of 1997, 26 February 1997*. Dublin: Stationery Office; also available http://www.irishstatutebook.ie/ZZA3Y1997.html [2003–06–08].

Ireland (1997b) *Decommissioning Act, 1997 (Independent International Commission on Decommissioning) regulations, 1997*. Statutory Instrument No. 400/1997. Dublin: Stationery Office; also available http://www.irishstatutebook.ie/ZZSI400Y1997.html [2003–06–08].

Irvin, Cynthia L. (1999) *Militant nationalism: between movement and party in Ireland and the Basque Country*. Minneapolis, MN: University of Minnesota Press.

Jackson, Alvin (1987) 'Irish unionism and the Russellite threat, 1894–1906', *Irish historical studies* 25 (100): 376–404.

Jackson, Alvin (1989a) *The Ulster party: Irish Unionists in the House of Commons, 1884–1911*. Oxford: Clarendon.

Jackson, Alvin (1989b) 'Unionist history (i)', *Irish review* 7: 58–66.

Jackson, Alvin (1990a) 'Unionist history (ii)', *Irish review* 8: 62–9.

Jackson, Alvin (1990b) 'Unionist politics and Protestant society in Edwardian Ireland', *Historical journal* 33: 839–66.

Jackson, Alvin (1993) *Sir Edward Carson*. Dublin: Historical Association of Ireland.

Jackson, Alvin (1995) *Colonel Edward Saunderson: land and loyalty in Victorian Ireland*. Oxford: Clarendon.

Jackson, Alvin (1998) 'British Ireland: what if home rule had been enacted in 1912?', pp. 175–227 in Niall Ferguson (ed.), *Virtual history: alternatives and counterfactuals*. London: Picador.

Jackson, Alvin (1999) *Ireland 1798–1998*. Oxford: Blackwell.

Jackson, Alvin (2003) *Home rule: an Irish history 1800–2000*. London: Weidenfeld & Nicolson.

Jalland, Patricia (1976) 'A Liberal Chief Secretary and the Irish question: Augustine Birrell, 1907–1914', *Historical journal* 19 (2): 421–51.

Jalland, Patricia (1980) *The Liberals and Ireland: the Ulster question in British politics to 1914*. Brighton: Harvester.

James, Robert Rhodes (1963) *Rosebery: a biography of Archibald Philip, fifth earl of Rosebery*. London: Weidenfeld & Nicolson.

Jenkins, Roy (1964) *Asquith*. London: Collins.

Jennings, Sir Ivor (1956) *The approach to self-government*. Cambridge: Cambridge University Press.

Jones, Greta (1997) 'Catholicism, nationalism and science', *Irish review* 20: 47–52.

Jones, Thomas (1971) *Whitehall diary: vol. 3: Ireland 1918–25*. ed. Keith Middlemas. London: Oxford University Press.

Jongman, Albert J. (2002) *World conflict and human rights map 2001–02*. Leiden: PIOOM, Leiden University; available www.goalsforamericans.org/publications/pioom/atf_world_conf_map.pdf [2003–05–27].

Kearney, Peadar (1928) *The soldier's song and other poems.* Dublin: Talbot Press.

Kee, Robert (1989) *The green flag: vol. 3: ourselves alone.* London: Penguin.

Kennedy, Liam (2002) 'Was there an Irish war of independence?', pp. 188–229 in Bruce Stewart (ed.), *Hearts and minds: Irish culture and society under the Act of Union.* London: Colin Smythe, for Princess Grace Irish Library, Monaco.

Kenny, Anthony (1986) *The road to Hillsborough.* Oxford: Pergamon.

Kiberd, Declan (1995) *Inventing Ireland.* London: Jonathan Cape.

Killen, John (1985) *John Bull's famous circus: Ulster history through the postcard, 1905–1985.* Dublin: O'Brien.

Kinghan, Nancy (1975) *United we stood: the official history of the Ulster Women's Unionist Council, 1911–1973.* Belfast: Appletree.

Kostick, Conor (1996) *Revolution in Ireland: popular militancy, 1917–1923.* London: Pluto.

Kotsonouris, Mary (1994) *Retreat from revolution: the Dáil courts, 1920–24.* Dublin: Irish Academic Press.

Laffan, Michael (1999) *The resurrection of Ireland: the Sinn Féin party, 1916–1923.* Cambridge: Cambridge University Press.

Lapping, B. (1985) *End of empire.* New York: St Martin's Press.

Larkin, Emmet (1972) 'The devotional revolution in Ireland', *American historical review* 77: 625–52.

Lawlor, Sheila. (1983) *Britain and Ireland, 1914–1923.* Dublin: Gill & Macmillan.

Lee, Joe (1973) *The modernisation of Irish society 1848–1918.* Dublin: Gill & Macmillan.

Loftus, Belinda (1990) *Mirrors: William III and Mother Ireland.* Dundrum, Co. Down: Picture Press.

Longford, Earl of and Thomas P. O'Neill (1970) *Eamon de Valera.* Dublin: Gill & Macmillan.

Lucy, Gordon (1989) *The Ulster Covenant: a pictorial history of the 1912 home rule crisis.* Lurgan: New Ulster for the Ulster Historical Society.

Lyons, F. S. L. (1968) *John Dillon: a biography.* London: Routledge & Kegan Paul.

Lyons, F. S. L. (1969) 'The two faces of home rule', pp. 99–124 in Nowlan, 1969.

Lyons, F. S. L. (1977) *Charles Stewart Parnell.* London: Collins.

Lyttle, Carl (1988) 'The development of political wall murals in Northern Ireland'. Unpublished HND thesis; copy in Linenhall Library.

McBride, I. R. (1998) *Scripture politics: Ulster Presbyterians and Irish radicalism in the late eighteenth century.* Oxford: Clarendon Press.

McBride, Lawrence W. (1991) *The greening of Dublin Castle: the transformation of bureaucratic and judicial personnel in Ireland, 1892–1922.* Washington, DC: Catholic University of America Press.

McCaffrey, Lawrence J. (1968) *The Irish question: two centuries of conflict.* Lexington: University of Kentucky Press.

McCartney, Donal (1984) 'The changing image of O'Connell', pp. 19–31 in K. B. Nowlan and Maurice R. O'Connell, eds, *Daniel O'Connell: portrait of a radical.* Belfast: Appletree.

Mc Cormack, W. J. (1988) *Battle of the books: two decades of Irish cultural debate.* Mullingar: Lilliput.

McCracken, J. L. (1971) *The Irish Parliament in the eighteenth century.* Dundalk: Dundalgan Press.

MacDonagh, Donagh (1945) 'Ballingarry', pp. 57–60 in M. J. MacManus (ed.), *Thomas Davis and Young Ireland.* Dublin: Stationery Office.

McDonald, Henry (2000) *Trimble*. London: Bloomsbury.

McDowell, R. B. (1979), *Ireland in the age of imperialism and revolution, 1760–1801*. Oxford: Clarendon.

McDowell, R. B. (1997) *Crisis and decline: the fate of the southern unionists*. Dublin: Lilliput.

McGarry, Fearghal, ed. (2003) *Republicanism in modern Ireland*. Dublin: UCD Press.

McGrath, Thomas (1999) *Religious renewal and reform in the pastoral ministry of Bishop James Doyle*. Dublin: Four Courts Press.

McGuinness, Frank (1986) *Observe the sons of Ulster marching towards the Somme*. London: Faber.

McIntosh, Gillian V. (1999) *The force of culture: unionist identities in twentieth century Ireland*. Cork: Cork University Press.

McIntyre, A. (2001) 'Modern Irish republicanism and the Belfast Agreement: chickens coming home to roost, or turkeys celebrating Christmas?', pp. 202–22 in R. Wilford (ed.), *Aspects of the Belfast Agreement*. Oxford: Oxford University Press.

McIntyre, A. D. (1965) *The Liberator: Daniel O'Connell and the Irish party, 1830–1847*. London: Hamish Hamilton.

MacIntyre, Donald (1999) *Mandelson: the biography*. London: HarperCollins.

Mackay, James (1996) *Michael Collins: a life*. Edinburgh: Mainstream.

McKittrick, David (1996) *The nervous peace*. Belfast: Blackstaff.

McKittrick, David and David McVea (2000) *Making sense of the troubles*. Belfast: Blackstaff.

McKittrick, David, Seamus Kelters, Brian Feeney and Chris Thornton (1999) *Lost lives: the stories of the men, women and children who died as a result of the Northern Ireland troubles*. Edinburgh: Mainstream.

McNeill, Ronald (1922) *Ulster's stand for union*. London: John Murray.

Maher, Jim (1998) *Harry Boland: a biography*. Cork: Mercier.

Major, John R. (1999) *John Major: the autobiography*. London: HarperCollins.

Mallie, Eamonn and David McKittrick (1996) *The fight for peace: the secret story behind the Irish peace process*. London: William Heinemann.

Mallie, Eamonn and David McKittrick (2001) *Endgame in Ireland*. London: Hodder & Stoughton.

Mandle, W. F. (1977) 'The Irish Republican Brotherhood and the beginnings of the Gaelic Athletic Association', *Irish historical studies* 20 (80): 418–38.

Mansergh, Nicholas (1991) *The unresolved question: the Anglo-Irish settlement and its undoing 1912–72*. New Haven and London: Yale University Press.

Marjoribanks, Edward and Ian Colvin (1932–6) *The life of Lord Carson*, 3 vols. London: Gollancz.

Marrinan, Patrick (1973) *Paisley: man of wrath*. Tralee: Anvil Books.

Marshall, Monty G. and Ted Robert Gurr, with Jonathan Wilkenfeld, Mark Irving Lichbach and David Quinn (2003) *Peace and conflict 2003: a global survey of armed conflicts, self-determination movements, and democracy*. College Park, MD: Center for International Development and Conflict Management, University of Maryland; also available www. cidcm. umd. edu/inscr/pc03print.pdf [2003–06–11].

Masterman, Lucy (1939) *C. F. G. Masterman: a biography*. London: Nicholson and Watson.

Maume, Patrick (1993) 'Aspects of nationalist political culture, 1900–1918'. PhD thesis, Queen's University, Belfast.

Maume, Patrick (1995) 'Parnell and the IRB oath', *Irish historical studies* 29 (115): 363–70.

Maume, Patrick (1998) 'Nationalism and partition: the political thought of Arthur Clery', *Irish historical studies* 21 (122): 222–40.

Melaugh, Martin (2003) Violence: differing approaches to statistics on deaths; available cain. ulst.ac.uk/issues/violence/counting.htm [2003–05–29].

Miller, Kerby A. (1985) *Emigrants and exiles. Ireland and the Irish exodus to North America.* Oxford: Oxford University Press.

Mitchell, Arthur (1994) *Revolutionary government in Ireland: Dáil Éireann, 1919–1922.* Dublin: Gill & Macmillan.

Mitchell, George (1999a) *Making peace.* London: William Heinemann.

Mitchell, George (1999b) *Statement by Senator George Mitchell in Belfast, concluding the review of the Northern Ireland peace process, 18 November 1999*; available http://cain.ulst.ac. uk/events/peace/docs/gm181199.htm [2003–06–08].

Moloney, Ed (2002) *A secret history of the IRA.* London: Allen Lane.

Moody, T. W., ed. (1968) *The Fenian movement.* Cork: Mercier Press.

Morgan, Kenneth (1989) 'Lloyd George and the Irish', pp. 83–103 in *Ireland after the Union: proceedings of the second joint meeting of the Royal Irish Academy and the British Academy.* Oxford: Oxford University Press.

Morgan, Kenneth O., ed. (1973) *Lloyd George: family letters 1885–1936.* Cardiff and London: University of Wales Press.

Morley, John (1918) *Recollections.* 2 vols. London: Macmillan.

Mottistone, Lord [J. E. B. Seely] (1930) *Adventure.* London: William Heinemann.

Mowlam, Mo (2002) *Momentum: the struggle for peace, politics and the people.* London: Hodder & Stoughton.

Murphy, Brian P. (1991) *Patrick Pearse and the lost republican ideal.* Dublin: James Duffy.

Murphy, Brian P. (1998) 'The IRA and its enemies: a review article', *The Month*, Sep-Oct: 381–4.

Murphy, Nancy (1985) 'Joseph K. Bracken, GAA founder, Fenian and politician', in Nolan and Whelan, 1985: 379–93.

Murphy, Richard (1986) 'Faction in the Conservative Party and the home rule crisis, 1912–14', *History* 71: 222–34.

National Graves Association (1985) *The last post.* 3rd edn. Dublin: National Graves Association.

Needham, Richard (1998) *Battling for peace.* Belfast: Blackstaff.

Ní Aoláin, Fionnuala (2000) *The politics of force: conflict management and state violence in Northern Ireland.* Belfast: Blackstaff.

Nolan, William and Kevin Whelan, eds (1985) *Tipperary: history and society.* Dublin: Geography Publications.

Nolan, William and Kevin Whelan, eds (1990) *Kilkenny: history and society.* Dublin: Geography Publications.

Northern Ireland Office (1996) *Northern Ireland negotiations, rules of procedure, 29 July 1996.* Belfast: Northern Ireland Office.

Northern Ireland Office (1998a) *Agreement reached in the inter-party negotiations.* Belfast: Northern Ireland Office; also available http://www.nio.gov.uk/issues/agreelinks/ agreement.htm [2003–06–08].

Northern Ireland Office (1998b) *Decommissioning scheme based on Section 3(1)(c) and (d) of the Northern Ireland Arms Decommissioning Act 1997.* Belfast: Northern Ireland Office; also available http://www.nio.gov.uk/pdf/1998decsch.pdf [2003–06–08].

Nowlan, Kevin B., ed. (1969) *The making of 1916: studies in the history of the rising*. Dublin: Stationery Office.

O'Brien, R. Barry, ed. (1910) *The autobiography of Theobald Wolfe Tone*. 2 vols. Dublin, Cork and Belfast: Phoenix.

Ó Broin, Leon, ed. (1996) *In great haste: the letters of Michael Collins to Kitty Kiernan*. Rev. edn, ed. Cian Ó hÉgeartaigh. Dublin: Gill & Macmillan.

O'Callaghan, Margaret (1994) *British high politics and a nationalist Ireland*. Cork: Cork University Press.

Ó Cuív, Shan, ed. (1927) *An dord féinne agus dánta eile. Réamhradh ó Éamon de Valera*. Baile Átha Cliath: Brún agus Ó Nóláin.

O'Ferrall, Fergus (1985) *Catholic emancipation: Daniel O'Connell and the birth of Irish democracy, 1820–30*. Dublin: Gill & Macmillan.

O'Halpin, Eunan (1987) *The decline of the union: British government in Ireland 1892–1920*. Dublin: Gill & Macmillan.

O'Halpin, Eunan (1998) 'Collins and intelligence, 1919–1923', pp. 68–81 in Doherty and Keogh, 1998.

O'Halpin, Eunan (1999) *Defending Ireland: the Irish state and its enemies since 1922*. Oxford: Oxford University Press.

O'Halpin, Eunan (2000a) 'Irish-Allied security relations and the "American Note" crisis: new evidence from British records', *Irish studies in international affairs* 11: 71–83.

O'Halpin, Eunan (2000b) 'MI5's Irish memories: fresh light on the origins and rationale of Anglo-Irish security liaison in the Second World War', pp. 133–50 in Brian Girvin and Geoffrey Roberts (eds), *Ireland and the Second World War: politics, society and remembrance*. Dublin: Four Courts.

O'Halpin, Eunan (2000c) 'Weird prophecies: British intelligence and Anglo-Irish relations, 1932–3', pp. 61–73 in Michael Kennedy and Joseph Morrison Skelly (eds), *Irish foreign policy 1919–1966: from independence to internationalism*, new edn. Dublin: Four Courts.

O'Halpin, Eunan, ed. (2003) *MI5 and Ireland 1939–1945: the official history*. Dublin: Irish Academic Press.

O'Hanrahan, Michael (1990) 'The tithe war in County Kilkenny 1830–1834', in Nolan and Whelan, 1990: 481–506.

O'Hegarty, P. S. (1952) *A history of Ireland under the Union, 1801 to 1922*. London: Methuen.

O'Leary, Brendan and John McGarry (1996) *The politics of antagonism: understanding Northern Ireland*. 2nd edn. London: Athlone Press.

O'Neill, Terence (1969) *Ulster at the crossroads*. London: Faber & Faber.

O'Neill, Terence (1972) *The autobiography of Terence O'Neill*. London: Hart-Davis.

O'Neill, Tim P. (2000) 'Famine evictions', pp. 29–70 in Carla King (ed.), *Famine, land and culture in Ireland*. Dublin: UCD Press.

Orr, Philip (1987) *The road to the Somme: men of the Ulster Division tell their story*. Belfast: Blackstaff.

Owen, Arwel Ellis (1994) *The Anglo-Irish agreement: the first three years*. Cardiff: University of Wales Press.

Palmer, R. R. (1959–64) *The age of democratic revolution*, 2 vols. Princeton: Princeton University Press.

Paterson, T. G. F. (1975) 'The sham fight', pp. 165–7 in *Harvest home, the last sheaf: a selection from the writings of T. G. F. Paterson relating to County Armagh.* Armagh: Armagh County Museum.

Paterson, Henry (1986) 'British governments and the Protestant backlash 1969–74', pp. 231–47 in Alan O'Day (ed.), *Ireland's terrorist dilemma.* Lancaster: Martinus Nijhoff.

Paterson, Henry (1997) *The politics of illusion: a political history of the IRA.* London: Serif.

Paulin, Tom (1987) *Hillsborough script: a dramatic satire.* London: Faber.

Pearse, Pádraic H. ([1922]) 'From a hermitage: VI', pp. 181–9 in *Collected works of Pádraic H. Pearse: political writings and speeches.* Dublin: Phoenix [first published 1913].

Petrie, Sir Charles (1939–40) *The life and letters of Sir Austen Chamberlain.* 2 vols. London: Cassell.

Philpin, C. E. H., ed. (1987) *Nationalism and popular protest in Ireland.* Cambridge: Cambridge University Press.

Phoenix, Eamon (1994) *Northern nationalism: nationalist politics, partition and the Catholic minority in Northern Ireland.* Belfast: Ulster Historical Foundation.

Pocock, J. G. A. (1975) 'British history: a plea for a new subject', *Journal of modern history* 47: 601–28.

Popplewell, Richard (1987): 'The surveillance of Indian "Seditionists" in North America, 1905–1915', pp. 49–76 in Christopher Andrew and Jeremy Noakes (eds), *Intelligence and international relations 1900–1945.* Exeter: University of Exeter.

Porter, Norman (1996) *Rethinking unionism.* Belfast: Blackstaff.

Pottle, Mark, ed. (1998) *Champion redoubtable: the diaries and letters of Violet Bonham-Carter, 1914–1944.* London: Weidenfeld & Nicolson.

Quinn, David and Ted Robert Gurr (2003) 'Self-determination movements and their outcomes', pp. 26–38 in Marshall et al., 2003.

Quinn, James (1998) 'The United Irishmen and social reform', *Irish historical studies* 31 (122): 188–201.

Redmond, John (1916) 'Introduction', pp. 1–14 in Michael MacDonagh, *The Irish at the front.* London: Hodder & Stoughton.

Rentoul, James A. (1921) *Stray thoughts and memories.* London: J. Parsons.

Robbins, Keith (1971) *Sir Edward Grey: a biography of Lord Grey of Fallodon.* London: Cassell.

Rodner, W. S. (1982) 'Leaguers, covenanters, moderates: British support for Ulster, 1913–14', *Eire-Ireland* 17: 68–85.

Rolston, Bill (1987) 'Politics, painting and popular culture: the political wall murals of Northern Ireland', *Media, culture and society* 9 (1): 5–28.

Rolston, Bill (1988) 'Contemporary political wall murals in the North of Ireland: drawing support', *Eire-Ireland* 23: 3–18.

Rolston, Bill (1991) *Politics and painting: murals and conflict in Northern Ireland.* Rutherford: Farleigh Dickinson.

Ruane, Joseph and Jennifer Todd (1996) *The dynamics of conflict in Northern Ireland: power, conflict and emancipation.* Cambridge: Cambridge University Press.

Ruane, Joseph and Jennifer Todd (2001) 'The politics of transition: explaining the difficulties in implementing the Belfast Agreement', *Political studies* 49: 923–40.

Sayer, George (1988) *Jack: C. S. Lewis and his times.* London: Macmillan.

Seldon, Anthony (1997) *John Major.* London: Weidenfeld & Nicolson.

Senior, Hereward (1966) *Orangeism in Ireland and Britain, 1795–1836*. London: Routledge & Kegan Paul.

Shaw, Bernard (1907) *John's Bull's other island and Major Barbara*. London: Constable.

Shaw, Henry (1844) *Shaw's authenticated report of the Irish state trials, 1844*. Dublin: Henry Shaw.

Shea, Patrick (1983) *Voices and the sound of drums*. Belfast: Blackstaff.

Shearman, Hugh (1942) *Not an inch: a study of Northern Ireland and Lord Craigavon*. London: Faber & Faber.

Singer, J. David and Melvin Small, with Robert Bennett, Kari Gluski and Susan Jones (1982) *Resort to arms: international and civil wars, 1816–1980*. Beverly Hills, CA: Sage.

Smith, Jim (1992) *The men of no property: Irish radicals and popular politics in the late eighteenth century*. Basingstoke: Macmillan.

Smyth, Marie (2000) 'The human consequences of armed conflict: constructing "victimhood" in the context of Northern Ireland's troubles', pp. 118–35 in Cox, Guelke and Stephen, 2000.

Stewart, A. T. Q. (1967) *The Ulster crisis*. London: Faber & Faber.

Stewart, A. T. Q. (1977) *The narrow ground: patterns of Ulster history*. London: Faber & Faber.

Stewart, A. T. Q. (1981) *Edward Carson*. Dublin: Gill & Macmillan.

Stewart, A. T. Q., ed. (1997) *Michael Collins: the secret file*. Belfast: Blackstaff.

Stoessinger, J. G. (1993) *Why nations go to war*. 6th edn. New York: St Martin's Press.

Street, C. J. C. (1922) *Ireland in 1921*. London: P. Allan.

Sullivan, A. M. (1927) *Old Ireland: reminiscences of an Irish KC*. London: Thornton Butterworth.

Sutton, Malcolm (1994) *Bear in mind these dead . . . an index of deaths from the conflict in Ireland 1969–1993*. Belfast: Beyond the Pale.

Talbot, Hayden (1923) *Michael Collins' own story: told to Hayden Talbot*. London: Hutchinson.

Taylor, Peter (1997) *Provos: the IRA and Sinn Féin*. London: Bloomsbury.

Taylor, Peter (1999) *Loyalists*. London: Bloomsbury.

Taylor, Peter (2001) *Brits: the war against the IRA*. London: Bloomsbury.

Thatcher, Margaret (1993) *Downing Street years*. London: HarperCollins.

Thompson, E. P. (1971) 'The moral economy of the English crowd in the eighteenth century', *Past and present* 50: 176–236.

Todd, J. (1999) 'Nationalism, republicanism and the Good Friday Agreement', pp. 49–70 in J. Ruane and J. Todd (eds), *After the Good Friday Agreement: analysing political change in Northern Ireland*. Dublin: UCD Press.

Townshend, Charles (1975) *The British campaign in Ireland 1919–1921: the development of political and military policy*. London: Oxford University Press.

Townshend, Charles (1983) *Political violence in Ireland: government and resistance since 1848*. Oxford: Clarendon.

Trimble, David (1988) *What choice for Ulster?* Lurgan: Ulster Clubs Movement.

Trimble, David (2002) 'Opportunists and tacticians, but poor strategists', *Spectator*, 14–21 Dec.

Ulster Society (1988) *Lillibulero!* 2 vols. Lurgan: Ulster Society.

United Kingdom (1997) *Northern Ireland Arms Decommissioning Act 1997 (c. 7), 27 February 1997*. London: HMSO; also available http://www.legislation.hmso.gov.uk/acts/acts1997/1997007.htm [2003–06–08].

Urquhart, Diane (2001) *The minutes of the Ulster Women's Unionist Council and Executive Committee, 1911–1940.* Dublin: Women's History Project in association with the Irish Manuscripts Commission.

Walker, Brian M. (1978) *Parliamentary election results in Ireland, 1801–1922.* Dublin: Royal Irish Academy.

Wall, Maureen (1966) 'Partition: the Ulster question (1916–1926)', pp. 79–93 in T. D. Williams (ed.), *The Irish struggle, 1916–1926.* London: Routledge & Kegan Paul.

Whyte, John (1990) *Interpreting Northern Ireland.* Oxford: Clarendon.

Winter, Sir Ormonde (1955) *Winter's tale.* London: Richards Press.

Yeltsin, Boris (1994) *The view from the Kremlin.* London: HarperCollins.

Young, G. K. ([1985?]) *Subversion and the British riposte.* Glasgow: Ossian Publishers.

Younger, Carlton (1968) *Ireland's civil war.* London: Muller.

Index